1. Franklin's ground squirrel and small white lady's slipper orchid at Chiwaukee Prairie

2. Migrating birds stopping off at the Magic Hedge on Montrose Point

3. Black-crowned night heron at Lake Calumet

4. Hog-nosed snake at Indiana Dunes National Lakeshore

5. Bobolink and controlled burn at Midewin National Tallgrass Prairie

6. Fawn at the Palos Forest Preserves

7. Bison at Fermi National Accelerator Laboratory

8. Migrating sandhill cranes

9. Chorus frog and red fox along the North Branch of the Chicago River

10. Fringed gentian and blue-spotted salamander at the North Branch Restoration Project

Hunting for Frogs on Elston

Hunting for Frogs on Elston

AND OTHER TALES
FROM FIELD AND STREET

Jerry Sullivan

Edited by Victor M. Cassidy

Illustrations by Bobby Sutton

Published in association with Chicago Wilderness

The University of Chicago Press
Chicago & London

Jerry Sullivan (1938–2000) was a career naturalist and journalist. He was an outreach naturalist and associate director for land management with the Forest Preserve District of Cook County. He also wrote *The Chicago Wilderness Atlas of Biodiversity.*

The columns reproduced in this volume appeared originally as a series in the *Chicago Reader,* under the title "Field & Street."

The University of Chicago Press, Chicago 60637
The University of Chicago Press, Ltd., London
© 2004 by The University of Chicago
All rights reserved. Published 2004
Printed in the United States of America

13 12 11 10 09 08 07 06 05 04   1 2 3 4 5

ISBN: 0-226-77993-9 (cloth)

Library of Congress Cataloging-in-Publication Data

Sullivan, Jerry, 1938–
    Hunting for frogs on Elston, and other tales from field and street / Jerry Sullivan ; edited by Victor M. Cassidy ; illustrations by Bobby Sutton.
        p. cm.
    The columns reproduced in this volume appeared originally as a series in the Chicago Reader, under the title "Field & street"—P.
    "Published in association with Chicago Wilderness."
    ISBN 0-226-77993-9 (cloth : alk. paper)
    1. Natural history.   2. Urban ecology.   I. Cassidy, Victor M. II. Title.
    QH81.S8784 2004
    508.31732—dc22

                                                2003022010

⊗ The paper used in this publication meets the minimum requirements of the American National Standard for Information Sciences—Permanence of Paper for Printed Library Materials, ANSI Z39.48-1992.

Contents

Acknowledgments ix

Introduction   *by Glenda Daniel* xi

1 › State of the Prairie

Prairie Cathedral 9/27/85 3
Fragmented Grasslands 5/22/87 7
Managing Nature 10/9/87 11
Too Many Deer 1/3/92 15
Middle Fork Savanna 7/9/93 19
Biodiversity 2/22/91 23
Transanimaling 6/26/92 27
Prairie September 9/25/98 31

2 › The Seasons

Spring Comes to Chicago 2/24/95 39
Early Spring 3/13/98 43
Early Risers 3/9/84 47
The Ephemerals' Moment 4/12/85 51
Cherries 7/11/97 55
Bees 7/3/98 59
Fall Flora 10/17/97 63
Turkeys 11/16/84 67
Winter Reading 12/20/85 71
Squirrels' Nests 1/27/95 75
Ice Fishing 1/20/84 79
Feeding Urban Birds 12/12/86 82

3 › Creatures Great and Small

Hunting for Frogs on Elston Avenue 5/16/86 89
Caterpillars 8/30/85 94
Woodchucks 3/8/91 98
Counting Butterflies 7/15/88 102
Sludge Worms 2/14/92 106
Rattlesnake Hunting 8/14/92 110
Ant Transplant 3/27/87 114
Searching for Bats 8/10/84 118
Fireflies 7/19/85 122
Migrating Monarchs 9/7/84 126
Badgers 11/23/90 130
Chorus Frogs 3/27/98 134
Coyotes in the City 2/2/96 137
Yellow Jackets 9/11/87 142
Reading Animal Tracks 1/25/91 146

4 › Birds and More Birds

The Bird Hunter 5/10/85 153
Woodpeckers 1/16/87 157
Looking for a Gyrfalcon 2/8/91 161
Sparrows 4/6/84 165
Red-Tailed Hawks 3/13/87 169
Birding in North Channel 7/17/92 173
Kestrels 1/18/85 177
Savanna Birds 2/19/93 181
Feathers 4/10/87 185
Winter Flocks 12/1/89 189
Christmas Bird Count 1/8/88 193
How to Find Nests 6/14/91 197
Mourning Doves 3/24/95 202
Goldfinches 9/28/90 206
The Passenger Pigeon 4/4/86 210

5 › Plants

Healthy Communities 2/27/98 217
Oak Trees 12/16/94 222

Sedges 6/27/97 227
Nightshade 6/13/86 231
Purple Loosestrife 9/5/97 235
Jewelweed 10/3/86 240
Hazels 10/11/96 243
Raspberries 7/17/98 247
Wild Onions 1/31/92 251
Eastern Prairie Fringed Orchid 10/1/93 255

6 › People and Places

Field Guides 9/8/89 263
Surveying Illinois 6/21/96 267
Inland Marsh 1/5/96 271
Women Naturalists 7/25/86 275
Bird-Watchers 8/28/87 280
Henry Chandler Cowles 11/6/98 284
Poplar Creek Preserve 9/6/91 288
Lichen Scholar 11/3/95 292
Dinosaurs and Birds 11/9/90 296
Roger Tory Peterson 8/16/96 300

Acknowledgments

When Jerry Sullivan died in 2000, several friends sent gifts to Chicago Wilderness in his honor. Without these generous donations, we would not have this book.

The *Chicago Reader,* which first published "Field & Street," was consistently supportive. We especially thank Kitry Krause, who was Jerry Sullivan's editor, and Patrick O'Neil, who was there at the office when we needed him.

Laurel Ross and Debra Shore gave their time and many good ideas as this book was planned. James McDonald also donated his time, and Rebecca Blazer of Chicago Wilderness very capably coordinated this project from beginning to end. Sheila Hoyos and Elizabeth Riotto did most of the keyboarding. Thanks to all.

Victor M. Cassidy

Introduction
Meet Jerry Sullivan (1938–2000)

He was a man with the body of a linebacker and the soul of a poet. He loved the world's great wild places and explored as many as time and a limited income would allow. Yet he was equally happy exploring the most banal, everyday aspects of nature visible from his own very urban backyard, the adjacent alley, or a nearby forest preserve.

For most of one growing season, he refused to let me remove a large tomato hornworm from the juiciest tomato in our garden because he wanted to observe its transformation from what surely must be one of the ugliest caterpillars in existence to a delicate brown-winged sphinx moth. Another summer, he spent a week of evenings at the height of baseball season (so you know just how serious this was) observing fireflies mating in our backyard and trying to determine their species from the color of their light and the timing of their flashes.

He had an amused appreciation for human nature with all its foibles, especially in relation to the rest of nature. He was struck particularly by the observation that most urban dwellers consider wild animals either pests or potential pets and either a serious danger or completely helpless. Among the many calls he took from citizens while working as a naturalist with the Cook County Forest Preserves, one of his favorites was from a woman concerned about a goose in a shopping center parking lot. She was afraid it might get run over. "Ma'am," said Jerry, "I think if you look closely at that goose, you'll find that it has wings."

He was serious about his work but never took himself too seriously. A running gag in his *Chicago Reader* columns was his inability ever to see species reported on the local Rare Bird Alert hotline. "There are two possible explanations for this. One is that I'm really not very good at this game. The other is that the whole edifice of organized bird-watching, with its guidebooks and magazines, its national organizations and local clubs, is an enormous hoax, a huge practical joke being played on me. While I'm shivering on some windswept cornfield or slogging through ankle-deep mud in search of imaginary rarities, the jokesters who concocted this jape are sitting around laughing until their sides ache."

He loved to tell the story of the time the late David Brower of Sierra Club/Friends of the Earth fame came to town and needed some hiking boots to take a tour of local natural areas. He wore size $13\frac{1}{2}$ shoes, and Jerry turned out to be the only local environmentalist anyone could find who had feet just as big. He was happy to make the loan. "Now," he said, "if anyone asks, I can say David Brower has walked a mile in my shoes."

His heroes were both professional and amateur scientists and naturalists, past and present, and he wrote about many of them, admiring them for the traits they shared of combining curiosity and awe of the natural world with patience and meticulous attention to detail. He felt a particular kinship with Margaret Morse Nice, the Ohio housewife who researched and wrote what has become the definitive work on the life history of the song sparrow. She made her observations on the floodplain behind her house while running a household and caring for her young children. Like Jerry, she appreciated the nature next door.

He claimed to regret having been born too late to meet (and fall in love with) Cordelia J. Stanwood of Ellsworth, Maine. Miss Stanwood gained immortality through her correspondence around 1910 with Arthur Cleveland Bent, published in his daunting series of bird life histories. With great thoroughness and an engaging, nonsentimental style unusual for her time, she described a pair of magnolia warblers building their nest in a spruce-fir forest over a period of several weeks in June. "I have been in spruce-fir forests in June," Jerry wrote, "and anyone who could sit through the onslaughts of mosquitoes to put together the precise and detailed notes she produces has my deepest respect."

Stories of the modern successors to these dedicated naturalists are told in many of the columns reproduced in this book. Originally published in the *Chicago Reader* under the heading "Field & Street," they include descriptions of particular projects pursued by such local heroes as

Ellin Beltz, who conducted a population survey of chorus frogs along the lower Illinois River, "surveying them on cold March nights, driving down back roads that sometimes vanished beneath her car and left her stuck in the sand. She drove about six miles an hour with the windows open, and listened. It was cold, arduous work."

Rich Hyerczyk, a botanist specializing in lichens who has completed several major reports on local lichens and, working with another prominent local botanist, Gerould Wilhelm, has identified 111 species in Cook County. Rich described the significance of lichens for "Field & Street," starting with a survey of the lichens on a picnic table in Harms Woods where the interview was taking place.

Ron Panzer, entomologist extraordinaire and steward of Gensburg-Markham Prairie.

John and Jane Balaban, a high school physics teacher and a pharmacist, respectively, who not only served loyally as stewards of Bunker Hill Prairie during the height of local opposition to native habitat restoration but who also continue generously to donate time to teach others.

Steve Packard, who successfully pollinated prairie fringed orchids using toothpicks and Styrofoam cups and then trained 20 other volunteers to continue the experiment.

Doug Taron, now Curator of Biology at the Peggy Notebaert Nature Museum, who in 1991 found some mysterious caterpillars inside the stems of mayapples on a remnant savanna in Elgin, took them home and successfully reared them to adulthood inside carrots in which he had drilled holes. He then was able to identify them as a rare moth called *Papaipema cerina*. When the Elgin savanna was slated for development, he led an effort to win approval from the Illinois Nature Preserves Commission to transfer them to the Bluff Spring Fen Nature Preserve not far away.

Along with the professionals, there were the hundreds of ordinary citizens, many of whom wrote Jerry with reports and inquiries that led to "Field & Street" columns. Jerry respected them because "they pay attention; they notice things." Among them was his brother-in-law, Dick Kaitchuck, who got him started researching the architecture of squirrels' nests with a simple observation. Dick pointed out how amazing it is that those balls of leaves stay anchored in the trees in the face of Chicago's fierce winter winds. "The stems on those leaves are not twister ties," he said. "How do they keep them together?"

Then there was the group of new Jamaican immigrants, teenagers lounging on a street corner at Granville and Winthrop at sunset one summer evening. As Jerry walked by, he noticed they were staring, fascinated, at a dense flock of chimney swifts flying out of a tall inactive chimney where they had rested while preparing for their evening's feeding foray. Nobody else on the block had noticed a thing. "Mon, what's goin' on up there?" one of them asked Jerry. He spent the next 15 minutes talking and answering their questions about swifts, the nighthawks on the nearby flat roofs, and other natural phenomena of the strange new environment they had just discovered.

People like these form a large and formidable constituency and make up the heart and soul of what has become Chicago Wilderness, a sponsor of this book. Chicago Wilderness is an unprecedented consortium of more than 160 nonprofit organizations and government agencies dedicated to restoring the rare ecosystems still present to a considerable degree in this grand metropolitan region.

Not content to advocate for restoration in a general way, Chicago Wilderness has organized itself into four separate teams: Science, Education and Communication, Land Management, and Sustainability. With the help of these teams, the consortium has developed and garnered widespread governmental and public support for implementation of a regional Biodiversity Recovery Plan. Chicago Wilderness has also produced a regional *Atlas of Biodiversity* (also written by Jerry Sullivan) and launched a successful quarterly, *Chicago Wilderness Magazine.*

Federal and state agencies such as the U.S. Fish and Wildlife Service, the USDA Forest Service, the U.S. Environmental Protection Agency, and the Illinois Department of Natural Resources have supported the effort since the beginning by providing funding to member nonprofit organizations and public agencies. These grants have stimulated scientific research and on-the-ground projects aimed at the restoration of native local habitats and public education about their value.

The strength of this movement in this location at this time in history can be attributed to many factors. Not least among them is the heritage that began with the local giants who were leaders in a national movement to understand and to protect natural areas at the turn of the 20th century—people like Stephen Mather, first director of the National Park Service; Jens Jensen and Dwight Perkins, who prepared the region's first open space plan in 1903 and laid the groundwork for formation of the Chicago Park District and Cook County Forest Preserves; and Henry Chandler Cowles, a founder of the science of ecology.

Their legacy has been passed down to each succeeding generation, fostering a continual awareness of the natural riches the region possesses even in the midst of massive urban growth. Much more recently, there have been Morton Arboretum staff members like May Watts, Floyd Swink, Ray Schulenberg, George Ware, and, later, Gerould Wilhelm, who were as dedicated to making natural history understandable and exciting to the public as they were to the work itself.

There have been the Northeastern Illinois Prairie Conferences, held periodically since 1979 and involving amateur enthusiasts as well as professionals, and local efforts like the North Branch Prairie Project (now the North Branch Restoration Project), initiated in 1976 by Steve Packard. The project built a network of volunteer stewards to restore degraded prairie, savanna, and woodland landscapes in a string of Cook County forest preserves along the Chicago River from Somme Woods in Northbrook south to Bunker Hill in northwest Chicago. The broader, region-wide Volunteer Stewardship Network evolved from these beginnings.

The stories told by people like Jerry Sullivan in his "Field & Street" columns have brought the work of the local natural scientists and amateur naturalists to a broader audience and helped build an interdisciplinary support network of the scientists themselves.

All of these factors and more set the stage for the founding of Chicago Wilderness in 1996 and have contributed ever since to its rapid growth and increasing activity on behalf of the region's natural riches.

Jerry characterized the appeal of the effort and the long but connected local tradition it represents in a column about a course he took on fall flora from John and Jane Balaban at the Field Museum.

> If you have no interest in trying to interpret the natural landscape, knowing the difference between tall goldenrod and Short's aster may not seem worth the effort. But I think we desire to learn things in order to make some sense of the world. When we look at nature we can be overwhelmed by all the simultaneous stimuli that hit us. There are so many different kinds of plants, and while we try to sort them out, grasshoppers are leaping about and butterflies are fluttering by and dragonflies are zooming past and birds are calling. To the extent that we can sort out all these impressions, we alienated, atomized, postmodern people can feel at home, connected to something beyond ourselves.
>
> Here in Chicago we can take lessons from the Balabans, who took lessons from Floyd Swink and Gerould Wilhelm, who took lessons from May Watts, who studied at the University of Chicago under Henry Chandler Cowles, one of the founders of the science of ecology. We can enjoy the riches of life in one of the world's great metropolises and still connect ourselves to the natural world.

Glenda Daniel (Sullivan)

1 › State of the Prairie

Prairie Cathedral

Bringing Back a Vanished Ecosystem

September 27, 1985

As a native-born Chicagoan, I grew up knowing that a prairie was any piece of land that supported neither buildings nor trees. Actually, I should amend that. In my neighborhood, it was any *large* piece of land. A small piece of open, treeless land—of which we had many—was a vacant lot. I lived in a suburban development that had been platted by a real estate man who went to jail before he could erect more than a handful of houses. I don't know what he did, but given the practices that passed as ordinary business in his line of work, it must have been pretty spectacular.

But thanks to his chicanery, I grew up in a neighborhood where the houses and their surrounding lawns were neatly tended little islands in a sea of tall grass. The vacant lots were big enough for us to turn a couple of them into ball fields—one for baseball, one for football.

And out beyond the last of our subdivision's two streets was the prairie itself. It seemed enormous to us, and I guess it did cover as much as 200 acres. We knew every foot of it with an intimacy that I am sure I will never achieve again with any piece of ground.

We played along the small creek that crossed a corner of it. The row of trees that bordered the creek we called the Jungle. The low spot that filled with water each spring and fall, we called the Pond, as if it was the only one in the world. We caught crawdads and tadpoles there in spring and took the tadpoles home to watch them change into frogs.

A farmer plowed a fraction of this prairie, growing sweet corn, which we pilfered for cookouts, and tomatoes, which we gathered late in the season when they were mushy and stinking to throw at each other and at the houses of people who didn't give out any candy on Halloween.

We built our own little houses on the prairie, too, using lumber stolen from construction sites. The developer's brush with the law meant that houses in our subdivision were built one at a time over a 15-year stretch, so there was always a foundation, as we called them, somewhere in the

3

neighborhood. I was 16 before I realized that most people had to go out and buy lumber when they wanted to build something.

If this little recital of the innocent thievery of childhood leaves you convinced that the developer wasn't the only person connected with the neighborhood who belonged in jail, I would respond that you ain't heard nothin' yet. Our worst crime was arson.

Every now and then, we would set fire to our prairie. Most of these blazes burned a little patch of grass and then went out, but one day when they were about seven years old, my friends Tom and Harold ignited a blaze that got so out of hand that the Des Plaines Fire Department had to come put it out. Not only did it endanger the whole neighborhood, it also fried some overhead electrical wires strung from pole to pole along the edge of the field.

I do not remember the punishment they got for this deed, although I'm sure it was ghastly. But looking back I realize that they were not really criminals. They were ecologists before their time. As near as I can determine from the available sources of information, that piece of open ground (it has long since vanished under a Wieboldt's warehouse and a hydraulic cylinder factory) actually was a prairie—not a prairie in the Chicago sense, but an actual remnant of the native landscape, a grassland of the sort that gave the Prairie State its nickname.

For that sort of prairie, the real prairie, fire is a life giver, a re-creation of the conditions that sustained the tall grass when it stretched from horizon to horizon. The flames kill off invading weeds and cottonwood trees, return minerals to the soil, and foster a rich growth of the hundreds of species of grasses and wildflowers that support all the special animals that can live nowhere else. Periodic burns have become the accepted

means of maintaining the few pitiful remnants of our native grasslands that remain in the state, and they are a powerful tool for driving out the weeds and restoring the prairie to land that it once dominated.

This spring and summer, I had a chance to do some legal burning with the North Branch Prairie Project, a volunteer organization that is upgrading and expanding several prairie remnants on Cook County Forest Preserve land along the North Branch of the Chicago River. The project, which started in 1975, is the brainchild of Steve Packard, my predecessor as writer of these columns. Most of the hundreds of volunteers who have worked with the NBPP are Sierra Club members, but several other environmental organizations help sponsor the project, and unaffiliated helpers are always welcome.

From north to south, the project areas are Somme Woods, at Dundee and Waukegan roads; Wayside, Indigo, and Miami Woods near Dempster Street between Lehigh and Waukegan roads; Bunker Hill Prairie near Devon and Caldwell; and Sauganash Prairie near Bryn Mawr and Kostner. In aggregate, these lands total about 200 acres.

Steve has gathered about a dozen regulars who serve as a sort of board of directors to decide what is to be done, and they direct the efforts of the hundreds who turn out to cut brush, gather and sow seeds, and assist at the annual fires. These decision makers are in the great American tradition of empirical-minded tinkerers, Edisons of ecology. They experiment—knowledgeably—until they find something that works, and the theoreticians can figure out why later.

This open-minded attitude is necessary, because the history of prairie restoration is quite short. The history of prairie destruction goes back to the first European settlement of this part of the country. The homesteaders found a garden here, sunlit meadows filled with a constantly changing wildflower display that can be equaled only in the richest of the alpine meadows of our western mountains.

But after a century and a half of intensive farming and the construction of many warehouses and factories, only a little over 2,000 acres remain here in the Prairie State, and the situation is almost as bad in the rest of the former realm of the tallgrass prairie. Imagine California with only 2,000 acres of redwoods and those scattered over the state in tiny clumps and groves.

Botanists at the University of Wisconsin in Madison began the first prairie restoration about 50 years ago, and the Morton Arboretum followed their example a few years later. Today, there are groups like the North Branch Prairie Project in every Midwestern state, and the zealots tending their prairie gardens gather at periodic conferences to compare experiences and spread the word on what worked for them and what failed.

Bringing back a vanished ecosystem is really an audacious project. Natural systems like prairies or forests are the most complex things in the universe. Think of hundreds of species of plants, each with its own mycorrhizal fungus growing symbiotically on its roots and helping it absorb nutrients from the soil. Think of thousands of kinds of bacteria, fungi, nematodes, protozoans, insects, spiders, mites, and other tiny creatures who, with the plants, support the frogs, salamanders, snakes, birds, and mammals—all of these interacting with each other, all influenced by the vagaries of weather and climate and the nature of the soil.

The fact is, nobody can understand it all, so if you want to create it you have to be open to experiment. Let's just scatter these prairie phlox seeds on the ground here. Over there, we will rake them into the soil, and on up the hill we will plant seedlings germinated in somebody's backyard. You plant some seeds in the fall and some in the spring. You burn one patch of prairie in the fall and another in the spring, and you keep track of what happens and when.

Mostly you wait. Prairie plants are botanical conservatives. They don't rush into flower. The first year after they germinate, you can scarcely find them. The tiny pale green leaves rise only an inch or two above ground. At this stage of their lives—they are almost all perennials that live for many years—they are working on their portfolios, growing a dense root system that will tide them over the inevitable summer drought.

Some of the seeds won't even germinate until the second or third or fourth year. We have selectively bred domesticated seeds to ripen at once and sprout at once, but wild plants hedge their bets. Maybe this year a late frost will kill off all the young shoots, or the August drought will be bad enough to wither them. Better save a few seeds for next year.

Touring the North Branch prairies, you can see the changes slowly accreting. Where nothing but imported weeds grew a few years ago, you can now see tall clumps of big bluestem grass. Crowds of bright purple blazing stars punctuate the green background. Pale creamy gentian hides in the grass, and huge yellow prairie dock flowers tower over everything else in sight. Grasses are now taking over places that were nothing but dense thickets of European buckthorn brush a few years ago. Like building a cathedral, Packard says. If you are in on laying the foundations, you may not live to see the topmost spire completed, but you will see enough to know that the project is on the way up.

Fragmented Grasslands
"Island" Ecosystems

May 22, 1987

I spent the first Saturday in May sitting in classrooms at Joliet Junior College, attending, along with a few hundred fellow enthusiasts, the eighth Northern Illinois Prairie Workshop.

The workshop organizers had provided us with 61 different classes to choose from, with topics ranging from "Prairie Management with Fire and Saw" to "Surveying Prairies for Reptiles and Amphibians" to "Seed-banks and Vegetation Establishment: Practical Considerations."

There was a heavy bias toward the practical, a bias that reflected the makeup of the crowd. Most of the people who came are working on prairies. They are managers of government or private preserves, or they are volunteers restoring or protecting places like the Wolf Road Prairie in Westchester or the Indian Boundary Prairies in Markham or the prairies along the North Branch of the Chicago River. They come to a workshop looking for some help in coping with purple loosestrife, European buckthorn, or other invasive alien weeds, or seeking advice on how to organize a prescribed fire.

The fact that you could get that many outdoor people to spend a Saturday in May inside classrooms suggests that prairie restoration and management have somehow arrived, that they are now legitimate outdoor activities, like bird-watching or destroying endangered species with off-road vehicles. Someday maybe we'll see a Mountain Dew commercial featuring a laughing gang of beautiful young people cutting down buckthorn shrubs.

There are restoration projects under way in all parts of Illinois, and all this activity produces a hopeful air at this meeting, which is quite different from the usual atmosphere at gatherings of environmentalists. The situation of the tallgrass prairie in Illinois has actually improved in measurable ways in the past 20 years.

Of course there was no way to go but up. Twenty years ago, almost nobody in Illinois knew what a tallgrass prairie was. They had nearly vanished from the landscape—we have four square miles left out of 40,000—and they had vanished from the public mind as well. They were also nearly unrepresented in the state park system, and that didn't bother very many people.

Today, although we have lost some more remnants, prairies are represented in the state park system and in the state nature preserve system; and restoration projects, some as big as 1,000 acres, are remaking prairies on land that's grown mostly corn and soybeans for the past century and a half. The Illinois Department of Transportation is even planting prairie grasses and flowers along the roads. There are some on the Edens Expressway. The tallgrass prairie is reentering public consciousness.

If it hasn't entered yours yet, I should explain that prairie is the French word for meadow. The French were the first Europeans to see the grasslands of Illinois, and they named this new thing after something familiar.

The grasslands of the North American interior began developing in the Eocene epoch about 50 million years ago after the Rocky Mountains arose in the west and threw a rain shadow across the heart of North America. With brief interruptions by glaciers, the prairie has been here ever since. With all that time to develop, the tallgrass prairie became a complex system of about 300 different plants and thousands of species of insects, mites, spiders, nematodes, birds, mammals, reptiles, and amphibians.

Periodic fires became part of the regular cycle of prairie life. The blazes burned away the dead plants from previous years, releasing nutrients into the soil, and also preventing trees from invading the grasslands.

The Illinois prairie was doomed as soon as settlers learned to plow it. The tallgrass prairie became the Corn Belt. The few unplowed prairies were invaded by alien weeds accidentally carried from Europe.

Prairie restorations are attempts to rebuild an ecosystem. The techniques are essentially agricultural. Gather the seed, clear the ground, plant, and then wait and hope. Ordinary farmers have the advantage of dealing with a small number of familiar domestic crops. Restorers are learning, by trial and error, to deal with the idiosyncrasies of a couple hundred wild plants, species that have never been broken to the regular rhythms of the husbandman.

My first class at the workshop had no apparent connection with prairies. Steven Apfelbaum and Alan Haney have been studying the forests of the Boundary Waters Canoe Area in northern Minnesota with particular emphasis on the jack pine woods.

A jack pine woods, like a prairie, is a fire-adapted community. The difference lies mainly in how often fire strikes. A prairie may burn nearly every year. A jack pine woods burns, on the average, once every 75 to 100 years.

The fires can be quite destructive, killing all, or nearly all, of the trees and reducing the detritus on the forest floor to ash. The soil is suddenly more fertile, the minerals locked up in dead wood and old pine needles released by the fire. The brilliant purple fireweed and other wildflowers spring up on a sunny forest floor. Woodpeckers invade to live on the beetles and other insects that are eating the dead tree trunks. Flycatchers, birds that catch flying insects on short sallies from exposed perches, can see their prey better on the open land.

Plants and animals succeed each other in regular patterns as the new forest grows. Chestnut-sided warblers like a newly burned area. Moose come in somewhat later when the woody browse they like to eat has grown bigger.

So a jack pine woods recycles itself. It is reborn in fire, returned to infancy with all the possibilities of life before it.

Think of that cycle spread out over space rather than time and you have the landscape of the Boundary Waters, with small patches of land that burned last year next to other patches that burned five years ago and still others that haven't seen a fire since 1910. The mosaic of even-aged communities constantly creates opportunities for all plants and animals. Black-backed three-toed woodpeckers can find newly burned tree trunks, and Cape May warblers can find tall trees to hunt in.

A cycle this grand is possible only because the BWCA is a million-acre wilderness bordered on the north by a Canadian wilderness of similar size. You could not accomplish a cycle like this if the unbroken forest was shattered into a few small, widely scattered fragments separated by pavement and other hostile environments.

But the remains of the Illinois prairie consist of just such scattered fragments. So our problem is to sustain an ecosystem that has been knocked to pieces. The difficulties involved in that project were central to the message Ron Panzer delivered in a class entitled "Managing Prairies and Savannas for Insect Conservation."

Insects are essential to the life of the prairie, and they are very vulnerable. They must reproduce successfully every year or they will disappear. They are often tied to host plants, individual species essential as food and shelter for both larvae and adults. Often, for reasons still mysterious, you can find a particular bug living on only one clump of host plants in an entire prairie, even though there are many such clumps all looking equally inviting.

So what happens if a fire sweeps through that one essential clump of plants? The insects will be killed. When the prairie covered thousands of square miles in an unbroken sweep, this local destruction would make little difference. Insects from neighboring areas that had escaped the fire would recolonize the devastated portions of the land. But when the neighbors are fast-food restaurants or split-level houses, the destruction is likely to be permanent.

Panzer offered us some suggestions for avoiding local extinctions of species. We should burn sparingly, he said, and never burn the entire preserve at once. But the most important thing is to have big preserves where large populations can exist and provide a cushion against catastrophe.

Panzer was talking about insects on small prairie preserves, but his remarks are more broadly applicable. Wild plants and animals are increasingly confined to islands of wildness in a human landscape. The Boundary Waters Canoe Area is big enough to provide a mainland for most species, but timber wolves, animals whose hunting range may exceed 100 square miles, are islanded even in the BWCA. So are the grizzly bears in Montana and the elephants on the Serengeti Plain. The fate of most of the world's creatures now depends on our ability to learn how to keep them alive on islands.

Managing Nature
Restoring Balance .

October 9, 1987

I spent last Saturday afternoon at a natural-areas conference organized by the Illinois chapter of the Nature Conservancy and jointly sponsored by the Conservancy and several other public and private conservation groups.

The conference drew more than 100 participants to Moraine Valley Community College in Palos Hills. The goal was to round up interested people to expand the Volunteer Stewardship Network, a group that works in the six counties of northeastern Illinois on the problem of how to keep our natural areas natural. The main focus was on the many natural areas in southern Cook County and in neighboring Will and Grundy counties.

Steve Packard, a field representative for the Nature Conservancy and the man who started the stewardship network, opened the afternoon with a look back at the glories of presettlement Illinois, a review of the grim recent history of nature in our state, and a look at the sort of work stewards do to protect the tiny fragments of natural Illinois that remain.

Two panel discussions followed, one featuring representatives of the public agencies that own most of the areas, and the other featuring experienced volunteer stewards, people who have signed up to devote their free time to maintaining, or improving, a natural area.

If you haven't been involved in this kind of activity, it may seem odd that people have to work to keep natural areas natural. Shouldn't nature keep on being nature as long as we don't interfere? Won't things remain as they always have if we just keep the bulldozers out?

Unfortunately, the answer is no. In case you haven't noticed, the war between humanity and nature is over. The humans won. However, our victory celebration turned a bit sour when we realized that fighting a war with nature was like engaging in a duel to the death with your liver. Having achieved total victory, we can stave off total defeat only by reviving our old adversary, and thanks to our unremitting assaults, it is desperately in need of reviving.

You may remember being told back in grade school about something called the balance of nature. The idea is that all the triumphs and catastrophes enjoyed or suffered by individual bobolinks or sunflowers or monarch butterflies would balance each other, producing a grand harmony.

Keeping this harmony alive has been a major goal of American conservationists for as long as there have been any American conservationists. Go back to the beginning of the century and you see conservationists creating the National Forest system, the National Park Service, the Fish and Wildlife Service and its wildlife refuges, and, locally, the Cook County forest preserve system.

In 1964, we created the national wilderness system. And we have private organizations—the Nature Conservancy is the largest of them—with extensive systems of their own.

Until quite recently, most of the lands in these systems were indeed managed as if everything from bunny rabbits to grizzly bears would prosper as they always had if we just gave them the space. If any management was done, it was usually applied to a small number of species, a particularly valuable timber tree, or game animals—especially deer—that hunters wanted to catch.

Bitter experience has revealed that noninterference just won't work much of the time. Rare species unaccountably disappear from preserves set up specifically to protect them. Land that has been prairie for thousands of years becomes, in a few decades, a young forest. Marshes where black terns or American bitterns had probably nested since the recession of the glaciers are suddenly devoid of these birds.

When biologists began to investigate the reasons for these disappearances, they discovered that our sanctuaries were really not places of safety. They were, in fact, under constant assault from an army of enemies. Some of those enemies were easy to see and understand, but others were so subtle that we could only learn of their existence by recording the harm they did.

So biologists and interested amateurs have been devoting increasing attention to what is called restoration biology or restoration ecology, and Chicago, for a number of reasons, is a major center for this kind of work.

Restoration biology treats an entire ecosystem, rather than a particular species, as the unit to be managed. Keep the ecosystem healthy and the individual species will do just fine.

The toughest problem, the one we can only ameliorate and not solve, is a direct result of Columbus's discovery of America. People have been living in Illinois for thousands of years, but they used to be here in much smaller numbers and they used to depend on a technology that was much less obtrusive than our present high-energy, high-production methods. Humans used to live on islands in a sea of prairie, savanna, and woodland. Now we are the sea and nature the island. The grand harmony will not continue to sound unless we can figure out how to keep it tuned up.

Chicago's prominence in restoration biology is partly based on the unpleasant fact that the assault on nature had gone farther here than it had in most of the rest of the country. Nature in northern Illinois had vanished not just from the ground but from historic memory as well. Thirty years ago, even biologists didn't know what prairies really were.

Since then we have seen a modest comeback. Many unprotected natural areas were destroyed, but a number of new areas were brought into one preserve system or other. Most important, our native prairies and savannas enjoyed a revival in the minds of the people, a revival sufficient to bring these 100 people out on a pleasant Saturday afternoon to hear what they might do to sustain and restore the native landscape.

The goals of their work would be very high indeed. Ecosystems are the most complex entities on earth, perhaps the most complex entities in the universe. Stewards are operating at the frontiers of human knowledge, just like high-energy physicists with their accelerators and astronomers with their radio telescopes.

Of course, the nice irony here is that the stewards are not working with expensive supertech toys but with shovels and scythes and lopping shears and handsaws. Those are the kinds of machines that we use to carry on this probe into places that no human has gone before. This highly intellectual enterprise is advanced mainly by manual labor.

As the stewards panel made clear, volunteers spend a good deal of time checking to see if vandals have torn a hole in the fence or ripped down the signs identifying the preserve. Garbage collection is always a major priority. We may have lost our lead in electronics to the Japanese, the Germans may make better cars, but we still lead the world in the production of garbage.

And then there is brush cutting. Our weakened little islands are all vulnerable to invasion, particularly by the pestiferous alien shrub called European buckthorn. My guess would be that cutting buckthorn consumes more hours than all the rest of a steward's tasks combined.

The rewards for all this stoop labor are slow in coming. You may have to wait three years or more for any visible change in the landscape of your preserve. But when it comes, it is wonderful. Steve showed us slides of Bluff Spring Fen near Elgin. Fens are very rare in this part of the world, and they support a distinctive flora, including plants that grow in no other kind of situation. Eight species of plants that live at Bluff Spring Fen are on the endangered or threatened list in Illinois.

A few years ago, Bluff Spring Fen was a dump. Dirt bikes and four-wheel-drive vehicles were gouging trenches where nothing grew. Abandoned cars littered the ground and brush was shading out the rare plants. Today, after thousands of hours of volunteer labor, it is a jewel, as it should be. And the people who did all that work have to feel that it was all worth it.

Too Many Deer

Eating Plants to Extinction

January 3, 1992

Busse Woods was among the first natural areas to be set aside as an Illinois nature preserve. The 440-acre hardwood forest, which is part of the Ned Brown Forest Preserve in Elk Grove Village, was also cited in the early '60s by the federal government as a uniquely diverse remnant of the native landscape. Only one other place in Illinois—Volo Bog—has received such recognition.

Busse Woods was famous for its spring wildflower display. In May the ground was carpeted with Dutchman's-breeches, spring beauty, red trillium, and large-flowered trillium. Rare orchids such as purple twayblade and the purple-fringed orchid added their delicate beauty to the scene. But by the late '70s the richness of this display was declining rapidly. The cause was an overabundance of white-tailed deer, which were eating many kinds of plants to extinction.

In 1983 scientists from the Illinois Natural History Survey began a systematic study of the effects of heavy deer populations on Busse Woods. At the same time they began removing deer from the preserve in an attempt to bring the population down to a level that would be within the carrying capacity of the land. Some of the deer were transported to new homes near Joliet, but most were killed with shotguns or netted and then killed by lethal injection.

A survey of the plants of Busse Woods conducted in 1983 revealed that 26 species that had grown there in the early '60s had disappeared. The famous spring wildflower display was almost completely gone. But now, after eight years of deer population control, there are some encouraging signs of regeneration. Dutchman's-breeches were rediscovered last year, and large-flowered trillium—which had hung on here and there in the shelter of downed logs—is appearing again out in the open.

But, according to Chris Anchor, a wildlife biologist with the Cook County Forest Preserve District, "regeneration has been painfully slow. The deer abundance continued for so many years that many plants were extirpated." The wildflowers of a woodland spring are perennials. Each year a bulb or other underground structure sends up new green shoots and new flowers. The bulbs live for many years, and they can survive a few years of having their leaves clipped by browsing deer. But if the clipping continues for six or eight years, the bulbs die.

The sad story of Busse Woods is unfortunately being repeated at other preserves throughout the area. The Lake County Forest Preserve District has had to set up a deer-control program to protect the biological diversity of the Ryerson Preserve, the magnificent old-growth forest on the Des Plaines River near Deerfield. This winter the Cook County Forest Preserve District will be taking similar actions in its portion of the Des Plaines River valley and in the Palos preserves around Camp Sagawau.

Just a few decades ago the spring wildflower display around the River Trails Nature Center, which is along the Des Plaines River between Lake Avenue and Willow Road, was as fine as anything at Ryerson. But then came the boom in deer numbers. They started on the trilliums, and when those were gone they switched to plants such as false Solomon's seal, which deer avoid unless they are very hungry.

The spring display at River Trails is now nothing but a few trout lilies and spring beauties. The situation elsewhere along the river is even worse. Around Dam Number One at the northern edge of Cook County, according to Chris Anchor, nothing grows in the forest understory except garlic mustard, buckthorn, and white vervain. The first two of these are aliens, the last is a native—but all three are regarded by deer as extremely unpalatable.

So over the next few months sharpshooters licensed by the Illinois Department of Conservation will be working along the Des Plaines and in Palos to reduce the deer populations. Nets will also be used, and the deer captured in the nets will be killed using methods approved by the American Veterinary Association.

A fundamental question for all those involved in controlling the deer herd is how many deer are enough? The answer needs to be tailored to the individual site. A good healthy woodland can support about 18 deer per square mile. In the Des Plaines River valley, where years of heavy deer browsing have seriously degraded the woods, five to seven animals per square mile would be an appropriate density. The preserves around Crabtree Nature Center near Barrington could sustain as many as 25 to 30 animals per square mile because there are still cornfields in the area to supply food.

Other portions of the Cook County forest preserve system will soon need deer-control measures too, including the preserves along the North Branch of the Chicago River. These preserves have received a lot of attention in recent years as volunteers from the North Branch Prairie Project have worked to restore the native prairie and savanna vegetation. Now increasing evidence shows that heavy deer populations are undercutting our efforts to increase the biological diversity of the preserves.

I spend a lot of time at Somme Woods, the northernmost of the North Branch preserves, studying the nesting birds, and my unscientific impression is that there are a hell of a lot of deer around. I have seen as many as 11 animals in a one-hour stroll around the 60 or 70 acres that lie between Waukegan Road and the Milwaukee Road railroad tracks. I am very cautious in counting the animals I see, since it is easy to flush the same deer more than once, so that figure of 11 could be too low.

The best scientific estimate, derived from an aerial census, shows that Somme Woods is currently home to about 54 deer per square mile, three times the ideal figure of 18 per square mile.

All those hungry animals are having a noticeable effect on the vegetation. Steve Packard of the Nature Conservancy offered me a litany of distressing details when I asked him for some specifics on what the deer have eaten.

Among the rarities sheltered at Somme were two milkweeds. One of these has disappeared completely; the other, which is not known to grow anywhere else in the state, is dwindling. An annual called maple-leaved goosefoot that grew under the oaks of the savanna has vanished completely. There may still be seeds in the ground that will sprout next year, but we don't know if this one will come back. Of course if it does grow next year, the deer will probably eat it again.

The cream gentian, a lovely savanna wildflower, grew at Somme in great abundance a few years ago. The plants are still there, but they have set no seed in the past few years because the deer eat the tops and prevent them from setting seed. The small white lady's slipper is an endangered orchid that was moved into Somme Woods from a site in Buffalo Grove that was about to be bulldozed. It did well initially, but now its numbers are declining.

The Canada milk vetch, a rare legume, is being eaten right down to the roots. Established plots that are censused every year are showing consistent drops in species such as woodland joe-pye weed, bottlebrush grass, and cow parsnip, all of which were planted in the Somme savanna as part of the restoration work. Places that used to support large numbers of trilliums and woodland phlox are now completely devoid of these spring flowers.

Chris Anchor says that at this point he does not have enough hard empirical data about Somme to support an application to the state to carry out a deer-control program. The hope is that enough such information can be gathered this year to make deer control possible next winter. Packard points out that there is good reason to concentrate efforts in places where the damage is not yet major. It may be too late along the Des Plaines, but moving quickly on the North Branch may deal with the problem before species have been extirpated.

We can expect deer-control measures to be a part of forest-preserve management for years to come. Deer herds all over the Midwest are at historic highs. Mild winters, the absence of predators, and low levels of disease and parasites are all contributing to this abundance.

Busse Woods is also showing us that controlling deer numbers can work. In addition to the return of some of the woodland plants, reduced numbers are producing larger, healthier deer. The whole ecosystem is benefiting from the control of the whitetails.

Middle Fork Savanna
What's Wrong with Brush?

July 9, 1993

Middle Fork Savanna is an image, a 550-acre miniature of northeastern Illinois as it looked in 1800. The image is blurred and distorted by alien plants and animals and by railroad embankments and drainage tiles, but we can still catch a glimpse of what Illinois was before the Potawatomi were thrown out.

The Middle Fork is in Lake County just west of Lake Forest. It occupies a strip of land split into eastern and western halves by a busy rail line that carries Metra, Amtrak, and assorted freight trains. The Tri-State Tollway is immediately west of the savanna and Waukegan Road is a short distance east. Illinois Route 60 forms the southern boundary, and a little hamlet called Rondout sits at the northern end. Rondout has body shops and landscaping outfits, places essential to the maintenance of Lake Forest but too gritty to locate there.

The middle fork of the North Branch of the Chicago River flows through the savanna. It has been channelized, and its local name is the Skokie Ditch. Turning the savanna into a protected preserve has been a joint project of the Lake County Forest Preserve District, Lake Forest Open Lands, and the Nature Conservancy, which for fairly obvious reasons chose to call the place Middle Fork rather than Skokie Ditch Savanna.

The preserve is a very diverse place, with four distinct habitat types within its boundaries. Lovely old oak groves are mixed with marshes. Along the eastern side is an extensive grassland that was a cow pasture until recently. And on the western side of the tracks is a combination of grasses, wildflowers, and low shrubs—the sort of place early settlers called a "brushy prairie."

I've spent several mornings over the past two months wandering through the Middle Fork trying to put together an inclusive list of the nesting birds that live there. I had originally planned to spend nearly every morning in June there, but the weather got in the way.

The weather also produced a mosquito crop that is easily the equal of Upper Peninsula levels. Since bird surveys require that one stand still for long stretches of time, I have taken to wearing a head net to keep the bugs away. The net—which, as it happens, I bought in a hardware store in da U.P.—makes me feel like I'm wearing the Tarnhelm, a wondrous helmet crafted by Mime for Alberich and eventually used by Siegfried, that had the power to make you invisible to your enemies. I am not literally invisible, but the bugs are kept far enough from me that they can't even annoy me by buzzing in my ears. Repellents keep the bugs from biting, but they don't keep them away. I also have tried to stay away from chemicals ever since the morning when a heavy application of deet—the active ingredient in most repellents—dissolved the plastic earpieces on my glasses.

But I digress. What I have found at Middle Fork is a highly diverse bird population. Each of the habitat types has its own distinctive community. One of those—the group of birds associated with the brushy prairie—raises some interesting questions about the way we have been managing our prairie remnants and restorations.

All but one of the oak groves at Middle Fork has a dense understory of the nasty alien shrub called European buckthorn. Buckthorn was originally introduced to this area as an ornamental. It escaped from cultivation, carried by birds that ate its fruits and defecated the seeds. It is now a major pest in all our forest preserves.

Savanna groves were once open places. The understory was grasses and such low shrubs as gray dogwood and brambles. A dense canopy of buckthorn—which typically grows 10 to 12 feet high—shades out all those native plants. The resulting environment does seem to benefit some forest birds. The buckthorn-infested groves at Middle Fork have wood thrushes and ovenbirds, species that depend on tall shrubs for nesting or for singing perches. I also have one record each for our two local species of cuckoos—the black-billed and the yellow-billed—and both are from groves with buckthorn. Our only singing male veery—a threatened species in Illinois—is also in a buckthorn grove.

The one grove that has been cleared of buckthorn and burned has a quite different character. Yellow warblers live in that grove, along with yellowthroats and indigo buntings. These are usually thought of as edge species, but they seem to be doing well in the interior of an oak grove with a ground layer of low shrubs mixed with grasses.

Up in the canopies of both the buckthorn groves and the nonbuckthorn groves, I find blue-gray gnatcatchers, wood pewees, great crested flycatchers, white-breasted nuthatches, and northern orioles. I have some evidence of nesting by a pair of Cooper's hawks, an endangered species that probably used to live in the presettlement savannas. But the grove where the hawks were is also the place where I keep seeing a great horned owl. Great horned owls do not like competition, and that grove was probably not big enough for both species.

Up until this year I had been working on a nesting survey at Somme Woods in Northbrook. Somme is a much smaller preserve—150 acres compared to 550—but it contains habitats similar to those at Middle Fork. Many nesting species are common to both places. But Somme has been the object of major restoration work over the past 15 years. Part of that work has involved girdling trees. You girdle trees by removing the bark in a strip a few inches wide all the way around the trunk. Girdling kills the trees, but it leaves the trunks standing.

Numerous birds use holes in standing dead trees as nesting sites. Woodpeckers dig them or natural processes of decay create them, and a variety of species move in. Somme's 150 acres have many more of such hole nesters as flickers, downy woodpeckers, black-capped chickadees, and house wrens than the 550 acres at Middle Fork.

The old pasture at Middle Fork has nice numbers of some prairie species. Bobolinks and eastern meadowlarks are there, and a few savanna sparrows. The marshes have green-backed herons, yellowthroats, swamp sparrows, and redwings.

Perhaps the most intriguing habitat at Middle Fork is the brushy prairie. The minds of those who manage prairie remnants or direct restoration efforts have been dominated by a vision of the prairie as a place with no wood. It's all grasses and wildflowers that die back to the roots in fall. Fires sweep over it regularly and prevent woody plants from ever taking hold. A prairie manager looking at the brushy areas at Middle Fork would almost certainly be thinking about using a combination of lopping shears and frequent fires to clear out those gray dogwood clumps. Give us a few years, he would say, and we'll have this looking like a proper prairie.

Buckthorn has inspired much of this kind of thinking. It is a nasty pest that has to be cleared out, and a sort of guilt-by-association process has made native shrubs—dogwoods, hawthorns, sumac, and others— into villains too.

But Middle Fork has me suspecting that proper prairies can have a substantial number of woody plants. Gray dogwood, by far the most common woody species there, grows in dense clumps that shade out any grasses that might provide fuel for a fire. When fire strikes, a few stems on the windward side of the clump get burned, but everything in the lee of that first rank survives. And the roots of the burned stems are unharmed so they can send up new shoots. Hawthorns, cherries, and even small oaks take advantage of that sheltered environment and grow right out of the middle of the dogwood clumps.

Bobolinks, meadowlarks, savanna sparrows, grasshopper sparrows, and Henslow's sparrows live in prairies where there is little or no wood. The brushy prairies support a completely different community. Put a patch of brush in the middle of a prairie and you will probably see yellow warblers, song sparrows, field sparrows, blue-winged warblers, willow flycatchers, catbirds, and yellowthroats moving in. Cedar waxwings will build their nests in the small trees in the middle of the dogwood clumps. Indigo buntings like the dogwoods as nesting sites, but they need some tall trees as singing perches. At Middle Fork, they nest in the brushy prairie near the tracks. The males sing from the power lines that parallel the railroad. In southern Cook County this kind of habitat would also be the place to look for Bell's vireo and the yellow-breasted chat.

Restoration and natural-areas management are applied ecology, and what makes them endlessly interesting is that there is always more to learn. It may be that a brushy prairie is not a degenerate form of the grassy prairie but an authentic community in its own right.

Biodiversity

Why Preserve Natural Variety?

February 22, 1991

What are muskrats worth? This is a complicated question. We can easily calculate their value as furs. About ten million muskrats are trapped every year in North America. Pelts bring an average of between three and four dollars each, so we could declare the value of muskrats to be between $30 million and $40 million a year.

Of course the pelts are only the beginning of the process. Individual pelts combined into coats are worth much more than raw furs. In their finished form, muskrat furs support manufacturers, wholesalers, retailers, and cleaners, whose combined contribution to the GNP is doubtless well over $100 million a year.

Live muskrats also have some value as experiences for humans. It is exciting to stand at the edge of a marsh or to paddle a canoe through shallow water and spot the head of a swimming muskrat just breaking the surface. Bureaucrats calculating the costs and benefits of major development projects try to turn that experience into dollars and cents. They survey citizens, asking them how much they would pay to see a muskrat, or, as a sort of semiterrorist alternative, how much they would pay to avoid the extinction of muskrats.

But any direct value to humans is only a small part of the total worth of muskrats. What about their ecological value? Muskrats are major actors in marsh ecosystems. They are food for bald eagles and minks. They eat huge amounts of cattails and other emergent vegetation, which helps prevent these plants from covering the entire marsh and produces areas of open water for mallards and blue-winged teal. They also build their low-domed houses of cattails in the water far from shore, providing protected nesting sites for black terns.

And muskrats make a more general ecological contribution, one they share with every species of plant and animal no matter how rare: they contribute to the biological diversity of their native ecosystem. Their presence puts competitive pressure on plants, on other plant-eating animals, and on the predators that hunt them. For example, many plants have evolved chemical defenses against herbivores. Muskrats might selectively feed on plants without defenses while leaving those with chemical weapons alone. In time these feeding habits could create whole populations with effective chemical protection. Other plant eaters might also be pressured into more selective feeding in order to escape competition with the gnawing incisors of muskrats.

The individual species in ecosystems with high levels of diversity are crowded ecologically. They constantly face competition, dangerous predators, and elusive prey. Crowding fuels the processes of evolution by promoting specialization that can lead to speciation as plants and animals seek secure niches. A high level of biological diversity creates an upward spiral as diversity produces even more diversity.

Do muskrats have some further value beyond their use to humans and beyond their various roles as constituents of an ecosystem? Is there some essence of muskratitude that gives them an intrinsic value, the sort of value we accord to human beings?

Questions like these are the focus of *Why Preserve Natural Variety?* by Bryan G. Norton (Princeton University Press). Norton is a professor of philosophy at Georgia Tech, and his book is a philosophical inquiry, not a scientific tract. It is a critique of various rationales for the protection of natural systems, with emphasis on the protection of rare and endangered species, and it offers Norton's thoughts on why the protection of nature is necessary. His arguments are complex, but his goal is to provide a basis for making public policy on the protection of nature.

He begins by distinguishing anthropocentric and nonanthropocentric arguments. Should we endeavor to save endangered species because their preservation will benefit us in some way, or should we save them because they have a value of their own completely separate from us and our wishes?

The benefits we derive from nature have to be looked at broadly. We can save natural things because we think they are pretty or because we can make fur coats from their hides. We can save them because experiencing wild places and wild creatures can transform us, change the way we think about our lives and our place in the world.

We can save them because natural diversity is essential to the functioning of ecosystems, and our lives—however much technology may insulate us from nature—depend on the functioning of natural systems. Diversity promotes diversity and simplicity promotes even more simplicity. When a species is removed from an ecosystem its absence ripples through the entire system.

We have some excellent local examples of how this works. With the native large predators removed from our forest preserves, deer populations boom. The hungry deer denude the forest floor, and so the absence of timber wolves eventually eliminates trilliums and other woodland wildflowers from the system. When the wildflowers go, the insects they support go too. The absence of the insects, combined with the physical changes in the forest-floor environment created by large deer populations, may wipe out wood thrushes, veeries, and ovenbirds, all insect eaters that feed on the forest floor. Plants eaten while they are young and green never have a chance to set seed. Seed eaters such as chipmunks may suffer, and with them owls and weasels, predators that feed on the seed eaters.

Ecosystems are so complex that we have no way of predicting how the removal of a single species will affect the rest of the system. It could cause a total collapse. The continuing loss of species poses what Norton calls a zero-infinity risk, the same sort of problem we face with nuclear reactors. Reactors may operate with perfect safety for years, but if one does melt down, the effects will be catastrophic. So we may take species from a system with little apparent effect, until we take one too many and disaster follows.

The effects of species removal may not be apparent for a long time. Norton points out that the mass extinction that ended the reign of the dinosaurs may have begun with a single event, the impact of an asteroid on the earth. But it took 40,000 years, the blink of an eye in geological terms but a very long time in human terms, for the effects of the collision to work their way through living systems.

An ecological view of life and our place in it, Norton writes, recognizes that humans are evolved animals and that evolution, the process that created us, "works within almost unbelievably complex and interrelated organic systems." Our awareness of that complexity should lead us to approach nature with humility and to seek harmony with it. "It is good, in this view," Norton writes, "to do things in a way that mimics nature's pattern; it is good to promote the natural processes that . . . produce greater diversity; it is good to introduce alterations slowly enough to allow nature to react."

Of course, some believe that we should protect other living things because they have the same intrinsic worth we do. They should be considered ethically as ends in themselves just as we are.

Norton sees two problems with this view. First, why are other creatures the same as us? Some animal-rights believers say it is because animals can feel pain and pleasure just as we do. This formulation leaves plants out of the ethical picture, even though they certainly can't be left out of ecosystems. Second, humans have rights as individuals. If other living things have the same rights, they must be treated as individuals and not as members of species. And then we cannot, for example, legitimately kill cowbirds to prevent them from parasitizing the endangered Kirtland's warbler, for cowbirds have as much right to live as Kirtland's warblers do. The animal-rights approach protects individual animals, but it provides no basis for protecting the ecosystems that sustain all life.

Ultimately, Norton's answer to our preservation problems is simple: We protect species by protecting habitats. Rather than compiling a list of endangered species and then working out protection plans on a species-by-species basis, we should seek to protect the full range of habitats within regions. In Illinois we would look to protect examples of the full range of prairie types, from the dry sandhill prairies to wet prairies. We would protect wetland types such as marshes and bottomland forests. We would protect oak savannas and, in the south, large blocks of forest.

Of course things are so bad in Illinois that we will have to create some of these places before we protect them. But if we can, by preservation and restoration, protect adequate acreage of all these habitat types, our multitudinous endangered species will no longer be in danger.

Transanimaling

Placing New Species in Nature Preserves

June 26, 1992

The Illinois Nature Preserves Commission, for only the third time in nearly 30 years of existence, has given its approval to the introduction of a new species into one of its preserves. So if Doug Taron can find a few caterpillars, a moth called *Papaipema cerina* will be released in the Bluff Spring Fen Nature Preserve near Elgin this September.

The commission's approval of this exercise in transplanting animals—you might say transanimaling—is in some ways a departure from previous policy and in other ways a continuation, or expansion, or older ideas. The issues raised by *Papaipema* illustrate many of the problems we face in our attempts to retain some vestiges of our native natural landscape in a state where humans are continually reshaping the land.

When the Illinois nature preserve system was created in 1963, the goal was to discover and preserve the natural gems that remained after a century and a half of wholesale destruction. Scientists scoured the state looking for prairies, wetlands, savannas, forests, and other communities that could reasonably be considered unchanged since settlement began in the early 19th century.

Not surprisingly, these places were all small. Of the 99 preserves created in the first 20 years of the system's existence, only four had more than 1,000 acres and half had fewer than 100. For the most part they were selected because of the presence of "conservative" species of plants, species that would be expected to vanish if their community was hit with a disturbance they weren't accustomed to. Because of their greater mobility, animals, especially vertebrates, are seldom thought of as good indicators of natural quality. So a prairie remnant with a high level of diversity and a good population of white-fringed orchid or a rich woodland with a population of nodding trillium would be considered for inclusion in the nature preserve system, while a field of bluegrass and Queen Anne's lace would not, even if that weedy field supported endangered upland sandpipers or Henslow's sparrows.

The Nature Preserves Commission has generally taken a very conservative approach to the management of its lands, and it is easy to see why. Managing tiny parcels of land containing the last remnants of natural Illinois is an awesome responsibility. There is no room for mistakes on a 20-acre prairie. The wrong move could doom the very things you are trying to save.

Dr. Brian Anderson, director of the nature preserve system, sees avoiding introductions as part of carrying out the goal of preserving presettlement communities. "We don't want species pollution," he told me, "so we don't do species loading."

Behind these phrases is the idea that the plants and animals that should be in a high-quality natural area are already there, and we shouldn't add a species just because it can be found in a similar community elsewhere. Preserves are often thought of as arks, and there is a tendency to want to load them up the way Noah loaded his. However, Noah's ark was designed for 40 days and 40 nights. You couldn't expect all those animals to live there forever.

About 15 years ago, the commission approved the introduction of Franklin's ground squirrels in the Gensburg-Markham Prairie in Markham, but that is the only instance of a species being allowed into a high-quality community thought to be in presettlement condition.

The one other instance of transplantation was at Bluff Spring Fen in 1990 when the entire Healy Road Prairie was moved into the preserve. Healy Road was a gravel-hill prairie that was about to be obliterated by its owner. As it happens, a portion of Bluff Spring Fen was a gravel hill whose natural cover had been destroyed, so the move seemed reasonable. Large numbers of free-flying insects, captured in nets, were moved at the same time.

Papaipema cerina is such an obscure little creature that nobody can be sure whether or not it is rare. Entomologists usually catch moths by setting up a black light in the evening. The light lures the moths into a trap whence they can be removed and studied. There is evidence that *Papaipema* are not attracted to black lights, so population surveys could miss them completely even if they were quite common.

The caterpillars live inside the stems of their host plants, so it is impossible to locate them by sight. To discover a caterpillar you have to look for a host plant that appears to be in a weakened and wilted state. You then carefully cut a slit in the stem and see if the larva is inside.

The caterpillars require at least two different host plants to complete their growth. They begin on *Hystrix patula,* commonly known as bottle-brush grass, and they continue on *Podophyllum peltatum,* mayapple. They may also use other plants as hosts, but these two seem to be the essential ones.

Obviously, *Papaipema* can live only where these two plants occur together. Mayapples are prominent in almost any forest or oak savanna in northern Illinois. They grow in dense clusters that are actually clones. The large number of stems arises from a single interconnected root system. Bottlebrush grass is much less common. It was a major component of oak savanna communities, but there are practically none of those left.

The only known Illinois population of *Papaipema*—until last year—was at the Nachusa Grasslands, a preserve owned by the Nature Conservancy near Dixon. Ron Panzer of Northeastern Illinois University, *the* authority on matters lepidopteran in northern Illinois, found it there. Then in 1991 Doug Taron, a volunteer with the conservancy's steward-ship network, slit open some feeble-looking mayapples on a remnant savanna in Elgin and found some mysterious caterpillars in the stem. He took them home and successfully reared them to adulthood inside carrots that he sliced open to make room for them. Once he had the adults—about two inches wing tip to wing tip and yellow with brown markings—he was able to identify them.

This year he discovered that the Elgin savanna is about to be developed. When the bulldozers scrape away the mayapples and bottlebrush grass, the moths will go with them. Hence the application to the Nature Preserves Commission for permission to transplant them to the Bluff Spring Fen Nature Preserve, where Taron is costeward.

Steve Packard of the Nature Conservancy praised the Nature Preserves Commission for acting quickly on the request. "They did a difficult thing in approving something that hadn't been studied to death first."

But Anderson says that the approval depended on the fact that the moths will be moved into a community that is in the process of restoration and not into a part of the preserve that contains a pristine presettlement community. "The two food plants occur in a degraded community at Bluff Spring," he says, "so this was consistent with current policy. And we decided it was worth taking a chance, since the alternative was to risk losing half the known population."

Packard is pushing for the creation of "landscape-scale restorations," where reintroductions could be done as a matter of course. "The tiny, gemlike preserves are too small for ecological processes to occur in them. We need to have some preserved land where everything that used to be there—even potentially—has a chance to be part of the mix.

"Conservation biology is a new scientific discipline with a strong element of urgency. It is more important to save than to understand. If we can only save what we understand, we will have impoverished systems. If we can save it, we can study it later."

For Anderson, the buffer zones that are being established around the gems in the nature preserve system can provide the opportunities for reintroduction. The buffers can be managed with restoration in mind to push them in the direction of the pristine community the buffer zone protects. Meanwhile, they can provide a refuge for rare species without creating species pollution in the pristine communities.

Right now the biggest obstacle in the way of the introduction of *Papaipema* is the lack of larvae. Doug Taron has been searching, but the drought of the past two months has slowed the growth of everything. So far he has found no bottlebrush grasses or mayapples with the stricken look that indicates the presence of a caterpillar in the stem. If he does find some, and can successfully raise them at home, they will emerge from their cocoons in mid-September. He will release the adults at Bluff Spring Fen, where they will mate. Then the females will locate bottlebrush grass and lay their eggs in leaf litter near the stems.

The eggs will either lie there all winter before hatching in the spring or they will hatch and the tiny caterpillars will spend the winter on the ground. So obscure is the *Papaipema* that nobody knows for sure which of these things will happen.

[According to Doug Taron, *Papaipema cerina* is still alive and well at Bluff Spring Fen.]

Prairie September

The Best Time of the Year

September 25, 1998

September is the kindest month. A month when electric bills are going down and gas bills have not yet begun to go up. A month when mosquitoes are dying off but butterflies are still with us. A time when migrant songbirds enliven every backyard and parkway and the last flowers of summer are in full and glorious bloom.

Prairies are showy now, and the richer Illinois woodlands are just as spectacular. Flowers and butterflies will not be with us much longer; now is the time to see them.

I spent a few hours recently walking the trails through Poplar Creek prairie. It was a sunny morning, and a cool breeze from the northwest rustled the tall grasses. They are all in flower now, golden yellow anthers releasing pollen to the wind. They are also truly tall now, with flowering heads more than six feet high. At one point I had to push aside the stalks of big bluestem crowding in from each side of the narrow path. This is a real Illinois experience, pushing your way through grasses higher than your head. It is an experience hard to come by in the contemporary Prairie State.

Migrating monarch butterflies accompanied me on my walk, flitting from goldenrod to sunflower in search of nectar. Yellow is the dominant color of the prairie flowers in this season, although a few rough blazing stars were around to provide a purple accent.

The bobolinks that nest on the prairie have already left for Argentina, but a few savanna sparrows and eastern meadowlarks were still around. A red-tailed hawk perched on a tall snag in the patch of trees at the north edge of the prairie. As the day warmed and the thermals started rising, the hawk soared over the prairie. He was joined by three turkey vultures, birds whose six-foot wingspans made the red-tail look tiny.

The vultures nest at the Max McGraw Wildlife Foundation near Elgin. Turkey vultures were long absent from Cook County, but within the past ten years they have returned. In addition to the McGraw birds, there are two or more pairs in the Palos preserves. It would be interesting to know what they are eating, or more precisely, where they are finding the dead bodies they are eating. Roads are the obvious places to look for dead animals in this area, but roads are heavily populated by large metal objects moving at speeds in excess of 60 miles an hour. A careless scavenger feeding on roadkill stands a good chance of becoming roadkill.

Crows can handle this dangerous job, but compared to crows vultures are clumsy and slow. They also don't like roads running through deep woods, where overhanging limbs might block their escape. Our resurgent vultures must be finding enough to eat on open ground away from roads.

The Poplar Creek prairie restoration began in 1989. The land selected for the project had been either cropland or pasture for almost a century and a half. A handful of prairie plants hung on along old fence lines, but the ground was dominated by Eurasian plants. Weedy as it was, the grassland was big enough—close to 150 acres—to support populations of prairie birds. Most prairie restorations have been small, and nearly all of our surviving prairie remnants are also small. You can't have an ecosystem on a scattered collection of postage-stamp refuges. Poplar Creek was among the few restorations that could operate on a landscape scale, with self-sustaining populations of both plants and animals.

In 1989 a farmer hired for the job plowed and disked a series of 16 strips in the old fields at Poplar Creek. The strips were 18 feet wide and 40 feet apart, and they curved in sinuous arcs across the landscape. Laid end to end, they would stretch five and a half miles.

In spring 1990 the strips were disked again before being seeded with a mix of prairie species with a heavy emphasis on grasses. Since 1990 the areas between the strips have been sown with prairie species with a heavy emphasis on wildflowers.

In September you can stand on the slope of the hill that rises at the northern edge of the prairie and plainly see the plowed strips. They are marked by the russet and gold of the prairie grasses. I am hoping to live long enough to see the strips and the unplowed land between them blend into a rich mixture of prairie plants.

In September the woods at Cap Sauers Holdings in the Palos area are alive with elm-leaved goldenrod, snakeroot, and joe-pye weed. I took a hike on the Visitation Esker, a lovely glacial feature deposited, according to some authorities, during the last advance of the Wisconsin glaciation into northeastern Illinois. Others date it much earlier.

Eskers are meandering ridges built of deposits left by streams flowing

under the ice. The flow of the water is usually not heavy enough or fast enough to carry sand and gravel, so these particles dropped out to form the esker. Few eskers survive, because mining them for sand and gravel can be very profitable.

The Visitation Esker was mined at its northern end, but the rest of it supports a lovely oak woodland bordered by marshes in the low spots along the ridge. A path winds along the crest of the ridge, and the woods are open enough to provide good views to either side. From the southern end of the esker the path climbs onto the high moraine through a grove of stately oaks before entering a small prairie. This prairie is one of the loveliest spots in the state of Illinois. It is one of the few places in Cook County where you can escape traffic noise, and if you catch the flight patterns at Midway and O'Hare just right you may not hear any airplanes.

When I visited, the prairie was rich with prairie dock, showy goldenrod, and Jerusalem artichoke. Small bur oaks and black oaks, hardy survivors of prairie fires, were scattered over the land. A turkey vulture, one of the Palos nesters, soared in the cloudless blue sky.

This has been a good year for big birds in the Palos area. The turkey vultures are increasing their numbers, and the ospreys successfully fledged three young. These fish-eating hawks nested near Bergman Slough in a snag—a standing dead tree—that toppled soon after the birds abandoned their nest. An osprey nest is a huge construction of sticks that might weigh several hundred pounds, so it is not surprising that the tree could not support it indefinitely.

The three fledglings are the first known osprey young produced in the country since 1855. Plans are now under way to provide nesting plat-forms for these spectacular birds next year. The Palos preserves are large enough and contain enough open water to support two or three pairs of ospreys.

This year also brought confirmation of nesting by sandhill cranes at Cranberry Slough Nature Preserve in the Palos area. Confirmation came in the form of a face-to-face meeting between Dennis Nyberg, the volun-teer steward at Cranberry Slough, and a three-foot, flightless baby sand-hill.

Entering the prairie at the crest of the moraine, I followed a path downhill into an oak woodland rich in late-season wildflowers. An in-termittent stream flows—when it is flowing—northward through the woods. Before large-scale settlement, watercourses like this one played a major role in shaping the landscape. They provided fire protection for areas in their lee and a humid environment for species that could not survive in the drier uplands.

Along this watercourse I found a lovely example of the shaping influ-ence of the stream. Within a meander bend where the stream provided fire protection to the south, west, and north grew the only sugar maples in the woods. They were big trees. They survived years of wildfires, and since 1981 they have survived prescribed burns deliberately set to main-tain the health of the woods.

If you put a stop to fires in these woods, they lose their connection with the land. In this particular woods the sugar maples would probably spread from the meander bend and eventually displace the oaks as the major trees. The small variations in the landscape that support small variations in vegetation would lose their distinctive qualities. The swamp white oaks growing in the scattered low, wet places would be re-placed by yet more sugar maples. The small openings in the woods where the clusters of tickseed sunflowers seem to turn the air golden would close in. The great spangled fritillary butterflies that accompa-nied me on my walk would find nothing to feed on. The variety that de-lights our eyes and ears on a sunny September day would be gone.

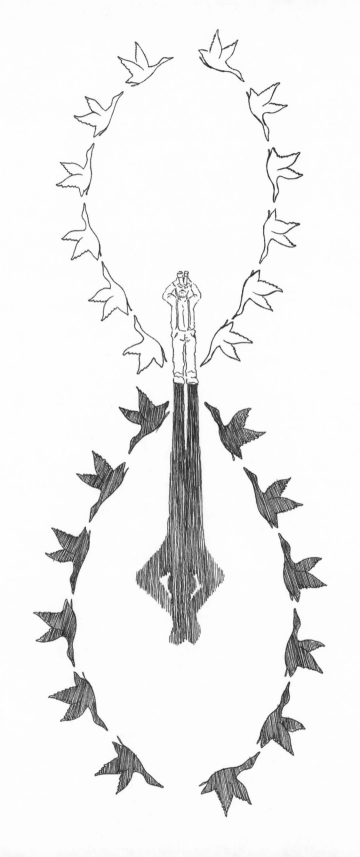

2 › The Seasons

Spring Comes to Chicago

It Seems to Take Forever

February 24, 1995

Spring has begun to push winter aside, although the signs are still very obscure. Two weeks ago, when the windchill hit 40 below, a few northern harriers passed through on their early migration, and an early canvasback duck was sighted at the Chicago Botanic Garden.

Birds we think of as typical winter species—northern shrikes, rough-legged hawks, snowy owls—also seem to show up in greater numbers now, perhaps because they have begun their northern movement, and birds in migration tend to be more visible than sedentary ones.

The earliest spring migrants fall into two groups: open-country birds and water birds. Harriers and rough-legged hawks both hunt by flying low over open ground. Treeless land loses its snow cover before forested land, so these hunters can move north very early in the year.

Water birds need only enough warmth to melt the ice off lakes and ponds. In a winter as mild as this last one there is open water to be found even in January.

A week ago a large flock of common mergansers was seen on Lake Calumet. We see three species of these big fish-eating ducks around Chicago, and common mergansers are our usual winter birds. As spring advances they will be replaced by red-breasted mergansers in the flocks on Lake Calumet, Lake Michigan, and other large bodies of water.

A pair of harlequin ducks, one a male in its gaudy breeding plumage, showed up off 53rd Street. These birds of rushing mountain streams have become fairly regular around Chicago in recent years.

By the time you read this the first small flocks of grackles and red-winged blackbirds may have arrived in the Chicago area. If they haven't, they will in a few days. The precise date of their arrival will depend on the weather. If we get a warm front carried on a southerly breeze we can rely on the birds to ride it into the rapidly thawing north.

I am really looking forward to the drama of the changing seasons this year. I spent last year in Seattle, where, meteorologically speaking, almost nothing happens. TV weathermen could record a couple weeks' worth of programs and then go on vacation—and I suspect that some of them do.

The long, slow agonizing shift from Chicago winter to Chicago summer takes months, and there is seldom a day between late February and the end of June when you don't feel just a little anxiety about whether we are going to make it this year. A front moves in from the gulf, bringing soft breezes, warm air, and flocks of migrating robins and killdeer. Then the temperature drops 40 degrees in 27 minutes, and four inches of snow fall in three hours. The robins and killdeer, frantically searching for snowless ground, gather on the highways and get squashed in large numbers. Crows and raccoons congregate to eat the robin and killdeer carcasses. Many of the raccoons become roadkill themselves, although the crows almost never do.

Our weather gives us drama, a quality that is usually absent from west-coast climates. They get the occasional flood, but our climate involves us year-round every year. You cannot be a spectator here. If you try you might get struck by lightning.

Along the Pacific they have freakish weather from time to time. Here in the middle of the continent our weather is always freakish. We are constantly going to extremes, turning the weird into the everyday. What would spring be without a snowstorm in late April?

Californians can convince themselves that this year's flood was an oddity that won't happen again for decades. Our climate has taught us that anything can happen at any time—and probably will within the next 24 hours.

Midwestern landscapes take on the quality of stage sets on warm, sunny days at the end of winter. The curtain has gone up, but none of the actors has yet entered. The sun warms the bare ground. The native trees, which have been dealing with the drama for millennia, lay low. Most of the birds are still in Mexico. The wings of a few insects shimmer in the sunlight, but most await the greater certainties of May.

In a matter of a few weeks this will all be transformed. Bright green will begin to cover the browns and grays of prairies and grasslands. Trees will leaf out and shade the ground beneath them.

And birds will arrive in large numbers. Only 13 species of wood warblers nest regularly in the state of Washington. One additional species occurs regularly as a migrant. Here we can expect to see about 36 species in migration every spring, and states like Wisconsin and Michigan, which have hardwood forests at their southern ends and boreal forests in the north, may have almost that many species nesting every year.

All these different kinds of birds produce a glorious variety of song. Take a slow stroll through one of our better forest preserves in May or June and the songs will come at you in such richness that you'll have trouble sorting them out. The forests of the northwest simply don't have the birds to make that kind of wonderful racket.

In Seattle I used to walk my dog in a county park near my house. It was a second-growth Douglas fir woods with the typical tree perhaps 18 inches to two feet in diameter. I went there regularly for almost a year, and almost nothing happened. The common songbirds were winter wrens, robins, bushtits, and black-capped chickadees, and all of them were year-round residents. They sang more in spring and early summer, but that seemed to be their only response to the seasons.

When I tell people that I didn't care much for Seattle and that I'm really happy to be back in Chicago I get a range of reactions. Some people—there are a lot of Seattle haters around—say, "I know exactly what you mean." Most Seattle haters are put off by the attitudes of northwesterners. "I can't imagine why anybody would rather live in Chicago than in Seattle," said a woman I met at a Seattle party one night. "That's the trouble with people here," I replied. "No imagination."

The scenery is always pointed out as one of the attractions of the place. But I used to look east from our house at the line of the Cascades and see not ruggedly beautiful mountains but a wall keeping me away from the rest of the world.

I seem to be getting very antiscenery as I get older. I react to the scenery of strange places much as I react to watching a Japanese No play. "I'm sure this is all very nice, but what does it mean? Why are they acting like that?"

Here in the Midwest I have several decades' worth of knowledge and experience to help me read the landscape. I can tell where the glaciers were, see what was an old field, get an idea of when fires began to be suppressed on the land, and even deduce whether this woodland was grazed at some time in the past. I can walk through a forest preserve in late February and tell you with a high degree of accuracy what birds are going to be nesting there in June.

My year in Seattle did teach me that if you want to enjoy that glorious scenery you need a weekend. When I was 25 I could have loaded up my backpack every Friday after work and set off for a two-night hike into the Olympics or Mount Rainier National Park. But at this point in my life I'm a householder and a parent and a busy worker. My weekends are mostly eaten up with obligations. What I need is a natural place where I can spend a Saturday or Sunday morning, leaving the afternoons free for shopping, cleaning out the basement, and taking the cat to the vet.

And the big secret of Chicago is that we have more of that kind of nature than almost any other city in the country. Seattle has mountains in the distance, but its city and county park systems ain't much. Thanks to our forest preserves, I will actually be able to see and hear and smell the vast changes that the coming spring will inaugurate.

Bioregionalists like to devise quizzes. They ask if you know what the local bedrock is or what kind of natural vegetation once covered the land where your house sits. But what they should ask people to do is tell the time of year by smelling the air. It really is possible. The temperature is 55 degrees. Is it an unusually warm day in early December? Is it the first stirring of spring in late February? Or is it one of those weird days in late May when winter seems to want to come back? If you have lived here a while and if you have been paying attention, you could take a couple of deep breaths, feel the breeze on your cheeks, and immediately know the answer.

Early Spring

Maple Sugar, Nesting Crows, Mergansers

March 13, 1998

The sap is flowing in the sugar maples. The crows have returned to the nest at the top of the tall ash across the alley. Listen closely and you can hear the bugling cries of sandhill cranes and, in the woods, the whispered note of the brown creeper. Raucous flocks of red-winged blackbirds and grackles add life to quiet winter landscapes, and mergansers dive for fish in the lakes. It's spring (which in Chicago means at least one major snowstorm).

For much of the past few weeks, temperatures have been below freezing at night and above freezing in the daytime. These are ideal conditions for stimulating the flow of tree sap. Sap is mostly water, but it includes small amounts of minerals and sugars as well. Sugar-maple sap is as much as 2 to 3 percent sugar, which is what makes the tree attractive to sugar tappers.

Native Americans were the first maple tappers, and we stole from them the secret—and for that matter, the trees. Their taps were hollow sticks inserted through small holes in the bark into the xylem, the vascular tissue that carries stuff from the roots up to the twigs and buds. We use steel and plastic for taps these days, but the principle is the same, and so is the joyfulness of the occasion. Indian families used to gather in the sugar grove to work together and party in celebration of this preview of warmth and sunshine. These days, nature centers near the scattered groves of sugar maples in the Chicago area hold special festivities—and pancake brunches—to mark the flowing of the sap.

At peak flow, a single tap in a large tree can deliver as much as eight quarts a day. Since the sap is flowing through the entire circumference of the tree and the tap is draining only one small spot, healthy trees can be tapped year after year without injury.

The sap from early in the period of flow is the choicest stuff. Late sap develops a woody taste and is definitely not something you would want to pour over pancakes.

The collected sap is boiled until enough water has been cooked off to turn what remains into a sweet syrup. Native Americans usually boiled off all the water, leaving behind maple sugar, which they used much as we use salt—as a universal condiment.

We have no sugar maples near our house, but the red flower buds on the silver maple that grows in the parkway are starting to open. Soon they will produce thousands of seeds, which will find their way, with unerring accuracy, into our gutters. One of the many advantages of oak trees is that their acorns fall directly to the ground, where they can be gathered with almost no risk of fatal injury.

Our neighbors the crows are beginning what is at least their third year in the ash tree across the alley. The nest was in the tree when we arrived in December 1996, which means they must have used it in the spring of 1996. They may have used it in prior years as well. Last year they fledged two young. If this year's nest users are indeed the same birds as last year, the young of last year are still with the family. Crows are traditionalists; the kids live at home until they get married.

The adults copulated two days ago. They will not begin incubating eggs until the whole clutch, which may include as many as six or seven eggs, has been laid. Both sexes sit on the eggs, with the female taking most of the time. The male brings food to the female at the nest. The whole process, from the beginning of incubation to the young leaving the nest, takes a little less than two months. By Memorial Day the clumsy young will be stumbling around the neighborhood begging from their parents.

I have written before about the resurgence in numbers of sandhill cranes. Nesting populations in Wisconsin and Michigan's Upper Peninsula seem to have occupied all the suitable nesting habitat there, so the birds are spreading south into northern Illinois. They currently nest in McHenry, Lake, Cook, and Du Page Counties. Now that the Canada goose has become an abundant year-round resident, the bugling cries of passing flocks of sandhills have replaced the honking of geese as major harbingers of warm weather and flowers.

Last Saturday I visited McGinnis Slough in Orland Park to check out the waterfowl. I was there for about 40 minutes and at least 200 sandhills passed over in that time. They flew in shallow Vs of 20 to 30 birds each. With their long necks stretched out before them and their long legs extended behind, they are unmistakable.

Sandhill cranes often pass over the city. You are more likely to hear

them along the river than along the lakefront, but if you live on a quiet street and have a window open, you can hear their cries a mile away.

A pair of mute swans was swimming in the inlet at the east end of McGinnis Slough. The presence of these Eurasian imports is an ambiguous blessing. They certainly are beautiful birds. They are also large and aggressive, and their increasing numbers in this area may not bode well for other marsh birds. When swans take over a marsh they expect everybody else to get out of their way. However, if the birds they drive out are Canada geese, it would be hard to get too upset.

McGinnis Slough is famous as a place to see waterfowl early in spring. On Saturday I saw ring-necked ducks and two species of mergansers, but no huge flocks of anything. Ducks are a varied group. Some eat plants almost exclusively; some specialize in crustaceans and mollusks; some are almost exclusively fish eaters. The dabblers—such as mallards—feed by tipping as they swim. Heads extended downward, tails pointed up, they grab what they can reach. Plants make up most of their diets. Diving ducks—like the ring-necked—can swim underwater, and some species actually reach depths of 150 feet or more. Mergansers are fish eaters whose long, slender bills have serrated edges that help them hold slippery prey.

The two species of large merganser, the common and the red-breasted, usually gather in large numbers along the lakefront in early spring. I assume that they are attracted by the smelt runs. Smelt numbers have been down during the past few years, so merganser numbers may follow suit.

I have always thought of the arrival of red-winged blackbirds as the real beginning of spring. Noisy, conspicuous, and aggressive, they have the uncontrollable vigor of nature in full cry. They will be arriving in waves during the next few weeks. They ride southerly winds from their wintering grounds in the mid-south. Sudden cold snaps, which are the result of major masses of cold air blowing in from the north, interrupt the migration.

The first redwings to arrive are always males, but the earliest birds seem to avoid display. Their fiery red epaulets stay hidden under the glossy black of their body plumage. But as more males and the first females arrive, the rituals of springtime begin. The males display to each other and to the females. The species is polygynous, and males try to get as many females as possible to build nests in their territories. The male acts as if all the females in his territory are his mates, but DNA tests have revealed that the females are messing around at a furious rate. The male in charge of the territory may not be the actual father of any of the offspring on his turf. Hey, it's spring.

Chicago springs are famous for cold weather, high winds, and all-day rainstorms chilly enough to induce hypothermia. The veteran resident learns to ignore the weather and concentrate on maple syrup, nesting crows, cranes, mergansers, and redwings. They are what spring is really all about.

Early Risers
Skunk Cabbage

March 9, 1984

Every year about this time, the newspapers can be counted on to run an item reporting somebody's sighting of the First Robin of Spring. This is of course a pseudo-occurrence, a media event. Robins actually live here year round.

The real, true first sign of a Chicago springtime—one that is utterly ignored by the media—is the magnificent flowering of the skunk cabbage, a plant that thrives in the black, mucky soils of our local swamps. Skunk cabbages bloom as early as mid-February, but most of the action is in March. The flowers have two parts: a spathe, which is a mottled, purplish cowl a few inches tall that grows right out of the ground, and a spadix, a short, thick, yellow stem that grows inside the shelter of the spathe. Clusters of tiny flowers cover the spadix. The jack-in-the-pulpit, a near relative, has the same sort of arrangement.

Amidst the hibernal slumber of a March woodland, the solemnly hooded skunk cabbages are the first heralds of the coming vernal season, making their announcement, if necessary, by melting their way right through the snow!

Melting? Exactly. Faced with the problem of March in the temperate latitudes, the skunk cabbage has solved it by generating its own heat. This is the same sort of strategy used by humans, cottontail rabbits, and ring-necked pheasants, but it is not the sort of thing we expect from plants.

Heat comes from respiration, from burning oxygen and expelling carbon dioxide. Most plants respire so slowly that they remain more or less the same temperature as their surroundings, but skunk cabbages can burn oxygen as fast as hummingbirds, burn it fast enough to keep the spadix at a comfortable 72 degrees for two solid weeks of near freezing temperatures and late winter blizzards.

Dr. William Burger, head of the botany department at the Field Museum, told me that the rate of respiration in plants is controlled by an enzyme. That enzyme is so abundant in the skunk cabbage that plant physiologists use a puree of skunk cabbage to speed up respiration in other plants so they can study the processes of energy transfer.

Generating their own heat allows skunk cabbages to bloom at a time when the competition is still snoozing underground. And a reliably warm place is a very big attraction for the few insects active at this time of year. Honeybees are usually grounded at temperatures below 65 degrees, but they have been seen visiting skunk cabbages when the mercury read 42. They warm themselves by clinging to the hot spadix, and along the way gather pollen to spread to the next flower they visit. There is even a species of long-jawed spider that uses the hot flower as a place to meet a mate and get a jump on this year's reproduction.

As with strange people, we can trace the origins of this strange plant by looking into its family background. *Symplocarpus foetidus,* the straight name for the skunk cabbage, is an aroid, a member of the family Araceae, a very eccentric bunch altogether.

All the aroids share the spathe-and-spadix floral structure, and in some species the flowers grow to enormous size. A Sumatran aroid engenders the largest inflorescence in the plant kingdom, growing a spathe up to 13 feet in circumference and a spadix 17 feet tall.

Aroids are also, as a group, into very bad smells. That Sumatran giant exudes an odor that has been described as a mixture of burnt sugar and rotten fish. The disgusting aroma is another clever piece of strategy.

We like to think of pollination as a poetic business carried on by pretty little butterflies and industrious bees flitting from one sweet blossom to another. But the stark fact is that many plants are fertilized by carrion flies, dung beetles, and fungus gnats, and these insects are not attracted by the perfume of the rose. There is a southwest Asian plant whose flowers mimic camel droppings in both appearance and smell. Some aroids produce volatile chemicals that scientists have assigned such vividly descriptive names as cadaverine. The putrid purple coloring of many aroid flowers is another big draw.

A Sumatran giant aroid, desperate to draw flies, can gain an edge on its equally gamy competitors by producing enough heat to excite its aromatics into greater activity, sending out pulsing waves of stench into the surrounding jungle.

Tropical flowers tend toward living fast and dying young. Insects are always around; success lies in raising enough commotion to attract their attention. The aroids in warm climates usually heat up for a day or so. The skunk cabbage could not get by on that strategy, flying insects being as scarce as they are in a Chicago March. To attract customers, you need to keep the sign blinking for a week or two. And this is apparently the selection pressure that pushed the skunk cabbage into being the champion oxygen consumer of the plant world.

You would expect a plant with the common name of skunk cabbage and the scientific name of *foetidus* to share the family bent toward bad smells, but out in the woods, a living skunk cabbage flower has a faintly sweet odor. However, tear a flower or a leaf, and you will be greeted by a stink that has been described as a mixture of skunk, rotten meat, and garlic.

The leaves, flowers, and roots of skunk cabbage are also filled with tiny needlelike crystals of a chemical called calcium oxalate, which is intensely irritating to tongue, lips, throat, stomach, intestines, and so on. All the aroids carry this poison as a protection against being eaten. It works very effectively. Skunk cabbage, and the jack-in-the-pulpit, are both left very much alone by deer, rabbits, and even insects. Dieffenbachia, or dumb cane, an aroid that is a popular houseplant, gets its common name from the ability of its calcium oxalate crystals to so inflame the tongue as to render a human speechless. Some especially sensitive people die when their tongues become swollen enough to cut off breathing.

However, people are more resourceful than other herbivores, and we have learned that boiling aroids in several waters will remove the irritants. This discovery allows tropical people to eat taro root, another aroid, and even enabled woodland Indians to eat skunk cabbage root.

Obviously that root has to be very nutritious. Since the huge elephant-ear leaves do not unfold until after the flowers have bloomed, all the energy for that intense floral cycle, for burning calories like a hummingbird through a March cold snap, has to come from the root. Skunk cabbages have a root—technically an underground stem called a rhizome—that may be several inches across and a foot long. It sticks straight down into the ground, and every year a new collar of smaller roots grows down into the muck from its upper end. The rhizome also grows at that end; each year, at the end of the growing season, the collar of roots shrinks, pulling the year's growth of rhizome under the soil.

The implications of this formidable subterranean apparatus are obvious. It may be possible to dine on skunk cabbage root, but the work of digging it out of the ground would use more calories than you could get from eating it.

Nobody knows how long a single skunk cabbage can continue this annual cycle, sending up flowers each spring and then leaves to make food, which is stored in the root until spring comes again. It could be for centuries. We can easily measure the age of trees, but herbs do not add annual rings. It may be that some of our skunk cabbages were breaking through the snow when the Potawatomi still owned Chicago.

The Ephemerals' Moment
High-Speed Flowers

April 12, 1985

It is hard for a seed to germinate in a forest. Animals eat many of them. Those that survive long enough to send out a feeble probing rootlet are likely to run into a rock, or into the well-established roots of a large tree, roots that efficiently pump all the available water out of the soil.

If the sprouts send a frail leaf up toward the sun, they find instead the Stygian gloom of a maple's heavy shade. It is tough getting started.

Trees evade the problem by living for a very long time. A mighty oak has centuries to produce the single tiny acorn from which its successor will sprout. Trees also reproduce vegetatively, as the botanists say, sprouting new trunks from old roots. If the main trunk goes down in a storm or fire, the sprouts can replace it. With a mature root system pumping for them, they are, like heirs to old money, guaranteed a good start in life.

The herbs that grow on the forest floor also rely on long life to balance the odds against offspring. But they have no tough wood, nothing that can survive winter above ground and unprotected. They are all green, all tender succulent tissue that couldn't endure an Illinois January.

They have dealt with this problem by going underground. In summer, they live as leaves and flowers, but during the cold months, they retreat to subterranean bulbs, tubers, corms, and rhizomes, fat little food storage organs where the carbohydrates that will fuel next year's flowering are kept safe during the winter.

Plants of the forest understory also have problems with light. In the dense shade of the canopy, it is very hard for a plant to get a square meal. Tree seedlings grow huge leaves to compensate for the dimness.

In the deciduous forests of eastern North America, the trees are bare in the early spring. The bright sun of April and May warms the forest floor with no curtain of leaves to get in the way. A whole group of flowering plants has taken advantage of this window of vulnerability, sprouting, flowering, fading away before the new leaves block the light.

Ephemerals, these high-speed flowers are called, and like the dormouse, they spend most of their lives asleep. April and May is their season. They sprout, pushing aside last year's dead leaves; they flower, and their bright colors relieve the tedium of brown and gray that dominates the woods. Their leaves make sugar while the sun shines; they tend to hold more chlorophyll than the leaves of flowers adapted to sunnier places. When the opening leaves shut off the light, the leaves wither; the seeds are set, and the plant is safely tucked away for the winter, snoozing in its bulb until next year.

Spring beauty is one of the first of the ephemerals to rise. The leaves and flowers—five-petaled, white to pale pink, and marked by darker pink veins—come up together, all in a rush. On rich soils, they might grow a foot tall, but they are usually shorter than that. Being short keeps them out of our April breezes.

Dutchman's-breeches grows in low clumps, the white bifurcated flowers rising above the leaves. The leaves are deeply cut into narrow lobes, a trait that also mutes the savage blasts of our typical spring.

Trout lilies are ephemerals that have added cloning to the tricks they use to avoid having to rely on seeds. The rhizome branches underground, and the new branch produces a pair of mottled leaves and a  graceful yellow flower. And next year, it branches again, and two sets of leaves and flowers grow. Cloning allows a single successful seed to expand, in effect to migrate from one place to another, and to reproduce without the need for further seeds. A study of a southern Wisconsin forest found one trout lily colony that was estimated to be more than 300 years old, and the average age of the colonies was almost a century and a half.

Cloning plants, as you might guess, grow in clumps of various sizes, and between clumps you may not see a single individual. Noncloning plants, like trilliums, tend to be randomly scattered rather than clumped. Trillium seeds—only about one-third of one percent of them will live to produce seeds of their own—are equipped with special handles that make them easy for ants to carry. The insects spread the seed.

Trilliums are favorite spring wildflowers. The white *Trillium grandiflorum* that is common in this part of the country has a three-petaled flower that sometimes grows four inches across, a bravura departure from the tiny, delicate style of most spring flowers.

Trilliums are not considered ephemeral because their leaves live well into the summer, carrying on low-level photosynthesis in the shade, slowly building energy reserves for next year's flowering.

There ought to be good displays of these heralds of spring in every woodland in the Chicago area, but many of our woods are degraded, depauperate. The spring sun warms nothing but creeping Charlie, a low plant of alien origin. People have picked some flowers. Along the Des Plaines River heavy deer populations have eaten them. Other woods were once grazed by sheep or cattle, and some are products of forest preserve reforestation programs that plant no herbs.

There are a few places around where you can still see a good show. Edgebrook Flatwoods at Devon and Central is one of the few high-quality natural areas left in the city. Black Partridge Woods in far southwestern Cook County near Lemont is also good.

In Lake County, try the Ryerson Conservation Area on Riverwoods Road just north of Deerfield Road. Much of this preserve is virgin forest, or nearly that, and the trilliums are everywhere.

Trilliums, like all successful plants, have made their peace with the odds. In an established woodland where populations remain roughly stable year to year, a trillium has one job: to rear a single successful offspring to replace itself.

But a trillium's life is full of hazard. Vicious, predatory deer, huge animals with jaws like vises, can snap off a year's growth with a single bite. The forest floor swarms with voracious little rodents—mice, chipmunks, voles—whose chisel-sharp teeth indiscriminately scissor leaves, stems, flowers, seeds, and even the very bulb itself.

I haven't mentioned the insects, and I don't think I will. It would just be depressing. And remember the obscure life forms—mites and nematodes and such—whose whole existence is dedicated to destroying trilliums.

And of course, there is the weather. Any plant that evolved as an early spring bloomer in northeastern Illinois is obviously accustomed to hardship, but some years it must get too mean even for these hardy types.

My recital of the vicissitudes of this lily is prelude to a plea to avoid picking *anything* you see in bloom. Pickers tip the odds, and the trillium's defenses collapse. But, you protest, how much difference can it make? I'll only take a few. But Kant says that it is categorically imperative for you to consider what would happen if everyone picked wildflowers—everyone in this case meaning the 31 million who visit the Cook County Forest Preserves every year—and this time, he is right. If you wouldn't steal an El Greco from the Art Institute, you shouldn't steal a trillium from the woods.

Cherries

Fifteen Species in This Area

July 11, 1997

We have picked three pies' worth of cherries from our two backyard trees, and more are ripening every day. The birds and the squirrels are taking their share, but so far their depredations are nowhere near as bad as I had expected them to be. I had fantasies of sitting on the back porch with a .410 shotgun in a futile attempt to defend our crops from clouds of starlings darkening the skies. More rationally, I looked into the possibility of draping netting over the trees to keep the birds off. In my wildest dreams I imagined a pair of Cooper's hawks building a nest in one of the many tall trees in our neighborhood and patrolling our backyard for us.

Our cherry trees are feeding a nice selection of neighborhood birds, including starlings, house sparrows, robins, cardinals, blue jays, and grackles. The regular grackle flock includes a bird just out of the nest that perches with dozens of ripe cherries in easy reach and begs its mama to feed it. She of course obliges. For all this activity, our trees appear to be just one of the stops on the birds' daily round, not the focus of all their efforts. Our neighborhood seems to be a rich environment, and that allows the birds to spread their demands. Also they mostly take the fruit at the very tops of the trees, and we can't reach them anyway.

Our harvesting equipment consists of an ancient wooden stepladder left behind by the previous owners of our house. It is eight feet tall and weighs—I would estimate—about 700 pounds. Despite its weight, it is very rickety. Climbing above the fourth rung is terrifying, so fear effectively sets the altitude limit on our cherry collecting.

Sour cherry trees bring back all sorts of happy childhood memories for me. We had a tree in our backyard, and my grandparents had a really large tree next to their farmhouse. When the cherries ripened I used to climb the trees and eat the fruit right off the branches. A cherry plucked from the stem and popped into your mouth is about as fresh as fruit can get. And then there is the challenge involved in seeing how far you can spit the stone.

When I talk about my childhood cherry eating, some people wrinkle their noses. They take the name of the fruit too seriously. The cherries are actually tart rather than sour, and when they are fresh they are wonderfully flavorful. And every once in a while you come across one that is really sweet.

Sour cherries were domesticated in Asia and brought here via Europe. They are *Prunus cerasus*. The genus *Prunus* also includes sweet cherries, plums, and peaches. The fruits of all these are classified as drupes, which means they have a fleshy outer layer surrounding a very hard inner layer, the stone. If the hardness of the stone does not deter animals from eating it, the prussic acid that many *Prunus* stones contain is a very good way to ensure that nobody eats more than one.

Plants of the Chicago Region by Floyd Swink and Gerould Wilhelm lists nine species of the genus *Prunus* that have been introduced into this area. Seven of these are from the Old World, and two are from elsewhere in North America. None of these is at all common in the wild, so if you come across a *Prunus* in the forest preserves the odds are that you will be looking at one of our six native species.

Wild plums—*Prunus americana*—are tall shrubs that were a major presence in native savannas and shrub lands. They are still around but probably less common than they were in presettlement times. Native shrub lands have become one of the rarest natural communities in our area. We have lands that are structurally similar—that is, they contain a mixture of shrubs, grasses, and scattered, usually small trees. But the precise species mix—wild plum, hazel, scarlet oak—of the old shrub lands is very hard to find.

Shrub lands have become a conservation concern in the Midwest. Shrub-land birds such as loggerhead shrikes, blue-winged warblers, and yellow-breasted chats are declining. The loggerhead is already listed as threatened in Illinois and is a candidate for listing at the federal level. The removal of fire from the landscape is at the heart of this problem. Without fire, Midwestern shrub lands rather quickly become woodlands; the invading trees alter the habitat enough to drive out the shrub-land species. But in the fragmented conditions of the contemporary landscape most woodland species cannot get to the newly created woodland habitat, so what we have is a weedy, impoverished community with a superficial resemblance to a woodland replacing both native shrub land and the structurally similar simulacra of recent times.

Just a few decades ago shrub-land species seemed to have all the habitat they could use. As conservation agencies took over old fields and turned them into forest preserves, state parks, and national forests, shrubs invaded the old croplands, opening up vast realms for chats, blue-wings, shrikes, and other shrub-land species. However, the days of large-scale land acquisition are mostly over, and the shrub lands are passing away.

One of the common trees in the new young woodlands is *Prunus serotina,* the black cherry. Black cherry fruits are clustered in long slender bunches that hang from the tips of twigs. The drupes are small; a large one might be a half inch in diameter. These fruits really are sour, but the birds seem to like them—and that is the secret to the black cherry's ability to invade young woodlands. Many plants have evolved seeds that can pass through the digestive tracts of animals without damage. Sprouting tomatoes are a fairly common sight on sludge farms. Some seeds even require exposure to digestive acids to soften their seed coats enough to allow germination..

In a fragmented landscape black cherries are as mobile as birds, a fact that gives them a competitive edge over many other species. Our drastic alteration of the landscape produces some changes that are immediately obvious. Others are more subtle and may not reveal themselves for many decades. When we alter the competitive balance among various trees in a woodland we can change everything from the soil chemistry to the amount of light that reaches the ground. These changes in turn can produce population increases for some species and declines, even extirpation, for others. The changes can happen in ecological time, and by the time the results are known it may be impossible for us to trace them back to their original cause.

Gastronomically speaking, the best of our local wild cherries is *Prunus pumila,* the sand cherry. This is a low shrub rather than a tree, and in suitable habitat it can form substantial thickets. Sand cherries are very common on the dunes along the shores of Lake Michigan. They sometimes actually invade the beach, but their more usual haunts are the low dunes dominated by shrublike bearberry or juniper. You can find them at both the Indiana Dunes and Illinois Beach State Park. Doubtless they were once common along the Chicago lakefront as well.

You can also find them inland on sand prairies and savannas. The Braidwood Dunes Nature Preserve in Will County has lots of sand cherries.

The fruits of sand cherries are large, succulent, and sweet. When ripe, their skin is darker than a Bing cherry. Unlike our sour cherries, they mature in late summer. I have a happy memory of a visit to Sleeping Bear Dunes National Lakeshore in Michigan when my daughter was six. We wandered over the high dunes on a sunlit day, cooled by a breeze from the lake and gobbling sand cherries until our hands were purple with the juice.

One of the best things about eating cherries fresh is that you can just spit out the stones. Cherries in pies have to be pitted, and this is a tedious process. We have a cherry stoner—also left by the previous owners—but I have to say that the design needs some work. It uses a plunger to poke the stone from the cherry, but often the stone does not fully detach, so I have to pull it off by hand. We are going to freeze most of these cherries in pie-sized batches for use this winter. We are not looking to add a chipped tooth to our memories of cherries.

Bees

Busy Building and Making Honey

July 3, 1998

These are the longest days of the year, and it seems like we need every minute of them to squeeze in all the stuff that is happening. During the past two weeks I have watched a pair of blue-gray gnatcatchers building a lovely nest of lichens bound together with spider's silk. I have watched Baltimore orioles feeding their young in hanging nests and discovered fire pinks blooming by the hundreds in my favorite oak woods.

The season advances. The spring flowers have all gone to seed. The flowers of high summer—the bee balm and blazing star, the obedient plant and brown-eyed Susan—will soon burst into bloom. In my backyard I am seeing small bumblebees, the first-born workers of the year.

When our cherry trees came into flower in late April, the bumblebees that fed on—and pollinated—the blossoms were giants nearly an inch long. These were the queens produced by last year's colonies late in summer. An entire colony of honeybees can live through the winter, but only the queens of the bumblebees survive. When they emerge from their winter shelters in April and May, the burden of carrying on their line rests entirely on them.

Bumblebee queens spend the winter underground, and when they wake from their hibernation they immediately start looking for another underground refuge where they can create a nest. According to the books, they look mainly for rodent burrows. My guess is that in the city they also find holes in foundations, wide cracks in concrete, and rotting corners of garages.

Once she has found a suitable location, the queen starts building. Using wax secreted by glands in her abdomen, she builds a shallow cup on the floor of the nest cavity. She places a ball of pollen in the cup and then lays eggs on the pollen. Finally she roofs the egg cell with more wax, sealing the eggs into the spherical chamber. Meanwhile, she is also building a honey pot near the entrance to the nest where nectar gathered from flowers will be placed.

The eggs will hatch into larvae that will be fed on pollen and nectar for the week to ten days until they are ready to pupate in cocoons, from which they will emerge as adult workers. While the first brood of young workers is developing, the queen must collect enough pollen and nectar to feed them; she also builds more chambers and lays more eggs. By the end of the season colonies of some species may contain as many as 400 workers.

Bumblebees belong to the genus *Bombus*—this Latin word refers to a low rumbling sound, which nicely describes the noise of their vibrating wings. Nearly all of the 200 or so species of this genus live in the northern temperate zone, although there is one species in the Amazon and a few others as far south as Tierra del Fuego. Two species occur on Ellesmere Island, which is far north of the Artic Circle.

The fact that only the queens survive the winter may be an advantage for these insects in cold northern situations. They do not need to find winter refuges for large numbers of individuals, as honeybees do.

The social organization of bumblebees is in many ways simpler than that of honeybees. The workers that hatch from the first eggs laid by the queen bumblebee are just smaller versions of her, and in some species the largest workers may be bigger than the smallest queens. In honeybees there are significant morphological differences between queens and workers.

There is some division of labor among bumblebees based on size. Very small workers are more likely to remain in the nest tending young and doing the housekeeping. The larger workers leave the nest to forage for pollen and nectar. However, the individual worker may move from one job to another during its life.

Bumblebee society can be seen as a dominance hierarchy, one that is maintained in part by brute force. Workers will sometimes try to steal and eat newly laid eggs. The queen attacks the would-be miscreants with feet and mandibles, and occasionally these attacks result in serious injury or even death. The attacked workers do not resist, but they try very hard to escape.

Egg-stealing behavior wanes quickly and, after a few hours of vigorous defense by the queen, stops altogether. The former thieves then become attentive nurses of the young. However, the queen will continue to be aggressive toward the workers, especially those whose ovarian development is nearly as great as her own. Head butting with mandibles agape is the usual tactic. Even though bumblebees have reusable stingers, they don't use them on one another.

In the highly developed society of the honeybee the queen keeps the workers in line with pheromones that she emits, which prevent any reproductive development by workers. Honeybee young are treated differently too. Each larva has its own individual cell where it is fed and tended by its nurses. Among bumblebees, small groups of larvae share an egg cell. Food is place in the cell, but it is up to each larva to find and eat its share. If food is scarce, there can be serious competition.

Bees as a group are the evolutionary descendants of predaceous wasps, but bees (except the rare egg-stealing worker) have gone totally vegan. Their sole foods are pollen and nectar gathered from the blossoms of flowering plants. Pollen is a rich food source. Grains are as much as 10 percent fat and 30 percent protein. From the plant's point of view, the purpose of pollen is to fertilize ovules and create a new generation. But nectar serves solely as an inducement, a reward for the pollinator. Nectar is mostly water, but it contains various sugars—fructose, glucose, and sucrose—as well as some proteins, fats, and even B vitamins.

A bee swallows the nectar it collects, using some for its own energy needs but shunting much of it into a special honey stomach. The swallowed nectar is regurgitated in the nest along with enzymes that carry on the conversion from nectar to honey. That luscious stuff on your morning toast is actually bee spit.

Raising one young bee to adulthood requires the nectar and pollen gathered during 3,000 flower visits. A bumblebee colony that grew from one queen in early spring to 400 individuals by the end of the summer would need 1,200,000 flower visits. Hence the term "busy bee."

Watch your neighborhood bumblebees at work. Their size and strength make them very good at pollinating flowers that hide their pollen and nectar. The bumblebee can muscle its way into a flower with a long corolla and get at the riches within. Look at a bee's hind legs. You will probably see large, pale masses clinging to the upper parts of the dark limbs. Bumblebees—and honeybees—have specialized structures called pollen baskets on their hind legs. The mass of pollen is held together with nectar. Thanks to these pollen baskets, a bumblebee can carry as many as 15,000 pollen grains. For the insect, this means longer foraging trips, with more time to collect food and less time spent commuting.

My experience has been that it is the bee you don't see that stings you. You can stand and watch a bee at work from just a few feet away without worrying too much about getting stung. If a bee takes an interest in you, perhaps checking out a shirt the same color as its favorite flower, the best strategy is to ignore it. It will go away. Still, you might want to take pains to breathe through your nose. I once accidentally inhaled a yellow jacket, with rather unpleasant results.

As the season advances and the queen adds more workers to her support staff, the colony will begin to produce young queens and males. The males of some species hang out near the entrance to the hive, waiting for an unmated queen to emerge. In other species, the males wait near flowers ready to approach anything that looks like an unmated queen.

The mated queens will start looking for underground locations to spend the winter. The males, this year's workers, and the old queen will pass with the coming of frost. When spring returns, the mated queens will rise from their burrows and start the whole process again.

Fall Flora

Goldenrods, Asters, Gentians

October 17, 1997

The last of the late-season wildflowers are fading. The petals have already dropped from the sunflowers. Only a few of the goldenrods retain the bright yellow of September. Even the asters, always the latest of our fall flowers, are past their prime. If you want to see the last of summer you had better get out this weekend. Next week at this time the only color in the landscape will be the turning leaves.

I got seriously into the fall wildflowers of this region over the course of the past month. I took a class called Fall Flora, offered under the combined auspices of the Field Museum and the Morton Arboretum and taught by John and Jane Balaban of the North Branch Restoration Project. John teaches at Saint Ignatius; give him a chance to conduct a class and he will lay on the rigor in true Jesuit style. Our plant list for this course included nearly 100 species. I thought I had a lot to learn when I signed up, and John and Jane let me know I was right.

We took three field trips during the course, one each to Bunker Hill Woods, Harms Woods, and Miami Woods. All three of these sites have been under active management for 10 to 15 years, and they all show the benefits. The sites were chosen because a fairly rich flora had survived there for 175 years. New species have since been planted, and existing plants are no longer suppressed by heavy shade and fire starvation. Here were places where we could actually see 100 species of wildflowers in a morning—and not just one or two specimens, but populations, abundances of flowers.

I did know a fair number of the species on our class list before I enrolled. But I was looking for a chance to systematize my knowledge, and I wanted to learn more about a few common genera that I knew only incompletely. I had a special interest in the genus *Solidago*, the goldenrods, and the genus *Aster.*

Goldenrods are everywhere around Chicago. They grow in the most pristine natural areas and in the median strip of the Eisenhower

Expressway. The golden yellow of their flowers is one of the most characteristic color of late summer and early fall. They are unfairly blamed for hay-fever symptoms that are actually caused by ragweed. Ragweed is a wind-pollinated plant that scatters huge quantities of pollen grains into the air. Some of them reach the ovaries of other ragweed plants; many of them reach the nasal membranes of afflicted animals—including humans.

Goldenrods are pollinated by insects. In fact, goldenrod flowers are good places to look for interesting ones. Soldier beetles—long, slender insects variously patterned in yellow and black or orange and black—are abundant on goldenrod flowers. From what I have seen, goldenrod flowers are the place that soldier beetles go in search of love.

Goldenrods all belong to the genus *Solidago,* which is almost certainly of North American origin. There are only a few species in Eurasia and South America. The eighth edition of Gray's *Manual of Botany,* by M. L. Fernald, lists 75 species and several common hybrids in the region bordered by the Atlantic coast, eastern Kansas, southern Canada, and Kentucky. Swink and Wilhelm, in *Plants of the Chicago Region,* list 21 native species and one introduced.

Real knowledge of goldenrods is one of the key distinctions between those who actually know things and those with only a superficial acquaintance with the natural world. For me, studying goldenrods is an attempt to overcome my deeply ingrained urge to be a dilettante by actually learning something.

Asters offer a similar opportunity. Fernald lists 67 species, some hybrids, and a number of distinctive subspecies. Swink and Wilhelm list 26 and 2 introductions. If I can get beyond the kindergarten level of "that's an aster" or "that's a goldenrod" I will have accomplished something.

There is more to it than that of course. Plants bring information with them. The presence of a particular species tells us something about a place. If we can't recognize the species we lose the information. Swink and Wilhelm have digitized this idea. Every plant in their encyclopedic compendium has a number called a "coefficient of conservatism." The number is a measurement of the tendency of the plant to grow only in relatively undisturbed, stable natural communities. The scale runs from zero to ten. Zero is reserved for opportunists like ragweed. If we find ragweed growing somewhere, about all we can say about that place is that there must be some dirt present. Hairy aster, *Aster pilosus,* is a zero. *Aster ericoides,* heath aster, is a five. It is usually found in prairies. If we come across this plant we can suspect that we are looking at a prairie remnant, and we might start hunting for other species typical of that sort of community. If our search turned up some *Aster laevis*, a nine, we could begin to suspect that we had discovered a prairie remnant of rather unusual quality.

We could verify that suspicion by looking for other plants on the Balabans' fall list. We might find the tall, waving plumes of Indian grass, one of the dominant plants of the tallgrass prairie and a five on the Swink and Wilhelm scale. On a really rich site we might find *Sporobolus heterolepis,* prairie dropseed grass—a ten—a plant that can survive only on the richest, least disturbed remnants of native prairie.

There are bits of this sort of community at Miami Woods. When this prairie was discovered 15 years ago, these species were embedded in a matrix of weeds. Now the remaining weeds are embedded in a matrix of prairie plants. And down among the grasses are the most stunningly gorgeous of the fall flora, the gentians. Swink and Wilhelm list seven species of gentians in our area. The lowest value is an eight. At Miami Woods and Bunker Hill Woods these beauties are all over the place. One of the gentians is pale yellow, but all the rest are a rich royal blue that leaps out at you as you scan the ground.

Fringed gentian has four broad petals spreading horizontally from a deep-blue cup. Bottle gentian flowers are closed and kept that way by a white membranous cap. Only a strong bumblebee can force its way in to capture the pollen of this plant.

The woodlands of northeastern Illinois are naturally open, rather sunny places where enough solar energy reaches the ground to support the growth of wildflowers that bloom in late summer and early fall. Where woods have been left unmanaged, the deep shade often kills off these species. At Harms Woods we could see elm-leaved goldenrod and blue-stemmed goldenrod growing with blue cohosh, white baneberry, and Short's aster. This was a late-season woodland where a hungry butterfly could have found a meal of nectar from many sources.

If you have no interest in trying to interpret the natural landscape, knowing the difference between tall goldenrod and Short's aster may not seem worth the effort. But I think we desire to learn things in order to make some sense of the world. When we look at nature we can be overwhelmed by all the simultaneous stimuli that hit us. There are so many different kinds of plants, and while we try to sort them out, grasshoppers are leaping about and butterflies are fluttering by and dragonflies are zooming past and birds are calling. To the extent that we can sort out all these impressions, we alienated, atomized, postmodern people can feel at home, connected to something beyond ourselves.

Here in Chicago we can take lessons from the Balabans, who took lessons from Floyd Swink and Gerould Wilhelm, who took lessons from May Watts, who studied at the University of Chicago under Henry Chandler Cowles, one of the founders of the science of ecology. We can enjoy the riches of life in one of the world's great metropolises and still connect ourselves to the natural world.

Turkeys

Huge Comeback in the Past Fifty Years

November 16, 1984

Our imaginations, inspired by grade-school history books, give the first Thanksgiving a Norman Rockwell flavor. We see Pilgrims neatly done up in New England's primary colors—black, white, and gray—and Indians with profiles like Crazy Horse gleefully watching the huge roast turkey being carried to the table by an apple-cheeked Pilgrim housewife.

The reality was a good deal more raggedy. The Pilgrims, until the successful harvest that the feast was celebrating, had been living on a total food ration of a peck of meal per person per week. The privation had been so severe since their landing that some had died and the survivors had all been sick a time or two. They must have looked rather pinched at this first Thanksgiving, and their clothes would have hung a bit slack.

The Indians may not have had the noble aquiline profile of the great Sioux warrior, but they were there in numbers. Chief Massasoit showed up with no less than 90 hungry braves in his train.

For two solid days—these people knew how to give thanks—they stuffed themselves with venison supplied by the Indians, wild ducks and geese shot by the Pilgrims, clams and eels from the sea, white bread, corn bread, and various greens, and for dessert, not pumpkin pie, but wild plums and dried berries. Their drinks were red and white wine fermented from local wild grapes and pronounced by the Pilgrims to be "very sweete & strong."

So far as we know, they did not eat any cranberry sauce, although the berries grew plentifully in nearby bogs. And if they ate any of the elusive, long-legged woodland birds they called "Turkies," the fact does not appear in their records.

Our common name for these birds, like so much in life, is based on a misunderstanding. They are New World creatures, a family with only two living species, one that ranges over North America as far south as central Mexico, and another that lives in southern Mexico and Central America.

Indians of the southwest and Mexico domesticated the North American form, and the Spanish had sent some of them home as early as 1519. The birds reached England in 1524, coming either via the Turkish empire or by some route that led people to believe they had come from there. When Europeans began to settle what is now the U.S., they brought their domestic turkeys with them. They did not capture local birds of the forest and tame them.

Domestic turkeys have raised stupidity to a level seldom achieved outside the Chicago City Council. There are stories of birds drowning in rainstorms because they were staring up at the source of these mysterious water drops and didn't have the sense to shut their mouths.

But the domestic turkey is about as remote from the wild animal as a Care Bear is from a grizzly. Wild turkeys slide around their woodland homes like wraiths. If you see any at all, it will be a glimpse of a flock vanishing over the hill when you are still a couple of hundred yards away. Would-be turkey hunters may wait years before they bag their first bird. Turkeys are much more difficult to see—or to hunt—than the white-tailed deer.

When the Pilgrims began trying their luck in the woods around Plymouth, the continental turkey population probably numbered in the millions. The big birds with their rich bronze plumage and their strange, naked, red-and-blue heads walked the woods and the forest edges, living on acorns, chestnuts, and various other fruits and seeds. Summers, they supplemented this vegetarian diet with insects and small snakes and lizards.

Their way of life was typical of the whole order of chickenlike birds to which they—along with pheasants, grouse, and quail—belong. They lived and ate on the ground, relying on their long, powerful legs to get them around.

They can fly, and surprisingly fast. One bird in Texas was reportedly timed at 55 miles per hour, and speeds in the 35- to 45-mile-an-hour range are common.

But flight for them is an emergency measure, a way to get away from an immediate danger. Their stamina quickly gives out, and they come back to earth. Looking at them, it is easy to see why. A large tom turkey may be four feet long, with a wingspread of five feet, and on the average it will weigh 16 pounds. The smaller hens average a bit over nine pounds.

The structure and physiology of the flight muscles actually adds to the difficulty of keeping all that bulk aloft. The turkey's legs are richly supplied with blood that can carry enough oxygen and food to sustain long-term effort. The breast muscles, on the other hand, are poorly supplied with blood, so a flying turkey quickly develops an oxygen deficiency and has to land. The rich blood supply gives the leg meat a dark color, while the impoverished breast is white.

In the spring, the males become hormonally inspired to gobble to attract females. Young toms utter high-pitched, hoarse gobbles, while older birds boom out their invitation in a deep basso. The older birds get most of the action.

When a female approaches the clearing where the tom had set up for business, he flares his tail into a broad fan and goes into a John Travolta number, performing a strutting dance that melts the lady's heart.

Copulation is all there is to turkey family life. Once he's had his bit of fun, the tom takes no further interest. The female incubates the eggs and cares for the young. They are precocial, able to run within 24 hours of hatching and to fly at two weeks.

During the autumn, the family group of mother and young breaks up, and the birds spend the winter in small flocks that are either exclusively male or exclusively female.

Wild turkeys suffered badly from the invasion of Europeans. Their woodland homes were converted to farms and cities, and like the bison, they were hunted unmercifully. When the explorer Henry Schoolcraft was visiting the Ozarks in the 1820s, he stopped to spend the night in a settler's cabin. The man of the house decided that a turkey dinner would be fun, so he and his son crept into the woods and shot 37 birds.

By 1930 turkeys survived in only 21 states, and the total population was down to about 20,000 birds. The last Cook County sighting was on March 23, 1878, and they were completely extirpated in the Chicago area by the late 1880s.

But in the last 50 years, turkeys have made a stunning comeback. The population has jumped about 10,000 percent to two million, and the birds are living in every state except Alaska. This marvelous population explosion depends on habitat improvement and the control of hunting, but it was made possible by large-scale restocking efforts carried on by state fish and game departments.

Early restocking efforts relied on birds raised on game farms. These birds carried a bit of domestic turkey blood, bred into them in the interest of tractability. A truly wild turkey is likely to respond to captivity by slamming into the fence until it kills itself. But eventually, game mangers learned that even a tiny admixture of domestic blood, as little as 5 percent, produced an animal almost as degenerate as a Swift Butter Ball.

Game farm turkeys, instead of slipping silently through the woods, tend to travel by road. Some are so tame that they will allow a human to approach within six feet before showing any alarm. They are useful only as cannon fodder in put-and-take hunting programs. They rarely survive in the wild.

When the failure of game farm birds became apparent, the wildlife managers turned to trapping wild birds and releasing them in turkeyless areas. This has worked spectacularly, so well that in some states, Missouri for example, all the suitable habitat is now occupied by wild turkeys. Here in Illinois, turkey are well established in the Shawnee National Forest at the southern tip of the state. In Jo Daviess County—where Galena is located—they are numerous enough to allow a hunting season.

But so far, we have none in the Chicago area. There were attempts beginning in the early '50s to stock the Palos forest preserves with game farm turkeys, but the birds met the usual fate of their kind. Peter Dring, naturalist at the Little Red School House Nature Center, claims that the birds were last seen following the yellow line down the middle of Willow Springs Road. Not behavior with much survival value.

But Dring would love to get some truly wild turkeys. The Palos preserves are fine habitat and quite large enough to support a population. The only obstacle is money. The money for the state's restocking program comes from hunters, so birds are released only in places where they can eventually be hunted, and this rules out the forest preserves.

Maybe we should start a fund-raising campaign to bring back the turkey. Imagine walking through a woodland literally in sight of the Sears Tower and catching a glimpse of a flock of these bronze ghosts disappearing into the trees.

Winter Reading

Bent's Life Histories of Birds

December 20, 1985

Now that the nights are getting longer and colder and the outdoors is becoming less appealing, I am again spending time with some of my favorite winter reading, a 26-volume work with the catchy title *Life Histories of North American Birds* by Arthur Cleveland Bent.

Bent's *Life Histories* are serious scientific tracts, compilations of the best available information on the ways of life of all of North America's birds. There are separate chapters not only for each species but for scores of subspecies as well. Each chapter is organized under the same series of headings. After a brief introduction, we learn about spring migration, courtship, nesting habits, eggs, young, the sequence of plumages to maturity, seasonal molts, feeding habits, flight, swimming and diving habits for water birds, voice, behavior, enemies, fall migration, and winter habits. The chapters close with condensed descriptions of breeding range, winter range, migration dates, and nesting dates.

If you are familiar with scientific literature in general, you are probably thinking that Bent's magnum opus is something only a certifiable bird nut could love. These days, anything written by a scientist serious about his reputation will be stated in the passive voice. The first-person pronouns, singular and plural, will be rigorously avoided. In the journals, nobody ever does anything: things just happen. My suspicion is that when scientists get married, they don't say, "I do." They say, "It is done."

Reference works are even worse than the journals. In them, passivity combines with compression to produce a prose devoid of both actors and articles. This stuff is like boot camp. It weeds out the weaklings. Only the truly dedicated will wade through enough of this to acquire the degrees that provide an entrée to respectable scientific endeavor.

But Bent is different. The 26 volumes of this mighty work are filled with charm. They are books on natural history, and they are also social history of a high order, a glimpse of the past as evocative as a good novel, and a revelation of the high adventure of scientific exploration.

Open the first volume—*Diving Birds*—to page one, and you discover a chapter on the western grebe that begins like this: "Where the sweet waters of Bear Creek empty into Crane Lake the bare shores . . . are transformed into a verdant slough of tall waving bulrushes . . . a green oasis . . . in the waste of bare rolling plains of southwestern Saskatchewan."

There follows a joyous account of Bent's visit to this place in the summer of 1905. He tells of wading waist-deep through the slough and discovering the nests of western grebes, along with the nests of 24 other species of water birds. Read it and you want to go there. Read it and you get a sense of the living bird in its habitat, a sense that you cannot get from a work in the contemporary style such as *The Audubon Society Encyclopedia of North American Birds*. The *Encyclopedia*'s entry on the western grebe starts like this: "Largest N. American grebe, common in w. U.S.; east to Man., Minn.; nests on inland fresh waters." All true, but it doesn't really sing.

Arthur Cleveland Bent came along just as the heroic era in American ornithology was ending. For a century and a half, beginning with Catesby in the early 18th century and continuing through the work of Wilson, Audubon, and many others, ornithologists were explorers wandering the uncharted wilderness in search of new birds. Science's first task was to enumerate the species, to find out what lived here.

By the end of the 19th century, that work was about done. Learned naturalists, as they were then called, had penetrated the western wilderness, charted the seabird colonies of Labrador and the Pribilofs, and collected specimens from the arctic tundra. The time had come for someone to sift through the vast and scattered literature of bird lore and find out just what we knew and what we didn't know about the ways of life of our native birds.

The first man to attempt this was a Major Charles Emil Bendire, an army officer who had fought the boredom of long years in frontier forts by studying the local birds. Bendire's thrasher, a southwestern relative of our brown thrasher, is named after him. Oology, collecting and studying birds' eggs, was a popular hobby among professional and amateur naturalists in the major's time, and he amassed a splendid collection, which is now in the Smithsonian.

When he retired from the army, the major became honorary curator of oology at the U.S. National Museum, now part of the Smithsonian, and began work on a two-volume compilation of life histories of North

American birds. He died in 1897 with the work unfinished, and in 1910 young Bent took over the task.

Arthur Cleveland Bent also started out as an egg collector, ransacking the fields and hedges around his home in Taunton, Massachusetts, as a boy, and traveling as far as the Bering Sea after he had grown to adulthood. He managed to write a 26-volume scientific work despite a permanent tremor in his right hand, a souvenir of a fall from a tree during a boyhood egg-collecting expedition.

Today, the idea of collecting rooms full of eggs seems grotesque, but in that era the hobby was perfectly acceptable. Oologists were among the founders of the first Audubon societies and were quite active in promoting conservation.

Once he took on the project, the *Life Histories* became Bent's life's work. The first volume, *Diving Birds,* was published in 1919 as a bulletin of the U.S. National Museum. The final installment in the series, the three-volume set on sparrows and other finches, did not appear until 1968. Bent died in 1954, his great work unfinished, and others had to carry it to completion.

Obviously, no one man could have personally acquired all the knowledge in these books. Bent took much from the published literature, and he also maintained an enormous correspondence, gathering unpublished accounts of bird life from both professional and amateur ornithologists. He thought of his project from the beginning as a community effort, and he closed the introduction to each volume with the same sentence: "If the reader fails to find in these pages anything that he knows about the birds, he can only blame himself for failing to send the information to—THE AUTHOR." By the end of the project, he had acknowledged by name the contributions of more than 800 persons.

Some of these contributors are merely cited as sources, but much of the charm of the *Life Histories* lies in the long quotations, many of a page or more, from his correspondents. A Mr. Frank A. Kleinschmidt, out "hunting bears for the Carnegie Museum," tells of his discovery on June 6, 1913, of the first known nest of Kittlitz's murrelet, a seabird of the auk family that lays its eggs high above timberline on Alaskan mountains. Miss Cordelia J. Stanwood of Ellsworth, Maine, describes a pair of magnolia warblers building their nest in a spruce-fir forest. Miss Stanwood is one of my favorites among Bent's informants. I have been in spruce-fir forests in June, and anyone who could sit through the onslaughts of mosquitoes to put together the precise and detailed notes she produces has my deepest respect.

Neil Gilmour, a game warden from Saskatchewan, submits a long, comic account of his attempts, on a spring day in 1922, to get near a whooping crane's nest. The birds are so wary that they fly when he is still a mile away, and the ground is so treacherous that Mr. Gilmour comes near to being sucked into the muck and drowned. "If . . . the reader has ever tried the experiment of wading through a muskeg with uneven bottom, without once daring to drop his eyes in the direction of his pedal extremities, he will have some idea of the task I had set myself."

And there is Frank Chapman approaching a South Carolina heron rookery in a canoe in 1908: "For two miles we paddled thus in a bewildering maze of sunlit, buttressed cypress trunks with shiny, round-headed 'knees' protruding from the water, and with every branch heavily moss draped. The dark waters showed no track, the brown trunks no blaze. We seemed to be voyaging into the unknown . . .

"We now approached the most densely populated part of the rookery. Thousands of Louisiana herons and little blue herons left their nests in the lower branches . . . their croaking chorus of alarm punctuated by the louder more raucous squawks of hundreds of egrets as they flew from their nests in the upper branches."

I could go on—almost forever. With 26 volumes to choose from, the books will probably last more winters than I will. All but a few of the Bent *Life Histories* are available in paperback editions from Dover Books. I had heard that the books were going out of print, but a check with the publisher revealed that the rumor was not true. They are even planning to bring back some volumes that had been unavailable.

Unfortunately, the two-volume set on goatsuckers and hummingbirds, the one hole in my collection, will not be available anytime soon. If anybody out there has a spare set, I'd like to hear from you.

[Dover Publications lists the following volumes by Arthur Cleveland Bent: *Life Histories of North American Marsh Birds; Life Histories of North American Wild Fowl; Life Histories of North American Gulls and Terns; Life Histories of North American Wagtails, Shrikes, Vireos, and Their Allies;* and *Life Histories of North American Flycatchers, Larks, Swallows, and Their Allies.*]

Squirrels' Nests
How They Hold Together

January 27, 1995

This time of year, when the trees are bare, you can begin to get an idea of how many squirrels live in your neighborhood. Look for a big ball of leaves wedged into a notch between branches. The leaves are the exterior of a squirrel's nest and each nest is home to one adult squirrel. In a few weeks the first young of this year will be born, so some of the nests will be home to a mother and her babies.

Not all squirrels make nests of course. Some look for shelter from the cold in cavities in tree trunks, and in cities others stay warm in attics, garages, and other havens inadvertently provided by humans.

I started to think about squirrels' nests last month when my brother-in-law pointed out how amazing it is that those balls of leaves stay anchored in the trees in the face of Chicago's fierce winter winds. "The stems on those leaves are not twister ties," he said. "How do they keep them together?"

I started looking at the Illinois Natural History Survey, where Edward Henske gave me an inside view of what he and other mammalogists call a "drey," a word of obscure origins.

The first point is that the leaves we see on the outside of the nest are not the structural supports that hold the thing together. Like Chicago's other famous Sullivan, Louis, squirrels use an internal skeleton to support their structures. Louis made his of steel. Squirrels use sticks and twigs and, of course, the living branches of the trees where their nests are located.

On this framework they weave a lining incorporating grasses, strips of bark, and shredded leaves. The best way to shred a leaf if you want to weave it into a structure is to skeletonize it. This means removing most of the blade of the leaf, leaving the sturdy central vein with just a bit of blade on each side of it.

Other authorities offer somewhat different accounts of how a squirrel builds its nest. A book called *The Wild Mammals of Missouri* says that "the leaf nest consists of a rough twig framework, from 12 to 20 inches across, and a bulky pile of leaves heaped upon layer and layer. The squirrel hollows out a nest cavity in the center of the leaves."

However, the authors agree that the outer leaves are woven into the twig framework, and they agree that material other than leaves and twigs—they mention "grass, roots, moss, corn husks, and other items"—may be woven into the structure.

A squirrel can build a drey in about 12 hours. In other words, in a pinch a squirrel evicted from a nest in the morning could have a new shelter built by nightfall. Nests usually last six to ten months, which means that a nest built in fall will last through the winter. But nests kept in good repair have been known to endure for two or three years.

The squirrel enters the nest through a hole in the side, and the hole is likely to be on the lee side to keep the wind and rain from coming in the door. Inside there is more or less one squirrel's worth of room. The animal curls up into a ball with its tail covering its face to maximize its insulation.

Dreys will keep a squirrel comfortable down to about 15 degrees Fahrenheit. Below that they will notice the cold, though they can survive a typical Chicago winter in a drey. Some squirrels might not make it through our coldest winter if they can't find a good tree cavity or somebody's attic.

Natural cavities in trees often form where large branches have broken away from the trunk. They can be enlarged by woodpeckers or by decay that enters through the hole. The tree grows new bark every year, and in the absence of any interference it will eventually seal the cavity. Squirrels keep their holes open by gnawing away the new growth.

January is breeding season for our local sciurids, to give them their official name, and if you pay attention you'll see lots of chasing about, hollering, and a certain amount of fighting. The usual stuff associated with romance. The young will be born six to seven weeks after mating. There will be another mating season in May and June.

We have two different species of squirrels in Chicago. Gray squirrels are the typical neighborhood squirrel. They are gray, which you may have already guessed, but you may find highlights of chestnut, cinnamon, or even orange in their fur. Their bellies are white, and their tails are fringed with white.

Fox squirrels are a bit bigger, and their underparts are reddish. I know of two populations of fox squirrels in the city. One is in Lincoln Park at the bird sanctuary behind the totem pole at Addison Street. The other is in Horner Park along the river between Irving Park and Montrose. There may well be others.

The distribution of fox squirrels and gray squirrels in Illinois is an unsolved mystery. In natural situations we generally expect to find gray squirrels in dense upland forests with well-developed understories. Fox squirrels prefer more open woods—the oak savannas of Illinois would have been perfect for them—with herbaceous rather than woody understories. Reading those habitat descriptions, you would expect that fox squirrels would be the essential city and suburban squirrel. City neighborhoods are places with scattered trees and lots of open ground in the form of lawns and flower beds. So why don't we have more fox squirrels and fewer gray squirrels?

Around Champaign, the traditional center of abundance for zoology graduate students in this state, the distribution of these two animals has been studied closely, but so far nobody has been able to figure out why they are where they are. In 1966 a student named Sharon Saari surveyed all the towns in Champaign County with populations larger than 150. There are 22 such towns, and 16 of them had only fox squirrels. The only towns with nothing but gray squirrels were Champaign and Urbana, the cities on the plain. Humans regard them as two towns, but squirrels show more sense and think of them as one.

Three towns had both fox and gray squirrels, and in two of these towns both species could be found in the same tree at the same time. In the third town, Ivesdale, the gray squirrels were in the heart of town, while the fox squirrels were in the woodlot out at the edge.

We might conclude from all this that gray squirrels are, for whatever reasons, better adapted to life in the city, but we don't know what it is that keeps the fox squirrels bottled up in our larger parks. It is something about the habitat, or is it something about their competitive relations with gray squirrels? We need somebody to spend long hours in Horner Park and around the bird sanctuary unraveling this mystery.

If you are in Lincoln Park or along the lake anywhere between Lincoln Park and Zion, you might keep an eye out for black squirrels. My only sighting in Chicago of one of these animals was on Stratford Place in the block between the Outer Drive and Broadway.

It was an absolutely, totally black squirrel, a deep inky black without a white hair on it. It looked like it had been dragged through a coal bin.

The animal was a melanistic gray squirrel, a genotype that turns up in various places and may be spreading. In Illinois most of our melanistic squirrels are on the North Shore, although there are a few along the Rock River.

Gray squirrels do wander some. In fact, there are historical accounts of large-scale migration. Robert Kennicott, writing in 1857, says that "immense numbers congregate in autumn, and move off together, continuing their progress in the same general direction, whatever it may be, not even turning aside for large streams." Unfortunately, that is one of those North American wildlife spectacles we were born too late to witness.

Ice Fishing
You Won't Catch Many Fish

January 20, 1984

The ice fishermen arrive at Montrose Harbor and the Lincoln Park Lagoon with the first hard freeze. Our ice blue Christmas set them up perfectly this season.

You are not supposed to walk on the ice unless it is ten inches thick, but some people stretch the season, especially late in the winter. I have seen fishermen peacefully sitting on cakes of ice whose attachment to the shore was so tenuous I expected them to drift off, angler and all, into the open lake.

Ice fishing is a sport born of desperation. You can only fish open water eight to nine months a year in these latitudes. Without ice fishing, the serious angler would have to spend the rest of the year indoors—and risk exposing him- or herself to the dreaded cabin fever. "What would we do at home?" an enthusiast asked me rhetorically. "Watch television?"

Last weekend, about 50 people a day were avoiding that horror on the ice at Montrose Harbor. They were a mix of families—parents and children of both sexes—and beer-commercial groups of young men with mustaches. Every group had its own ice auger.

An ice auger is a wonderful piece of gear that can take you through 18 inches of solid ice in less than a minute. It looks like a giant brace-and-bit combination. Five feet long overall, it is tipped with two razor-sharp blades that do the cutting. The broad blades of the auger spiral the finely shaved ice out of the hole. When you break through into the water below, it is like hitting a gusher. Very cold water explodes out of the hole, and if you are not careful, it can soak you to the knees.

With that hazard out of the way, you settle down for some ice fishing. The technique is simple: bait your hook with a minnow or an artificial lure, lower it to within six inches of the bottom, and wait. You can jig the line a bit now and then, but nothing too violent. Fish are cold-blooded and they slow down when the water gets really cold, so you wouldn't want to scare them off with sudden movements. This sluggishness also means that fish caught through the ice don't have much fight in them. "They come up through the hole pretty easy," one man told me.

The ice anglers' rig, since it need do nothing beyond hauling the hooked fish through the hole, is very simple. A few use their summer tackle, but most employ stubby little rods two feet long or less. The rods serve as a base to tie a line to; many have no reels at all. A few have reels the size of a kitchen clock. With the rod mounted on a tiny bipod, the ensemble looks like a Wehrmacht-surplus automatic weapon.

Some rods are outfitted with bells to draw the attention of the fishermen away from conversation and toward their fishing hole. On an average day, you won't get interrupted too often. In addition to being more sluggish, winter fish are also more scarce. In other words, it doesn't matter too much that they don't fight, since you won't catch many of them anyway.

One of the pleasures of ice fishing is standing around on every cold days completely exposed to the Fury of the Elements. It is hard to find a place more exposed that the middle of a lake, and even the middle of a harbor is breezy enough. Since they are likely to get no exercise once their hole is drilled, ice fishermen dress very warmly.

For some, mere clothing is not enough. The ice is dotted with tiny shelters ranging from the primitive—a sheet of wood-framed canvas set up to block the wind—to the highly sophisticated—an actual ice fishing tent, clear plastic shelter for one with an internal aluminum frame, the sleek aerodynamic shape of something you could take up Everest, and no floor. Sitting inside, out of the wind, with the clear plastic greenhousing the sunshine and a Coleman lantern hissing in a bucket, the owner has even taken off his coat and gloves.

But what he gains in warmth, he loses in society. He and another cocoon owner are set up side by side. The condensation on their plastic walls keeps them from seeing each other. They talk to each other in loud voices and miss everything around them.

They are better off, however, than the lonesome man hunkered down in a homemade wood-and-canvas hut. He has only one tiny window to look through, and he looks morose.

Ice fishermen do have stories, but none of them is about Lake Michigan. I have heard of Wisconsin lakes where slumbering giant northern pike try to snatch a meal on reflex and find themselves hooked by the wily ice fisherman. I have heard of clear tarns in the Colorado Rockies where four feet of spring ice hides whole shoals of voracious trout. I have heard of frantic anglers hacking at their fishing holes, desperately trying to enlarge the opening to let through a gargantuan lake trout.

But mostly what we have in Chicago's harbors and lagoons is people catching perch. And very small perch at that. We are talking key chain size. The ice is littered with fish that it would take a sushi grand master to fillet. Of course, Lake Michigan being what it is, there are positive advantages to small meals of very young fish.

Trout are caught here. Tales of them circulate through the assembled anglers. But they are like winning the lottery; you can't expect them.

So you don't catch many fish. And those you get are very small. And even the occasional big one is too cold to fight. And the winds howl across the open ice. But the air is certainly fresh. You can kibitz with your friends or talk to your daughter with very few interruptions from hungry fish. Your ostensible occupation is respectable. If anyone asks, you can say you are fishing. You don't have to admit that you are standing around in the subzero windchill just to be sociable.

And you can stare at the skyline. If you are properly dressed, you can feel the cozy inexpressible joy of one who is warm in a cold place. And you can dream about how good it will be when the ice is gone.

Feeding Urban Birds

Sparrows Are Inevitable

December 12, 1986

If you live below the fourth floor, you could be feeding birds this winter. You could hang a feeder on your kitchen window, hang one from your back porch, or just scatter seed across your backyard. You will almost inevitably attract birds.

But what kind of birds, you ask? If I put out some seed, will I be besieged by pigeons until April? It is certainly possible, and we'll get back to that later, but you might also get cardinals and chickadees. A survey of 266 members of the Chicago Audubon Society showed that nearly all of them (93 percent) reported cardinals at their feeders in 1985–86, and 82 percent had chickadees.

This survey is much more suburban than urban, but I would estimate, basing my estimate on a combination of long experience and wild guesses, that if you live in the *Reader*'s lakefront circulation area either north of Chicago Avenue or south of Congress, you can probably get cardinals and chickadees at your feeder. Nothing is guaranteed here, but I think the odds would favor you.

Both chickadees and cardinals perch to feed, so you can get them with the little feeders that stick to your windows, with tall, slender tube feeders, or with peaked roof boxes with troughs at the bottom to dispense the seeds.

It is possible to spend an enormous amount of money on a bird feeder. You can even get feeders with counterweighted perches. If something the size of a cardinal, or smaller, settles on the perch, it can feed all it likes. If something heavier, a blue jay or—Heavens forfend!—a pigeon, lands, the perch swings down and a door closes over the food.

It is also possible to get by very cheaply. Scattering seed on the ground works quite well. I bolted an old hunk of plywood to the monkey bars on a swing set to provide a feeding shelf out of reach of cats. Chickadees and cardinals feed there, and so do mourning doves and juncos, birds that don't like to perch as they eat.

Chickadees are a particular treat to watch. They are very active little birds, constantly in motion. The black-capped chickadee, our local variety, has to get enough food every day to sustain both all that activity and a body temperature of about 104 degrees in the face of January in Chicago. It can stand some help.

Most people feed the sort of standard seed mix you can get at the supermarket. If you want to move up in the price a bit from that, sunflower seeds are a favorite. If you want to buy your seed in bulk, and at considerable savings over the supermarket, you can go to the Evanston Environmental Association's Ecology Center at 2024 McCormick Boulevard in Evanston.

There are various other kinds of seeds available for special purposes. Thistle, for example, is the special favorite of the goldfinch.

If you get into feeding, you have to be patient. The birds may not instantly discover the presence of this new food source, and you may have to wait a while before anything shows up. Once they start, they are likely to keep returning for more, so if you start feeding, stay with it.

You should also recognize that living in the city does put certain limits on how many birds you can expect to attract. I don't think that buying expensive thistle seed—$36.75 for a 25-pound bag—is worth the money. Goldfinches are not common in the city, and the chances are that your expensive seed will be eaten by house sparrows.

The banes of everyone who feeds birds are squirrels, pigeons, and house sparrows. The problem with squirrels is that they eat so much. They are a whole lot bigger and heavier than chickadees, and they need a lot more food. My daughter once made a pinecone bird feeder in her after-school program. The kids rolled pinecones in peanut butter and then coated them with birdseed. When she brought it home, we put it out on the feeding board for the birds. A squirrel almost immediately stole the whole thing, including the red yarn loop for hanging the feeder on a tree.

There are several "squirrel proof" feeders on the market and also several "squirrel proof" ways of hanging them. They work pretty well, but squirrels are resourceful, persistent, and acrobatic, and they have been known to break through the toughest maximum-security precautions. I think the thing to do is figure out just how many you are actually feeding. For the past two years, I have been supporting just two animals, and I'm willing to put up with that. It does my heart good to see them looking plump and sleek in the foulest of winter weather.

Many feeders are designed so that only small birds can use them. Pigeons can't contort themselves sufficiently to stand on the perch and get

their heads in the feeding ports. You may get pigeons from time to time mopping up under the feeder. There is always a certain amount of spilled seed there.

You will probably have to resign yourself to feeding house sparrows. They are also quite resourceful and small enough to feed in any feeder.

I would argue that feeding sparrows and pigeons is not all that bad. People whose backyards abut national parks can get really fussy about what they are willing to feed, but here in the city we should be a little less restrictive.

My friend David Standish follows this philosophy in his feeding operations in Lakeview. David has the usual tiny backyard of the city householder. He has a honey locust tree on one side of the yard and the western branches of the elm tree next door on the other side. He stocks two seed feeders and a suet feeder (for woodpeckers) and scatters seed on the deck outside his kitchen window. He feeds squirrels, pigeons, house sparrows, and anything else that shows up. The view out his kitchen window is a strong argument for feeding trash birds.

Imagine a typical winter day in Chicago. The view out your kitchen window is bounded at the top by a grim, iron gray sky. The ground is covered with pale gray snow. A dull brown brick wall and parts of your porch—which is, of course, painted gray—complete the view.

In this kind of environment, it is a pleasure to contemplate the animation in a flock of sparrows, David is convinced that at least two tribes of the birds come to his feeder. One of the tribes is marked by some white flight feathers. The presumed patriarch of this tribe is an old male whose rakishly upswept white wing feathers have led David to call him Cadillac Jack.

You can get interested in sparrows if you look at them day to day. You start to notice who pushes whom from the choice perches. You notice who shows up with whom. David and I talk half-seriously about getting a permit to band his sparrows so we can find out where they live and how many of them nest in a square block and how large their feeding territories are.

If you are willing to put up with the sparrows, you can see lots of interesting stuff. David has seen 16 different species at his feeders, including downy woodpeckers, white-throated sparrows, purple finches, and even a kestrel that came to feed on one of the birds that was feeding at the feeder. Once we sat at David's kitchen table and counted 24 American tree sparrows, high-class sparrows feathered in rust and pearl gray, arctic birds who think that flying to Chicago is going south for the winter.

If you get into feeding, you will almost inevitably want to expand as David has. More feeders bring in more birds. David's suet feeder has brought him regular visits from downy woodpeckers and one appearance from the larger, and rarer, hairy woodpecker.

I once met a lady in Streamwood who had a large backyard with 31 feeders scattered over it. She fed mixed seed and sunflower seed and thistles and pecan butter, and a whole lot of stuff I had never heard of. Her backyard was constantly filled with birds. From her kitchen window you could see flocks of redpolls, goldfinches, cardinals, and mourning doves. They were in constant motion around the yard. Looking at them could make winter almost bearable.

3 › Creatures Great and Small

Hunting for Frogs on Elston Avenue

In the Forest Preserves and Elsewhere

May 16, 1986

I have been a sucker for frogs since I was a kid. Every spring from about age seven until I got old enough to realize that girls were even more fun than amphibians, I would snatch a few empty mason jars from the fruit cellar in our basement and go in search of tadpoles.

My hunting ground was the pond. It needed no other name since it was the only pond in my world. I would remove my shoes and socks at the edge of the water, roll up my pants legs—never quite far enough, of course—and wade in.

Tadpoles are easy to catch. I would stand quietly, bent over far enough that I could hold the mason jar under water. Soon, a tadpole would swim within scooping range and fall victim to my trap.

When I had three or four, I would take them home and install them in an old fishbowl. I am a little vague about what I fed them. It may have been goldfish food left over from the unfortunate piscine that had briefly inhabited the bowl before going belly up. Whatever they ate, they grew very nicely, sprouting hind legs first and then growing front legs as their tails got shorter and their heads got flatter.

When they were fully adult, I took them back to the pond. My dream was to have a huge aquarium where I could keep adults, but I was as far from that as I was from the 2.5-inch reflecting telescope that I also wanted desperately.

I have no idea what kind of frogs these were. To me they were just frogs, no additional adjectives required. I'm not sure I even knew that there were many different kinds of anurans—to give them their formal name. But of course, there are many. Twenty-seven hundred different kinds worldwide, and 81 in North America north of the Rio Grande. Here in Illinois, we have 20 species: 3 toads and 17 frogs, including our eponymous endangered subspecies, the Illinois chorus frog.

89

Times have been hard for wildlife in this state for the past century or two, and frogs have suffered as much as if not more than other sorts of creatures. The draining and filling of wetlands combined with the pollution of our waterways are very tough on animals that breed in water.

This year, the state Department of Conservation is using some of the money citizens have donated through the nongame checkoff on our state income tax forms to finance a modest survey of Illinois' frog and toad populations.

On the evening of May 5, I went along with a party of six frog surveyors whose territory is the northwest side of Chicago and adjacent suburbs. Party is the right word here. You put seven people in a van and send them in search of frogs along Elston Avenue, and a certain hilarity is almost bound to result.

The methodology of the census is based on breeding-bird surveys. The surveyors travel a ten-mile route, stopping every half mile to listen for singing males. This way of doing things makes a lot of sense for birds, because there are at least some birds in almost every kind of situation, from high rises to cornfields to suburban yards to virgin forests. But frogs are more specialized. You could lay out a ten-mile route almost anywhere this side of the Okefenokee Swamp and miss every frog along the way if the ponds happened to fall between the stops. The problem is especially acute in a city, where the frogs are likely to be scattered in the few remaining natural areas.

Fortunately, Alan Anderson had laid out our route in so artful a manner that we were able to hear something singing at a grand total of 3 of our 20 stops.

Alan; Laurel Ross, the naturalist from North Park Village Nature Center; Elaine Vercruysee of Chicago Audubon; Wayne Swoboda, a professor at Northeastern Illinois University; Allen Feldman, an aquarist at the Shedd Aquarium; and Karen Furnweger, a reptile fancier who keeps an assortment of turtles and crocodilians in her apartment, made up our party.

We started at North Park Village, where American toads were trilling in the marshy pond near the nature center. Toads spend their adult lives on dry land, zapping insects on the forest floor with their extendible tongues. But in spring when they emerge from hibernation, they hop toward water to find mates. The males trill their songs in the evenings to attract females.

American toads are slow-moving and easily caught in their woodland homes, but they are not without defenses. Glands on either side of their necks secrete a poison that inflames the mouth and throat of a would-be predator and causes nausea, irregular heartbeat, and even death. Few predators try eating toad more than once.

We got our second species, the western chorus frog, at stop number four, the northeast corner of LaBagh Woods Forest Preserve. We also began to appreciate just how noisy the city is. Just a thin strip of woods separated us from the Edens Expressway, and the din nearly drowned out every other noise. I started wondering how frogs, or birds for that matter, managed to hear each other singing in the midst of all this racket.

Chorus frogs are tiny creatures. A very large individual might be an inch and a half long. The male's song sounds like the noise you get by running your fingernail over the tips of the teeth on a comb. The males sing in classic frog fashion, sitting upright on a lily pad or other floating vegetation.

Once we turned onto Elston Avenue, our chances of hearing frogs dropped to about zero. One of our stops was right in front of the secretary of state's driver testing facility, where, needless to say, we heard no frogs. Since the secretary of state will be up for reelection soon, we might consider asking him just what he plans to do about reintroducing a healthy amphibian population to his branch offices.

We didn't hear another frog until the last stop on our itinerary, a forest preserve north of Oakton Street along the North Branch of the Chicago River. These were chorus frogs again, and we sat along the roadside to enjoy the music. Our presence attracted the police, but after Laurel offered the sensible explanation that we were counting frogs, the policeman drove off, his expression suggesting that we were nuts but probably harmless nuts.

By this time, it was past midnight, and all of us were growing a bit weary. But my fatigue was tempered by a sense of peace that was almost euphoric. For on this night, the curse was lifted. All of our froggers are also birders, and at all the likely stops along the route, Alan Anderson played a tape of screech owls and great horned owls in hopes of getting a response.

Screech owls are common birds all over the eastern U.S., but I had never seen one that I could put on my life list, and I didn't expect to see one on our frog count. Long ago, when I was seven or eight years old and spending the summer on my grandparents' farm, I had shot an owl. In those times, owl, like frog and pond, needed no qualifiers, but I now know that what I shot was a red phase screech owl. (Screech owls come in two colors, gray and rusty red.)

My grandparents hated owls. Given the bird's eating habits, this dislike was irrational and self-destructive, but it was nonetheless common among farmers.

It was a clear, cool summer evening. The sun had just sunk below the distant horizon, but the western sky still glowed a fiery orange. The bird landed on a limb about ten feet up in the old oak in the yard. The tree was ancient, far older than the farm, and it was barely hanging on to life.

I had a Daisy Red Ryder carbine, a BB gun new that summer, and my grandpa told me to get it and shoot the bird. My first four or five shots must have missed, because the bird didn't move a feather. But the next one hit. The bird fell and hung upside down, holding onto the branch with one talon while its wings flapped futilely. I pumped four or five more shots into it, and it fell to the ground. Grandpa finished it off with a hoe.

I had always figured that this sordid little incident had permanently scotched my chances of seeing another screech owl, just as George Halas could never make it to the Super Bowl after letting Dick Butkus play when his knees were bad. Other birders could call up owls by the flock, but though I worked for years perfecting my screech owl imitation, no birds ever responded to it.

But at Miami Woods, the penultimate stop on our frog run, Alan had wandered a little ways into the woods while the rest of us stood listening by the roadside. Suddenly, he ran up, excitedly telling us that a screech owl had landed in a tree about four feet over his head.

He grabbed his tape recorder from the van, and we all followed him into the woods. When he played the tape, *two* owls responded, landing silently in a tree at the woodland edge. We could see them silhouetted against the vague gray of the suburban sky.

They stayed briefly and then flew, but when I tried my screech owl imitation, the birds came back and again posed for us. We watched them for a moment and then left to avoid disturbing them further. I felt a great weight lifted from my soul.

Caterpillars
Eating Machines

August 30, 1985

This story starts with the caterpillar on the parsley stem. Actually, it starts with the parsley, and the parsley is the result of our moving, after years in apartments, into a house with a proper backyard. It is a city backyard. You couldn't put a tennis court in it. A couple of pool tables, maybe, but not a tennis court.

But it is big enough for a modest garden with tomatoes and broccoli and green peppers and onions and cucumbers and green beans and, of course, herbs. We have basil and fennel and oregano and mint and the aforementioned parsley. Far too much parsley in fact. So much parsley that I am thinking of going into the garnish supply business. We could decorate every surf-and-turf in Cook County and scarcely dent our crop.

I saw the caterpillar on one of my frequent strolls around the estate. Stretched out along the stem, it was almost invisible. Its pale green body blended nicely with the color of the stem, and the black transverse stripes that decorated each of its 13 body segments could have been bits of earth showing through. When I knelt for a closer look, I noticed yellow spots along the border of each of the stripes.

I have written before about how difficult it is to deal with unknown insects. Field guides to birds, mammals, and reptiles are meant to be definitive. If it lives here, it is in the book. But insect guides are like public opinion polls. They supply the gross outlines of the subject, but a lot of the nuances get lost. Lepidoptera, the order of insects to which butterflies and moths belong, is represented by 12,000 species in North America. A field guide that included all of them would outweigh most of its readers. So when my quick search through the caterpillar pictures turned up nothing remotely like my specimen, I sighed at the depth of my ignorance and went on to other things.

But then last Sunday morning while I was standing on our balcony surveying the grounds—I handle most of the surveying; my wife Glenda does most of the weeding—I saw a huge butterfly flutter into the yard. It landed briefly on a zinnia blossom. It was a swallowtail, a member of the family of butterflies named for the long, slender streamers that extend back from the hind wings and remind people of the forked tail of a swallow. Its dark wings were decorated with yellow spots and, along the inner edge at the rear, a bit of blue and red.

I ran down the stairs and out the back door, hoping for a better look, but it was gone by the time I got outside. I opened the field guide feeling certain that I would find either nothing remotely like it or seven totally different species that could be the one I was looking for. But this time the force was with me, because the picture of the eastern black swallowtail was very much like what I had seen, and when I turned to the text, I read: "Caterpillar is green with black head and a black band on each segment incorporating a series of golden spots." And under the heading "Food" it told me: "Caterpillar eats foliage of plants in the carrot family, including wild and cultivated carrot, celery, and *parsley*." Well, doggone.

I walked back outside and surveyed my parsley crop a little more closely. The caterpillar was quite close to the stem he had been sitting on before; searching carefully through the dense foliage of our bumper crop, I found two more. We are infested with black swallowtails.

The book also said that these caterpillars can become serious pests, and I suppose if I were counting on the sale of the carrot crop to pay the bills, I could see it that way. But I could go the rest of my life without a taste of parsley and never miss it. If I have to make the choice, I'll take the butterflies anytime. As a city person, my previous experience with insect infestation involved cockroaches running through the butter dish, and compared to that these gorgeous creatures don't seem very menacing. Can you imagine one of those creepy, nature's-revenge horror movies called *Swallowtail*?

I've been watching the caterpillars for the past two days, stretched out on my stomach, peering through a magnifying glass. Caterpillars have a very limited repertoire of behavior. They are eating machines, and their daily routine consists of eating everything in reach and then moving within reach of something else to eat. But it is amazing to see how efficiently they chow down.

A caterpillar's head consists of two simple eyes, two very short antennae, and a jaw with a cutting edge like a razor. Next time your *sole bonne femme* comes garnished with a sprig of parsley, don't just look at it. Try to take a bite out of it. Clomp your incisors onto it, and chances are you will not neatly slice the leaf in twain. You will either have to hold the leaf in your teeth and yank on the stem with your hand or slide the whole problem along to your molars, where you can grind it to death.

Caterpillars that weigh a gram or so and have almost no jaw strength can slice a parsley leaf as neatly as a brain surgeon. They eat like 12-year-olds attacking corn on the cob, starting at one side of the leaf, swiveling their heads a bite at a time to the other edge, and then—carriage return—back to the starting point for another run.

Internally, caterpillars are mostly intestine. Their job is to eat enough to provide the energy to create an adult butterfly. They start life as an egg that has been laid by an adult female on the underside of a leaf of an appropriate food plant. A newly hatched black swallowtail caterpillar is about three millimeters long. It is black with a white saddle that gives it a useful resemblance to a bird's droppings. Its first act is to eat the eggshell. Then it starts on the leaf. In the course of its larval life, it will shed its skin—actually its exoskeleton—five or six times until it attains the inch-and-a-half length and bright coloring of the bugs that are eating my parsley.

A caterpillar's 13 segments consist of a head, a thorax of three segments, each equipped with a pair of clawed legs, and nine abdominal segments, five of them outfitted with stubby little Long John Silver appendages called prolegs. As a proper insect, a caterpillar has only six real legs, but these prolegs serve to help the animal get from leaf to leaf.

When it is finished growing, the caterpillar attaches itself to a stem and then turns into a pupa. Unlike the pupae of moths, butterfly pupae are not sheltered in a silken cocoon; but inside their pupal skin, they can ride out a Chicago winter if need be. The larval tissues of the caterpillar literally dissolve—the inside of the pupa is mostly liquid—and reconstitute themselves as an adult butterfly.

Black swallowtails produce two or three generations in a summer, and I will be watching my caterpillars to see if they are going to metamorphose into adults before the cold weather or spend the winter hanging onto the dead remains of my parsley crop and wait until spring to assume the responsibilities of adulthood.

The question that really arouses my curiosity is how mom knew where to lay the eggs. The relationship between a butterfly or caterpillar and its food plants is very precise. Black swallowtails feed on a whole family of plants, but some of their relatives are tied to a particular genus or even a single species of plant. Parsley leaves are not a balanced diet, so the insect's physiology must be exactly tuned to the mix of chemicals it gets from the plant.

Plants don't just sit there and let themselves be eaten. They have evolved a grand assortment of chemical defenses, deadly poisons in some cases, alkaloids that will make you very sick in other cases. Humans have discovered that many of these chemical defenses will get you stiffer than a billy goat before they kill you, leading us to cultivate coffee, coca, and opium poppies, but a caterpillar has to be immune to its host's defenses. If it bites into the wrong plant, it may die.

Butterflies and flowering plants evolved at about the same time, and many swallowtails—one of the oldest butterfly families—feed on members of the magnolia family, a mostly tropical group of great antiquity with a distribution that matches well with the bulk of swallowtail species. Sassafras, a temperate-zone member of the magnolia family, contains an oil with the same chemical structure and scent as an oil in fennel, a plant of the parsley family. Some swallowtails have switched from parsleys to sage, especially green sage, *Artemisia dracunculus*, a plant whose domestic form is known as tarragon. Tarragon, fennel, and anise all contain an aromatic substance called anesic aldehyde.

So we can at least speculate that these chemical affinities have led the swallowtails from the tropical magnolias to the temperate-zone parsleys and sages, and we can guess that the caterpillars are immune to the defenses of these plants and that adult butterflies let scent guide them to the right place to lay their eggs. All of which means that my herb garden is probably doomed.

Woodchucks
A.k.a. Whistle Pigs

March 8, 1991

So far as I know, the groundhog is the only rodent to have its own official day. It also has its own song, an old southern Appalachian banjo tune about an epic hunt. It is only fitting for banjo players to sing about groundhogs—or whistle pigs, as alternative name that shows up in some versions of the song—since groundhog hide was commonly used to make the heads of homemade banjos.

The groundhog has other names as well. Woodchuck is the most common. This name has fed endless speculation on the amount of timber a groundhog would hurl if it were capable of throwing logs around. The question, as so often in philosophy, resolves itself into a semantic argument. "Woodchuck" is actually a corrupted version of Cree or Chippewa words that sound something like "wuchak" or "otchig." These words have nothing to do with either lumber or throwing. For that matter, they have nothing to do with woodchucks. They actually describe another small mammal, the fisher. However, since nobody but some of Cecil Adams's daffier correspondents would wonder how much wu a wuchak would chak if a wuchak could chak wu, we may consider this conundrum settled.

You might think I am about a month late in writing about woodchucks, since Groundhog Day is traditionally celebrated on February 2. But the fact is, Groundhog Day is far too early. In most of this animal's range, it is sunk in deepest slumber in early February. March is a far more likely month for ground hog emergence in Illinois.

Still, it is at least possible that a woodchuck might awaken from hibernation and take a look around in February. For reasons unknown, even the deepest hibernators wake up from time to time during the winter. Some species of ground squirrels store food in their burrows and periodically get up to eat. Woodchucks do not store any food, but some scientists think they get up to pee, since urination is an almost invariable action of an awakened woodchuck.

The general consensus among woodchuck students is that there must be an important reason for the animals to get up. Coming out of hibernation uses large amounts of energy—the process takes about three hours—so selection pressure would probably act against it if it didn't offer some compensating advantage.

Hibernation is a strategy for conserving energy, for riding out difficult times with a minimum expenditure. There are all sorts of variants of this strategy. Physiologists who study it usually reserve the term "hibernation" for really deep slumbers. The less extreme forms are called "torpor." Torpor can be very slight and short-lived. Camels and some other desert mammals can reduce their body temperatures slightly during the cold desert night and raise them back up in the morning.

Bears experience torpor rather than true hibernation. In winter a black bear has a rectal temperature of 90 to 95 degrees Fahrenheit. Its heart rate is about 10 beats to the minute, compared to 40 a minute for a sleeping bear in summer, and its overall metabolic rate is 50 to 60 percent of summer levels. Bears can awaken quickly from this state, so one must admire the bravery of the biologists who obtained those rectal temperatures. Wouldn't it be great if Bill Kurtis would do a show on these people? Can't you imagine Bill, thermometer in hand, creeping up on a snoring bear while maintaining a constant whispered voice-over?

An animal is not considered a true hibernator unless its body temperature drops below about 40 degrees. This sort of profound slumber is most highly developed among the rodents, especially the sciuromorphs, the group that includes squirrels and woodchucks. As it happens, the woodchuck is the largest true hibernator in existence. When it lies down in October or November, its heart rate begins to get slower. It may skip beats as it slows down. Next oxygen consumption declines, and finally body temperature. Once it is fully in its winter sleep, its body temperature drops from a summer level of 97 degrees to hover just a few degrees above freezing. Its heart slows from about 80 beats a minute to about 4. Its breathing rate slows from about 25 to 30 breaths per minute to about 1 every five minutes. It is living on the fat reserves it built up during the summer, but it is not using them very fast.

This turns out to be very helpful to the animal. When it emerges from its slumbers in early spring, most plants will still be dormant. There will be no new growth of leaves yet and certainly no flowers or fruits. Woodchucks have to get by on dried stuff left over from last year and on bark.

They need energy right away because reproduction is the spring's first activity. Woodchucks are generally solitary animals. Each one digs a large and ramified burrow system that usually has at least two entrances and may have as much as 75 feet of interconnected tunnels. Within the burrow will be one or more nests, areas where the tunnel is widened and deepened. These nests—hibernacula, nurseries, and sleeping areas—may be as much as five feet underground, which puts them well below the frost line. Woodchucks also dig a separate defecation chamber in the burrow.

In spring a male woodchuck will move into a female's burrow for a brief time. This is the only portion of the year when the adults depart from their usual solitary mode of life. The young are born in April after a 32-day gestation period. An average litter consists of four or five animals. They weigh about an ounce each at birth, and they are naked, blind, and helpless. They don't open their eyes until they are about a month old, and they don't go above ground for another couple of weeks after that.

Food has to be the major interest of young woodchucks. Between April and November they have to grow from one ounce to about six pounds in order to sleep comfortably through their first hibernation. They won't reach full adult size until their second year, when the males will average close to nine pounds each. The females will be slightly smaller. Woodchucks have been known to weigh as much as 14 pounds.

They achieve this impressive size on a diet of grasses, clovers, leaves, fruit, and bark. They feed mostly on the ground, although they can and do climb trees when they need to. According to various studies, they are able to get enough to eat while feeding only a few hours a day. Even in summer they spend most of their time in their burrows.

Woodchucks are easily recognized. They are thick-bodied animals, much chunkier than squirrels. Their ears are short and rounded. Their fur is reddish brown tipped with white, a combination that produces a grizzled appearance. Their tails are thick and bushy, but not nearly as long as a tree squirrel's.

You can see woodchucks in lots of places. If you get out in the country, you may see them along country roads. The few hours they spend above ground are always in the daylight. They seem to want to take advantage of the little chance they get to absorb some rays, so you'll often see them just sitting in the sun. When they see you, they may give a loud whistle before heading for their burrows.

Woodchucks benefited from the changes in the Illinois landscape that accompanied settlement. Robert Kennicott, writing in 1857, noted that they had been rare in northeastern Illinois in the past, but they were then becoming quite common. They are edge animals. You can often find their burrows where woodlands meet grasslands. You probably would not have found them on the unbroken prairie.

The entrances to burrows are large—up to a foot across—and there is likely to be a large heap of earth next to the entrance. In late summer when the grass is tall, trails radiating out from the burrow entrance may mark the customary paths the woodchucks follow to get to feeding areas.

Woodchuck burrows have some importance to the ecosystem. Other animals—rabbits, skunks, opossums, even foxes—use them for shelter. In building the burrows the woodchucks also help turn over the soil, bringing minerals up from the subsoil and depositing—especially in those defecation chambers—organic matter deep below the surface. Somebody one calculated that woodchucks in the state of New York rearranged 1,600,000 tons of soil every year.

In the Cook County forest preserves, woodchucks are likely to be hanging around the borders between woodlands and open fields, and they're more likely to be out in the middle of the day that at sunrise or sunset.

Counting Butterflies
Monitoring in the Prairie

July 15, 1988

The first dog face butterfly of the morning scudded by as Ron Panzer was introducing us to Gensburg-Markham Prairie. Two inches across, bright yellow, marked with heavy black at the wing tips, the dog face soared and swooped, dancing in the sun. Later, Panzer caught one in his long-handled net and showed us the details of the wing pattern that give the insect its common name. The scalloped edges of the black at the wing tips outlined the profile of a poodle's head in the yellow of each wing. A black "eyespot" within the yellow added to the illusion.

Last Saturday, Gensburg was filled with dog faces, and by the end of an hour's walk, all nine of Panzer's students could identify a passing dog face. The mystery of the world of butterflies had been slightly reduced.

We nine students are all volunteer butterfly monitors recruited by the Nature Conservancy to keep track of wild lepidopterans on nature preserves in Illinois. Most of us will be working in natural areas in the forest preserve systems of the six counties of metropolitan Chicago. So far as we know, we are the only volunteer butterfly monitors in the U.S., a position of leadership that is just what one might expect from this area.

Butterfly monitoring is a first step into the realm of the invertebrates, the animals that hold the living world together. We vertebrates like to think of ourselves as the earth's dominant creatures. We are big, beautiful, noble, stately, and filled with dignity. But we are like Louis XIV and his courtiers. We stand around admiring each other's finery while the invertebrates, the peasants of the animal world, do all the work. Bald eagles may inspire our awe, but they are less important than bumblebees to the functioning of ecosystems.

Invertebrates pollinate almost all the flowers, aerate and fertilize the soil, and break down dead plant and animal matter, releasing minerals for another cycle through the system. They far outnumber vertebrates in numbers of species, in biomass, and in energy consumption. A study of a ten-acre piece of Maryland forest discovered 73 nests of a single mound-building ant species. The total population of workers was estimated to be 12 million. At an average weight of about 11.5 milligrams, those 12 million workers represent an biomass of about 300 pounds. These numbers account for only one of several species of ants in the woods, and ants represent only a tiny fraction of the total population of invertebrates.

In addition to their need for pollinators, many plants have other kinds of symbiotic relationships with invertebrates. A local prairie ant, *Formica montana*, carries the seeds of various native plants into its nests. The seeds are coated with ant candy, a substance the ants enjoy eating. The ants eat the candy, keep the seeds underground for a time—perhaps until they are ready to germinate—and then carry them back to the surface.

Invertebrates, especially insects, are a major source of food for creatures with backbones. We would have few songbirds without insects. Even seed-eating species often feed their developing young on a high-protein insect diet.

Nature preserves are supposed to be high-quality examples of native biotic communities, and they can't be that without healthy, diverse, and abundant populations of animals without backbones. Surveying all the tens of thousands of species of insects, spiders, nematodes, annelids, and centipedes is way beyond our resources. Surveying butterflies is a place to start, a way to begin checking the health of our preserves. Butterflies are relatively conspicuous and easy to identify. They occur in a manageable number of species—about 100 in the northern part of Illinois—and they are annuals, short-lived creatures whose numbers respond very quickly to changes in the environment. If something is going wrong, the butterflies will let us know right away.

Ron Panzer is the logical person to teach us how to survey butterflies. He is the site manager of Gensburg—the land is owned by Northeastern Illinois University—and he supplements that job with contract surveys of insect life for various conservation agencies. He is also a patient and enthusiastic instructor, the sort of person who makes the daunting task of learning all the local lepidopterans seem manageable, even easy.

We began our formal instruction in the small gravel parking area at the edge of the Gensburg prairie. Panzer showed us the chief article of equipment we would need, a heavy-duty net mounted on a long wooden handle. He also recommended some guidebooks and showed us a few cases of mounted specimens.

The specimens raised some questions, the principal question being, should we take any ourselves? We may be dealing with very rare animals, and none of us wants to have our activities make them any rarer. Panzer tells us that we may have to take a few individuals of species that are very difficult to identify, but we should keep our collecting to a minimum. For most species, it will be enough to net them, examine them carefully, and release them—and we should be striving to develop our eyes to the point where we can identify the local butterflies on the wing without disturbing them in any way.

Panzer has got to that point himself. Like a skilled birder, he has assimilated all the details of shape, size, color, and behavior that make each species distinctive. He has assimilated all this so thoroughly that sometimes when we ask him how he knows that a particular fluttering insect is, for example, a wood nymph, his first response is "Well, it looks like one." He has to think for a moment to remember which visual clues he is responding to.

Even in the parking lot, his eye is active. He notices a byssus skipper on a milkweed flower next to his truck and excitedly points it out to us. The byssus is a true rarity, one of the specialties of Gensburg that you can't see in many other places.

Skippers are the shorebirds or fall warblers of butterflies. There are many species, and they all look alike. They are small—wingspans usually range from an inch to an inch and a half—and colored in various shades of brown and tawny orange arranged in obscure patterns. When you can make quick identifications of skippers, you have arrived as a butterfly expert.

The caterpillars of skippers feed on grasses and sedges. Some are quite catholic in their tastes, but others are tied to a particular genus or even a single species. The byssus, Panzer thinks, feeds exclusively on big bluestem grass, a dominant plant of our native prairies. Two hundred years ago, when big bluestem was one of the most common plants in Illinois, the byssus skipper was probably one of the most common butterflies. The nearly total destruction of our native grasslands has made it rare.

The heart of our morning lesson was a walk through the prairie. Panzer took the lead, and his partner Don Stillwaugh brought up the rear. Gensburg is famous for its great assortment of butterflies, and they were out in numbers for us. We counted—thanks to two pairs of expert eyes—15 species in the course of an hour, along with four interesting moths, some nice beetles, and a very rare katydid.

We saw two kinds of fritillaries, orange-and-black butterflies that are among the largest and showiest we have. Panzer told us of a girl who came along on a tour he gave of the prairie. She was wearing orange socks, and the fritillaries were all attracted to the color. She walked surrounded by butterflies.

We saw a viceroy, a species that mimics the monarch. Birds avoid eating monarchs because they taste bad. The viceroy's mimicry presumably saves it from being eaten.

One short stretch of path was bordered by Indian hemp, a species of dogbane, that was just coming into flower. For whatever reason, this was butterfly central. The two-spotted skipper—which may soon be declared endangered in Illinois—was there, and so were the silver-spotted skipper and the peck's skipper. A big black swallowtail, a coral hairstreak, and an American painted lady flew by.

We found two species of hummingbird moths feeding on the dogbane flowers. These moths hover in front of flowers in the manner of hummingbirds, inserting their long proboscises into flowers in search of nectar.

Panzer trotted up and down the line of dogbane, calling out the species, while the rest of us followed after, trying to remember the names and field marks of everything we saw. I felt the scales falling from my eyes. My perceptual universe was beginning to change. Creatures that had been part of the visual background for me were acquiring distinctive forms, moving into the foreground. When next I look at a prairie, I will see more than I saw before.

The effects of the drought were quite noticeable at Gensburg. Many of the plants were little more than half their usual size; flowers were relatively scarce, and most of the blooms were smaller than normal. Prairie plants are very long lived, and their strategy for dealing with hard times is to hold back, to cut down the demands they make on the environment, and to wait for things to improve. However, they evolved under conditions of recurrent drought, and even this year they look quite green.

Insects cannot hunker down and wait for rain. They have to reproduce now or not at all. It seems likely that this year's drought will cut insect populations next year and perhaps for several years to come. Butterfly monitoring gets us started on the job of tracing the changes the drought is producing.

Sludge Worms
They Indicate Pollution

February 14, 1992

Down in the mud at the bottom of Burnham Harbor and Montrose Harbor and Calumet Harbor and all the other shallow sheltered waters along our lakefront lives a bright red worm, an animal so interesting they named it twice: *Tubifex tubifex*. It lives in a tube it fashions out of the bottom mud. The tube straddles the water-mud interface, extending a few centimeters down into the mud and a few centimeters above it.

It is not alone down there. It has an equally bright colored relative named *Limnodrilus hoffmeisteri* that is probably even more common in the mud of our harbors.

Both worms live upside down. Their bright red tails extend out of the tops of their tubes. The tails wave and wiggle almost constantly. If you were scuba diving in one of our harbors, you might find the entire bottom practically coated with these tiny bright red writhing tails. Recorded population for *Tubifex* range up to 8,000 worms per square meter.

Of course, if you are scuba diving someplace where the bottom is coated with *Tubifex* and *Limnodrilus*, you should seriously consider getting back to dry land as soon as possible. Both of these worms are what ecologists call indicator species, species whose presence tells us something significant about the environment. And what these worms tell us is that there is a whole lot of sewage in the water. The common name for both species is sludge worm.

When sewage or other kinds of organic wastes are dumped in water, all sorts of organisms get involved in breaking them down into their constituent elements. Bacteria are the most important of these decomposers. Decomposers, like the rest of us, need oxygen. The heavier the load of sewage, the more oxygen they need.

In a shallow harbor full of clean water, oxygen saturation can reach 100 percent; that is, the water is holding all the dissolved oxygen it can. Add sewage, and the decomposers begin to multiply. Oxygen levels start to go down. As they drop, animals sensitive to oxygen deprivation start to vanish from the local fauna. *Limnodrilus* and *Tubifex* populations go up. *Tubifex* can live in water with saturation levels of oxygen as low as 10 percent. In laboratory experiments one-third of test populations have survived up to 48 days with no oxygen at all. *Limnodrilus* is not quite as tolerant of low oxygen levels, so in the most heavily polluted situations *Tubifex* may be the only living thing present bigger than a bacterium.

Indiana Harbor, generally regarded as the most polluted place in the Great Lakes, is paradise for *Tubifex*. In that environment it has no predators and no competitors.

The bright red color of sludge worms is a result of their strategy for surviving in low oxygen levels. The color is created by a chemical very like the hemoglobin in our own blood. Like hemoglobin, it is an oxygen carrier, and these worms have so much of it that they can both collect oxygen from nearly stagnant waters and store oxygen in their bodies for future use.

Sludge worms belong to a family of annelids called the oligochaetes. The name means "few chaetae." Chaetae are hairlike bristles that extend from the sides of the bodies of these worms. Earthworms are oligochaetes, and *Tubifex* and *Limnodrilus* feed just as earthworms do, ingesting dirt, digesting all the digestible material in it, and excreting the rest. If you wade in water with a muddy bottom and feel the mud squishing between your toes, what you are squishing is mainly worm doo-doo, the castings left by oligochaetes.

In 1974 and '75 a graduate student at Northeastern Illinois University named David M. Heffernan collected samples of bottom mud from 19 locations in southwestern Lake Michigan. Ten of his locations were near shore in Burnham Harbor, Calumet Harbor, and near Navy Pier. The other nine were offshore, ranging from a spot one-half kilometer from Navy Pier to a location 40 kilometers out. He found the pollution-tolerant oligochaetes at 13 of his 19 locations, and overall the worms made up 39 percent of the total animals collected. Our protected near-shore waters—harbors and waters inside breakwaters—are polluted.

But oligochaetes are not the only bright red bottom dwellers in our harbors. We also have bloodworms. Bloodworms are not worms at all. They are the larval stage of a family of nonbiting midges called chironomids. Chironomid larvae burrow into the bottom. They eat mostly detritus, the bits of dead plant material that constantly rain down on the lake bottom.

Some chironomids spin nets of fine filaments across the entrances of their burrows. They wait a few minutes to allow the net to collect whatever is floating by, and then they eat the whole business, both the collected particles and the net. Then they spin another net.

Chironomid species vary in their tolerance for low oxygen levels, so we can get an indication of pollution levels by identifying the species of bloodworms that live in it.

Our harbors are also home to large numbers of clams. If you dig up some bottom mud, you will almost invariably find clam shells in it. The shells endure long after the animals in them have died, so shells will be much more abundant than living clams. Snails of various species are also common in shallow water.

Offshore, where the water gets cleaner, Heffernan found a different sort of fauna living on or near the bottom. The dominant animals here were tiny crustaceans. There were amphipods, also called side-swimmers or scuds. And there were aquatic sow bugs, relatives of creatures that live under rocks and in damp leaf litter on land.

Pontoporeia is the most typical scud genus in the Great Lakes. It lives only in cold, clean waters, so its presence is an indication that away from shore Lake Michigan is still in pretty good shape. Pontos, as limnologists call them, are vertical migrants. They spend the day on the bottom and then rise into the water at night. They never get to the surface, but they do get high enough to feed on plankton.

Another clean-water indicator in Heffernan's collection was *Mysis relicta,* commonly called an opossum shrimp. This is another vertical migrant that spends the day on the bottom and the night in the water. In winter opossum shrimp may rise all the way to the surface. In summer they stay in the deeper, colder water.

Heffernan's results reveal the great variety in communities of benthic (bottom-dwelling) animals in Lake Michigan. To learn something about how all these communities sort out, I talked to Dr. Jerry Kaster of the Center for Great Lakes Studies in Milwaukee. According to Dr. Kaster, the benthic communities of the lake can be classified by the nature of the bottom and by the amount of pollution present.

Mud bottoms feature oligochaetes, clams, and chironomids. Bottoms of hardpan clay have lots of snails, some pontos, some chironomids, and usually leeches. Sand bottoms feature chironomids almost exclusively— the abrasiveness of the sand seems to eliminate almost everything else. A fourth kind of bottom, which Kaster calls cobble reef, is paved with rocks ranging in size from Ping-Pong balls to VWs. Cobble reefs have the richest benthic fauna in the lake, including freshwater sponges, hydras, and bryozoans. Bryozoans (the name means moss animals) are colonial creatures that live attached to rocks and feed by filtering edible matter out of the water.

Cobble reefs are the cleanest benthic environment in the lake. The exposed rocks on the bottom show that waves and currents are preventing runoff from accumulating. Mud bottoms include the most polluted waters in the lakes. However, there are unpolluted mud bottoms far from shore where wind and currents combine to allow particles to settle. Oligochaetes are common in such places, but the genus is likely to be *Stylodrilus* rather than *Tubifex* or *Limnodrilus*.

The benthic communities of the Great Lakes didn't get much attention until quite recently. In the past decade we have learned that persistent toxics such as PCBs, DDT, and polyaromatic hydrocarbons collect in the bottom mud. This was once thought to be a very good place for them, but now we know it isn't.

Oligochaetes and chironomids take in toxics from the mud as they feed. Present estimates are that a given molecule might be recycled 100 times through living organisms before it gets buried deep enough to be out of reach. Bottom-feeding fish take up the toxics when they eat a bloodworm or an oligochaete. Bottom-feeding fish include obligate bottom feeders like bullheads and carp as well as species like perch and lake trout that feed on the bottom sometimes and higher at other times.

Scuds feed on the bottom during the day and carry their load of toxics up at night, providing food for small trout and salmon. And when a trout that has been eating toxic food all its life finally dies, its body washes ashore and gets eaten by a bald eagle. Toxic loadings in bald eagles that live near the lakes are much higher than in inland birds, and as a result their reproductive success is much lower. Things on the bottom can rise up to haunt us.

Rattlesnake Hunting
Cutting-Edge Herpetology

August 14, 1992

I went rattlesnake hunting last Saturday. Guided by Tom Anton, who works in the fish department at the Field Museum and pursues snakes as an avocation, I wandered through several forest preserves along the Des Plaines River peering under hummocks of grass and turning over logs. I am still trying to decide whether this was a rational activity.

I am mildly phobic about snakes, probably as a result of being raised by a mother who can't stand to look at even a picture of a snake. In my career as an outdoorsperson, I have gone to some lengths to avoid contact with dangerous snakes. Most of my outdoor time has been spent in the great north woods, a land of bears and dangerous weather but no venomous reptiles.

My first real experience walking around in snake country was in the early '70s, when I did some hiking and backpacking with my wife in Arkansas. All the books said timber rattlers liked rocky hillsides, and that happened to be almost the only kind of place there was in the Ouachitas and Ozarks. My steps were short and slow. To get a better look at the ground I walked bent at the waist, and I lifted my feet so high between steps that I looked like a man trying to see if there was dog shit on the sole of his shoes. With steady application I could cover about a mile an hour in this style, so Glenda began to take the lead on our hikes. She grew up in the Ozarks and didn't seem to be bothered by the fact that she was walking over ground where the ranges of the timber rattler and the western diamondback overlap. Where copperheads slithered along the ridges. And down in the creek bottoms—cottonmouths.

Finally, moved by that deepest human terror, the fear of looking silly, I started to walk around with an assurance I usually didn't feel. But along the Des Plaines last Saturday, I was deliberately breaking the rules of snake avoidance, going out of my way to get close to a pit viper. I was picking up large boards, two-by-tens and old sheets of plywood, and flipping them over. Sticking my hands—or at least my fingertips—under those boards to prize them out of the ground.

Our search was unsuccessful. We found three garter snakes—two with the opaque, sightless eyes of serpents about to shed their skin—one masked shrew, and lots of ants and other insects. But no rattlers. I was hoping Tom would find a snake for us and spare me the tachycardia that would follow my discovering one. But I was also hoping I would find one and establish myself as a fearless snake hunter.

Massasaugas are small rattlers. The biggest are only a little over three feet long—about half the size of the biggest timber rattlers. Anecdotal evidence says their fangs cannot stab through the leather of an ordinary hiking boot. There is no known instance of a human dying from the bite of a massasauga, and very few instances of anyone being bitten. Anybody who has hung around them much says they are very unaggressive snakes, animals that defend themselves mainly by keeping still and hoping you don't see them.

The massasauga is the only venomous reptile native to the Chicago area. I should note that "venomous," not "poisonous," is the correct term. A poisonous snake would be a snake that killed anything that ate it. Venomous snakes poison the things they eat. When settlement began, massasaugas probably lived along the Des Plaines (as they do now), in Du Page County (where they have been extirpated), and in extreme southern Cook County (where they may still survive). The last sighting by a biologist at the southern site was in 1989, but local residents say they have seen some since then. Ken Mierzwa, who has been studying local reptiles for years, says that the possibility of a snakebite tends to blunt people's observational powers. "Fox snakes vibrate their tails. Hitting dry leaves, they can sound like rattlers. People say they saw a rattlesnake, but then they show you an out-of-focus Polaroid of a fox snake."

Our local massasaugas seem to have rather precise habitat requirements. They live along the borders between bottomland forests and wet prairies, or along the edges of a distinctive type of northern Illinois forest called a flatwoods. Mierzwa says they are found only in soils underlaid by a clay hardpan, and they appear to be dependent on the prairie crayfish to provide them with places to hibernate. The crayfish digs a burrow six feet deep with an enlarged chamber at the base that is big enough to hold a sleeping snake.

There are three subspecies of massasauga in North America. The eastern can be found in ever-declining numbers from southern Ontario and western New York to western Iowa. The western is the typical form in the area from western Iowa south and west through Kansas, Oklahoma, and Texas. The desert form lives in west Texas, New Mexico, and southeastern Arizona.

Massasaugas have been unfortunate in their habitat preferences. In Ontario and New York they live in wetlands. Some hibernate under sphagnum-moss hummocks in northern bogs. They are excellent swimmers, as evidenced by their presence on islands in Lake Huron. Of course we know what has happened to most eastern wetlands.

Here, as I said, they like places where bottomland forests meet wet prairies. One of their big problems throughout Illinois has been the lowering of the water table, a change that has come about both through heavy use of groundwater and through the effects of drainage projects. Many formerly wet areas are now dry and either plowed or paved. The range of the massasauga in Illinois has been reduced by two-thirds since settlement began, and within that range the animal maintains only small, scattered populations.

The western snake lives in the tallgrass prairie, especially along watercourses, so it too has lost much of its habitat. The desert massasauga is an animal of the desert grassland, a community that has been devastated by overgrazing and fire protection.

Animals of wetlands or river bottoms can easily develop a scattered, islanded distribution. Floods can carry them for miles, allowing them to create new population centers far from their original homes. But the naturally patchy distribution of the massasauga suggests that it is a relict, an animal that spread across its considerable range in a time when a different climate produced different vegetation. Climate changes over the past few thousand years could have shrunk the favored habitats and left much less room for this snake.

The accelerating decline of the massasauga has led to proposals that it be listed as an endangered species. It is on the "watch list" in Illinois, and biologists with the U.S. Fish and Wildlife Service are currently reviewing the possibility of a listing at the federal level.

There are definitely political considerations involved in putting a rattlesnake on the endangered list. Tell people there are venomous snakes in that forest preserve just behind their houses and many will start fantasizing about eight-foot cottonmouths coiled in their baby's crib. Conservatives will have great sport with the airhead environmentalists who have all sorts of ideals and no common sense. The commonsense approach, of course, is to ruthlessly exterminate anything that might possibly annoy you in any way. As late as the '60s people were still running rattlesnake roundups in Wheeling.

The massasauga is a predator that feeds high on the food chain. Voles and mice are its main foods. It grows slowly, and females reproduce only every other year. It is never going to be as common as, say, garter snakes. It is so shy and retiring that you would have to make a serious effort to get one to strike at you. The chance of it being a menace ranks just below the chance of being bitten to death by a huge pack of Yorkshire terriers.

Still, I am glad that we have the massasauga as at least a possible danger. Motorcycle gangs are the only scary things in most of our forest preserves, and we should have something natural that can command respect. Knowing there are snakes around raises your level of concentration. It suggests the power that resides in nature. Americans are traditionally devoted to taming or conquering nature, hence our murderous ways. If we were willing to recognize nature as a genuine great power, we could work out accommodations rather than seek conquests. Which means we could leave the snakes alone and stay alert enough not to step on one.

We were very alert last Saturday, but it did us no good. The weather was working against us. It got very hot early, so that the snakes were coiled up in the coolest, shadiest places they could find. With their cryptic coloration, they would be practically invisible to a human searcher. Tom Anton is a serious student of this snake—a friend called him the Jane Goodall of the massasauga. If he couldn't find any, they must have been lying very low.

Anton has observed these snakes so carefully and for so long that he has devised a way to identify individual animals. The pattern of spots on a snake's back is, he says, "like a thumbprint." In one snake the 24th and 25th spots, counting from the head, will be joined together. Another animal might have no joined spots, and another might have the 15th and 16th fused. Ellin Beltz, who is currently preparing a report on massasauga populations for the Illinois Department of Conservation, calls Anton's work, including the identification system, "cutting-edge herpetology."

Anton has been studying the snakes along the Des Plaines for years, watching their behavior and charting their movements using his ability to recognize individuals. His work will provide another insight into the complex workings of ecosystems, the real building blocks of life. But he can keep doing that work only as long as the ecosystem and all its parts continue to exist.

Ant Transplant
Four Shovels and a Pillow Case

March 27, 1987

On first hearing, you might think that *Formica montana* was some sort of western subsidiary of Plywood Minnesota, but it is in fact an ant and, more that that, it is a prairie ant, perhaps the most common species in our native grasslands.

F. montana is a mound-building species. Its nests are all in the ground and may extend three to four feet under the surface. The mounds that crown these nests are as much as six inches high and a yard across; the mounds are built of miscellaneous vegetation, dead plant stems, leaves, etc. that are piled up by the ants to form a sort of thatched roof over the nest.

This time of year, on warm sunny days, the worker ants move the colony's developing pupae—and often the queen as well—into chambers in the thatch to let the sun help warm them.

Last year about this time, some volunteers from the North Branch Prairie Project used their knowledge of the ants' habits to perform the first recorded ant transplant in Illinois history. Or should the word be "transanimal"?

They discovered the ants living on a tiny prairie remnant in Deerfield that was about to be destroyed by a highway-widening project. They collected a total of 11 mounds and moved them to Wayside Woods Prairie at Dempster and Lehigh streets in Morton Grove, one of the degraded prairie remnants that the North Branch Prairie Project is restoring. *F. montana* had been extirpated from Wayside at some unknown time in the past.

Transanimaling is a tricky business, especially when you are dealing with ants. You can't shoot a few with tranquilizer darts and ship them off. The North Branch Prairie people used a crew that consisted of four persons with shovels and one person with a pillow case. The four shovel wielders stood in a tight square, their shovels poised. At a signal, they all pushed their shovels into the earth and then lifted out a square plug of dirt and dropped it into the pillow case.

They had to be quick, because the ants would react to any disturbance by moving the queen and the pupae from their penthouse under the thatch to a place of safety deep in the soil.

All 11 colonies seemed to be doing well last summer at Wayside Woods, and if they thrive again this year the operation will be counted as a great success.

The new inhabitants of Wayside Woods Prairie will certainly have a very large effect on their new home. Ants are probably the most abundant land animals on earth. In tropical regions they replace earthworms as the principal movers of the soil—the Amazon basin has been described as a giant ants' nest—and even in temperate regions their excavations have a powerful effect. A study made in a Massachusetts woodland concluded that each year ants carry 50 grams of soil to the surface of every square yard of land area. This amounts to enough stuff to add an inch to the topsoil every 250 years.

The leaf-cutting ants of tropical America make agriculture truly impossible in the areas of their greatest abundance. They can cut up and carry off a whole garden in a night.

Ecologists like to identify the dominants in any ecosystem, the plants and animals that exert the greatest effect on the system as a whole. On the tallgrass prairie, big bluestem grass is a dominant plant. It is among the most common and widespread species and an aggressive colonizer of open ground. Big bluestem dominates the landscape by taking up a lot of space and by controlling some of the conditions—such as the availability of light—that other plants live in.

When they are designating dominant animals, ecologists generally favor large animals, especially mammals. On the prairie, they would consider the bison a dominant.

But they might overlook ants, even though sober scientists have suggested that on a typical tallgrass prairie, the biomass, the amount of living stuff, of an abundant ant species like *F. montana* might exceed the biomass of the local bison herd. Ants are weighed in milligrams; a bull bison weighs a ton. There must be a lot of ants around.

Their presence changes everything. Most ants are carnivorous, and insects and other arthropods are their major food. They also like nectar. Many plants have developed organs called extrafloral nectaries, which is to say places outside the flowers where the plant exudes nectar. The nectaries attract ants, and the payoff for the plant is that the ants eat insects that eat, lay their eggs in, or otherwise parasitize the plant.

Don't underestimate the importance of this exterminating service. A study done on sunflowers in a southwestern prairie found a direct ratio between seed production and proximity to an anthill. The closer to the ants, the more seed the sunflowers produced. Plants more than ten feet from an ant mound were so heavily preyed upon that they were rarely able to produce any seeds at all.

This sort of relationship reaches a peak of development in the bull's-horn acacias, tropical trees with thick, hollow thorns. Ants build their nests in these thorns, and the trees feed them on nectar and on tiny, detachable bits of stuff that grow at the tips of leaves. These growths are called Beltian bodies (named for Thomas Belt, an early student of ants) and they are rich in protein and fat. The ants break them off and eat them.

Ants of the genus *Azteca* who live on bull's-horn acacias repay this handout by aggressively going after other insects and anything else that gets close. Humans in the tropics who make the mistake of leaning against an acacia can get furiously stung by hordes of attacking ants.

The value of this to the trees was established in some studies done in Mexico in the 1960s. An entomologist named D. H. Janzen removed the ants from some acacias. The unprotected trees were invaded by bugs, beetles, and assorted caterpillars, and various competing plants began to sprout around their roots.

On protected trees, as much as one-fourth of the ant population was on patrol at any given moment, scouring the tree for pests. Plants that sprouted too close to the host were chewed and mauled by the ants until they died.

After a year of study, the unprotected trees were lagging far behind those infested by ants. They looked in such a sorry state that Janzen expected them to die shortly.

A colony of *Formica montana* consists of worker ants (sterile females who make up nearly all the population), one or more queens, and a few winged males. New queens and males are produced only be well-established colonies and only in summer. The virgin queens and the males engage in a nuptial flight, copulating in the air. The males then die and the queen comes to earth, loses her wings, and either founds a new colony or is adopted by an established colony whose queen is growing old.

F. montana workers are a rather pallid brown in color and a few millimeters in length. The queen is a similar color, but she is about the size and shape of a honeybee and much larger than anything else in the nest. The queen's sole job is laying eggs. She is fed and tended by the workers and never leaves the nest.

As those colonies at Wayside Woods Prairie divide and expand, and the ants extend their influence over the entire prairie, we can expect some unexpected consequences. An enormous number of insects and other arthropods live in ant colonies. Some of them feed on ants; some of them, for reasons we can't fathom, are fed by the ants.

There were a number of mysterious larvae in those transanimaled colonies. The ants were tending them closely. And there were beetles and springtails and a considerable assortment of other creatures, perhaps prairie species, now introduced to a restored prairie along with their hosts, the ants.

Searching for Bats
Physiology and Folklore

August 10, 1984

Jack Schmidling is a tireless proselytizer for the virtues of bats. He travels the Midwest, in a van called (what else?) the batmobile, talking to Audubon societies, schools, and museums, bringing a live bat along, and showing a film he made in the bat caves of Texas.

Some of the film was shot upside down, turning hanging bats into upright bats. The transformation amazes audiences. "People can't resist them," Schmidling says. "They are so cute. They look like Mickey Mouse." The climax of the show is a bat hunt undertaken with the help of a bat detector (it is impossible to talk about this without sounding like a comic book).

The bat detector is a piece of apparatus designed by a bat expert from the Milwaukee Museum. It consists of a microphone capable of hearing the supersonic squeaks bats use to navigate. The microphone is mounted in a parabolic reflector and connected to an amplifier and tiny speakers. Bat squeaks are transformed to clicks. Schmidling pans the sky with the reflector. When he picks up some clicks, a floodlight flashed in the same quarter of the sky usually finds the beast itself, wings beating furiously as it searches the night for flying insects.

I went along on one of Schmidling's bat hunts early this week. The night was hot and muggy, great bug weather, and therefore great bat weather. We were hunting the woods at North Park Village, the old Municipal Tuberculosis Sanatorium at Pulaski and Peterson, and the place was alive with bats. Every time Jack pointed the bat detector at the sky, it obediently started clicking. A constant procession of bats flickered overhead as we walked the paths. They swooped low over us and climbed again to the treetops. Two animals who were doing something with each other—fighting? playing? courting?—crossed above us again and again.

Jack's batmobile is decorated with bumper stickers that read "Bats Need Friends" and his message is one of conservation. Bats are innocuous at worst and, as prodigious mosquito eaters, probably helpful. They are also unique, the only mammals that actually fly, and as animals who have learned to live with humans, they are easy to see. There really are bats in belfries, and in attics and garages as well.

One hopes that Jack has some success with the message, because bats need some good press. For whatever reason, they have always given people the willies. The fact that they fly at night has something to do with it, but owls do that too, and people love owls. Have you ever heard of anyone collecting ceramic figurines of bats?

Bats hang out with witches. The vampire bat of South America becomes associated with the Central European undead. Sullivan's Law states that if you mention bats in any group of four or more people, at least one person will start spouting lines like "Thank you, Mr. Renfield, I do not drink wine," in a dime-store Hungarian accent, and Bela Lugosi will rise again.

My grandmother told me that bats flew into people's hair, a fairly widespread bit of folklore. Of course, there is no reason why a bat would want to fly into your hair, but it is true that they sometimes come close. Flying insects cluster around the heads of people—and animals—and bats swing in close to snatch them. And once in a while, one might accidentally bump into somebody.

Bats are famous for using echolocation to navigate the night skies. While they are not blind as bats, their eyes are generally small and weak. So they use sonar, squeaking at very high frequency and listening to the echoes as they bounce off the objects around. They can squeak at up to 60 squeaks a second at frequencies ranging from 30,000 to 100,000 cycles per second—all well beyond the abilities of our ears. But with the bat detector, we can follow a cruising bat. The first clicks we pick up come at regular intervals with less than a second between them. The animal is apparently scanning the area looking for a blip that says bug. As it begins to home in on a possible meal, the speed and frequency of clicks pick up, etching a clearer picture of where the insect is and how fast it is flying. As the bat closes on its prey, one last outburst of sound locates it precisely. On the bat detector, the clicks rise to a rattling buzz that could be politely described as a Bronx cheer.

Bats have very large ears, as you might expect. Big-eared bats—we have two species in Illinois, neither near Chicago—have big ears even for bats. They look like something created by Steven Spielberg, with pointed, erect ears three times as long as their heads. Inside the ear of most bats is a spiky structure called a tragus. Of uncertain function, it is presumed to help the sonar system in some way.

Echolocation enables bats to live in completely dark places—such as caves. With it they can hunt, find suitable roosts, and even migrate long distances. But it is not quite so precise as vision—among other reasons because sound waves travel much more slowly than light waves—and this could be the reason for the rare collisions between bat and human hair.

Jack made a guess that the bats we were seeing at North Park Village were big browns, but identifying bats on the wing is a rather inexact science. He has identified four different species at North Park Village, big and little brown bats, red bats, and hoary bats. The hoary is the biggest of these, and it is only about six inches long and weighs about an ounce. The smaller species are no bigger than mice.

They do have formidable teeth, however. Our bats are all insect eaters with teeth like needles, excellent for crushing beetle carapaces and other such exoskeletal matter.

They are insatiable eaters, gobbling more than their weight in insects each day. Catching insects on the wing is a very high energy way to make a living, and the way bats are put together gives them even greater energy requirements than birds who follow the same mode of life. A bird's wing—the skin, muscle, and bone—is a spindly thing. Most of what we see as wing in the living bird is feathers. Feathers don't need to be kept warm; in fact, the plumage actually keeps the bird insulated. But a bat's wings are all skin stretched over the bones of the hand and arm. The wing membranes are richly supplied with blood vessels. Add the large ears and the tiny body, and you have a creature that is all surface, an animal perfectly designed to radiate heat. They need to eat a lot, especially in spring and fall when the air is cool.

Bats breed in the fall, but the sperm remains in the uterus through the winter. Fertilization doesn't happen until spring, and the young bats are born about two months later. When they are very young they cling to their mothers, but as they get bigger they are left hanging at the roost while mom forages. This late in the summer, the young are flying on their own.

Come fall, the bats of Chicago will both migrate and hibernate. Their migration may be to central Illinois or all the way to the gulf states. Their destinations are hibernacula, refuges that may be caves, mines, abandoned buildings, or hollow trees, depending on the species.

Once they find their refuge, bats hang upside down and drift off to dreamland. Their respiration, heart rate, and body temperature all go down. They stay in a stupor until spring. The ideal refuge for a bat would be a constant 33 degrees: cold enough to keep them dormant—and thus using little energy—and warm enough to avoid freezing.

Bats are at their most vulnerable during hibernation, since the temperature renders them almost completely helpless. Humans sometimes kill them in large numbers, wiping out whole caves with blowtorches or other mass destruction methods. Some of this is pure vandalism, and some is justified by the supposed danger that bats pose to the public health.

Bats do carry rabies, but then again so do raccoons, animals that are much more likely to encounter people. Certainly, the modest danger bats pose doesn't justify slaughter.

Summer is a good time to see bats in the city, even if you don't have a bat detector. All the parks and cemeteries support considerable numbers, and quiet residential streets with large trees are often home to a few. Dusk is a good time to look. Just keep your eyes on the sky. Check around streetlights too, since bats are often drawn to the bugs that are drawn to the lights.

Fireflies
Why They Flash

July 19, 1985

Sitting on the back steps enjoying the cool of the evening one night last week, I began to follow the flight of the fireflies. Lightning bugs are not as common in the city as they are in the leafier suburbs, but there are enough to provide a little show for an hour or so after sundown.

As I watched the pulses of light from the flying insects, I noticed another pulse from down in the grass. One of the bugs in flight noticed it too. He began to circle the spot, emitting a flash of pale green. Again the firefly in the grass answered, and this time the flying insect dropped down and landed on a blade of grass about six inches from the source of the flash.

Aha, I said to myself. I know what this is. This is a "Field & Street" column. So I crept over on hands and knees and watched as the newly landed insect flashed again, and again got a response. This time, he flew in a small circle and landed directly on the back of the other insect. There he remained for a time, his antennae waving, his head moving from side to side. And then, he flew away.

What I was witnessing, in case you haven't guessed already, was the mating of a pair of fireflies, beginning with the use of their lights to locate each other and ending with mounting and copulation.

Turning this experience into a column required some research at the Field Museum. The museum has an excellent library and vast collections overseen by friendly scientists who are always happy to show an inquiring nature writer some preserved specimens of whatever he is interested in.

Frankly, when it comes to insects, I need all the help I can get. Insects are daunting. There are so many of them. According to current reference works, there are 136 species of fireflies in the U.S., most of them living in the eastern half of the country. They are a part of the order Coleoptera, the beetles, the largest order in the animal kingdom with about 300,000 species worldwide and 30,000 in North America!

When I want to write about a bird, I can find detailed accounts of its life history rich in the sort of anecdotal detail that journalists need. With an insect, even an insect living near large universities with departments of entomology, basic information—like what it eats—may simply be unknown.

But you have to start somewhere, so the next night I was ready with my collecting equipment, which consists of an empty peanut-butter jar with several holes punched in the lid. I'm sure that a firefly (or should I say firebeetle) would take hours to breathe all the oxygen in a peanut-butter jar, but when I was eight years old I always punched holes in the tops of my collecting jars, and I see no reason to stop now. With the aid of this quality gear, I quickly secured a specimen.

Entomologists kill their specimens with chloroform or some such poison, but I have nothing against firebeetles, so I just stuck mine in the fridge. This is a trick that photographers use with invertebrates and with cold-blooded vertebrates like frogs and snakes. Cool them off and they get sleepy and slow moving, so you can pose them—or examine them—at leisure. When you are finished, put them in a warm place, and they are soon as good as new.

After consulting my field guide, I decided that my firebeetle was a *Photuris pennsylvanicus,* a Pennsylvania firefly. Of course, the field guide describes only two of the 136 species, but presumably the authors picked the two most common and widespread. They also picked two that look remarkably alike. My other choice, *Photinus pyralis,* is slightly smaller, but its colors are virtually identical. Beetles possess a scaly plate called a pronotum that extends forward from the back to cover the head. The pronotum of *pennsylvanicus,* according to the *Audubon Society Field Guide,* is "dull yellowish . . . with a black spot surrounded by reddish ring." On the other hand, the pronotum of *pyralis* is "rosy pink with dull yellow edges and black spot in center." How's that for a clear choice?

The color of the light they produce is another piece of evidence. Firefly experts can name species just by looking at the color and timing of their flashes. According to the book, *pyralis* produces a yellow light, *pennsylvanicus* a green light. I think I am seeing green, but it is a very chartreusey green that, at the apex of the flash, could almost be taken as yellow.

Ultimately, it may not matter whether I made the right identification, but to the beetles themselves it is literally life and death. The pattern of flashes that a flying male firefly emits, the number and length of pulses and the intervals between them, are unique to his species. The females—

in most species, they are flightless—hide down in the weeds waiting for the flash that will open their hearts. When they see it, they respond, also in a way unique to their species, and the males react to the response by approaching.

However, things can get tricky. *Photuris* females have learned to mimic the *Photinus* response well enough to attract *Photinus* males. These unwary gents, instead of getting laid, get killed and eaten.

The females are not safe either. To a spider, the flashes in the grass mean dinner, and the flightless beetles have little chance for escape.

The flashing lights of the Lampyridae, to give them their proper family name, are produced by a chemical process involving a substance called luciferin, an enzyme called luciferase, and ATP, otherwise known as adenosine triphosphate, a complex chemical involved in energy exchanges in many living things, including us. The chemistry of the reactions involved is very complex, but the result is light, produced with such high efficiency that there is almost no waste heat generated.

Many different kinds of animals glow in the dark, but the process in the Lampyridae is probably the most thoroughly investigated and understood of any. *Photinus pyralis* is even harvested commercially for the extraction of luciferin for experimental purposes.

If a pair of lightning bugs can avoid the dangers in the process, they will breed, and the female will lay her eggs on moist ground. The larvae that hatch from the eggs look rather like caterpillars. They are predators, eating a variety of other insects as well as slugs and snails. They are also slightly luminous. In fact, in some species, even the eggs are slightly luminous.

Firefly larvae are long-lived. Those born this year will not become adults until two years from now. In the meantime, they will spend their days hiding under debris on the ground or in cracks in the bark of trees. Nights, they will come out in search of food.

As a tomato grower, I have a strong affection for anything that will eat slugs. Once, in the days when I lived on the shores of Lake Superior, I lost a whole crop to these slimy critters. My current garden also shows signs of supporting a variety of leaf-eating caterpillars. Presumably, firefly larvae eat these pests, but I don't know if I have any larvae. So for the past several nights, I have been creeping through the foliage hunting for firefly larvae. Catching one would also give me some more evidence to verify my identification of the species that is living in my backyard. The larvae are somewhat more distinctive than the adults.

I look first for the luminosity—no flashes, just a dull glow. But this is

Chicago, and the level of ambient light from streetlights and houses is probably so high that it would drown out the larva's glow. So I am using a flashlight to help me search. I haven't found any yet, but I will keep looking—at least until the neighbors start complaining about this weird man who spends half the night crawling around his backyard shining a flashlight on his tomato plants.

Migrating Monarchs

They May Fly 2,000 Miles

September 7, 1984

In September, you can see monarch butterflies almost everywhere. In fact, one just flew by my window as I was typing that sentence. They are in the parks, where you might expect them, and on Michigan Avenue, where you might not.

They look to be in no particular hurry to get anywhere. They flutter lightly from tree to tree or soar on wings cocked into a shallow vee. But their laid-back style belies their purpose, because these languid-looking insects are in fact heading south for the winter. Butterflies bred amid the cornfields of Illinois are on their way to the Gulf of Mexico and beyond on an epic flight that may reach 2,000 miles.

The monarch is the one butterfly that *everybody* knows. Their gaudy orange-and-black wings, spotted with white, and their slow, soaring flight make them easy to see, and they are common all over North America except in the far north.

Their caterpillars are garish, slow-moving creatures vertically striped in black, yellow, and white. Their chrysalises are green, albeit a very bright green spotted with gold, and as they mature, the colors of the adult begin to show through.

When an animal makes itself that conspicuous, you begin to wonder how it got to be common in a world full of hungry kingbirds and voracious shrews. Life tends to favor the drab, especially in the open environments that monarchs prefer.

The reason for this immunity to predation is the monarch's diet. Monarchs live on milkweeds, or more formally, plants of the genus *Asclepias*. Twenty-five species of milkweeds grow in eastern North America. The most common is, appropriately enough, the common milkweed, a plant that Linnaeus named *Asclepias syriaca* under the mistaken impression that his specimen came from the Middle East rather than the Middle West.

Common milkweeds are everywhere, thriving in virgin prairies and on roadsides and railroad embankments. Their luxuriant flower clusters are smoky purple and they smell as sweet as lilacs. Their presence in weedy corners of the city gives us our own breeding populations of monarchs.

Milkweeds are named for their sap, which is milky white, and which is also bitter, acrid, and mildly poisonous. Monarch caterpillars, feeding exclusively on milkweed leaves, and monarch butterflies, sipping nectar from milkweed flowers, are also bitter, acrid, and mildly poisonous.

There is solid experimental evidence that birds don't like monarchs. A young bird with no experience trying its first monarch will often spit it out still alive. And there is further experimental evidence that birds remember these unpleasant experiences. Once exposed, they will avoid monarchs from then on.

So effective is this Star-Kist strategy ("Charlie, Star-Kist doesn't want tunas with good taste; they want tunas that taste good") that it has even inspired an imitator. The viceroy butterfly is an orange-and-black stunner that looks enough like a monarch to fool experienced blue jays, but it feeds on sweet willows and poplars, and inexperienced birds will swallow a viceroy with relish. Viceroy caterpillars are effectively protected by a shape and color scheme that make them look like bird droppings on a leaf. Humans can recognize a viceroy by its habit of soaring with wings held flat; monarchs soar with their wings in a vee.

It takes about a month to produce a new generation of monarchs. Females lay their eggs, the caterpillars hatch and eat and spin themselves into a chrysalis, and the adults emerge. At the northern end of the monarch range, up around Lake Superior, there may be time for only one generation a year. Farther south, as many as five will hatch.

As early as July, adults in the north may begin a persistent movement south. Feeding part of the day, waiting out bad weather, they make a slow and often interrupted progress. As the season advances, more monarchs join the movement. The peak flights through Chicago are in September, but some will remain into October.

Each night, the migrating butterflies roost in trees, and sometimes these gatherings are large enough to cover a tree like a second set of leaves. I have seen them in Lincoln Park in September so thick that a green maple looked from a distance as if its leaves were already turning brown.

Entomologists have marked monarchs in the north and then tracked them by recapturing them farther south. They discovered that the leisurely monarchs may average 80 miles a day. An insect marked in

Ontario north of Lake Erie on September 18 was in Mississippi, over 1,000 miles away, just 17 days later. The long-distance champion so far is a butterfly marked on September 18 in Ontario and recovered on January 27 in Mexico, 1,870 miles from its starting point. That averages out to 14 miles a day for 130 days. That average is almost certainly too low, since it assumes a straight-line journey and it assumes that the insect was captured as soon as it arrived in Mexico, when in fact it may have been there for weeks.

These marked insects proved that migrating monarchs fly a long way, and they also proved that single individuals make these long flights, a fact that was in doubt. Some insects do a multigeneration migration. The Oriental armyworm moth, for example, makes a summer-long migration from Canton to Manchuria that takes four generations to complete. Each generation of adults flies part of the way and then lays its eggs. The new generation then carries on, performing the next leg of the journey before laying its eggs.

We now know that monarchs don't do that—at least in the fall. The butterflies that are passing through Chicago now will spend the winter hibernating in trees in Florida, Texas, Mexico, and California. On warm days, they will move around and feed, but they will not breed. As spring approaches, the females begin to develop eggs, the sperm matures in the males.

The trip north seems like a desperate, hurried affair after the leisurely pace of autumn. The butterflies move as fast as they can, even flying at night. But many apparently do not make it all the way back. They stop along the way to breed and lay their eggs, and their offspring, like Oriental armyworms, continue the flight.

But some at least may make it all the way. The researcher who marked the monarchs in Ontario said that some of the insects he saw returning in spring had the slightly worn and nibbled look that age brings to us all. But none of his marked monarchs returned.

The profoundly unknown thing in the case is how they find their way. We know that birds can navigate by the stars and the sun, and that they can somehow read variations in the earth's magnetic field. These are, of course, all compasses of a sort, direction finders. We don't have any idea what they use for a map.

Our ignorance of the ways of insects is even more profound. Birds have small brains, but they are Einsteins compared to insects. Where would a monarch butterfly store the information it would need to make a 2,000-mile flight? We don't know. But the magic show is fun even when you don't know how the trick is done.

Badgers
Born to Dig

November 23, 1990

The people in Villa Park put up with the strange animal in their toolshed for about as long as they could. They didn't know exactly what it was, but they knew that anytime they opened the door of the shed they heard nasty growls and hissing noises. And the smell, a powerful musky odor, was enough to drive you off all by itself. They had reason to believe that the animal, whatever it was, had raised a litter of young in the toolshed.

When they had finally had enough, they called the animal control people to come and get whatever this nuisance was. The call led directly to the involvement of the Illinois Department of Conservation, because the surly, smelly animal was a badger, and having a badger in your backyard is a sort of distinction.

Of course, you might react like the man who was being tarred, feathered, and run out of town and say, "If it wasn't for the honor, I'd just as soon forget it." But most Illinoisans go through their entire lives without seeing a real wild badger, so the honor of having one living in your backyard is not something you can dismiss lightly.

You could describe a badger as a sort of king-size skunk with an attitude problem. A big male badger may reach a weight of 25 pounds, although most are smaller than that. They look even bigger, because their skin is very loose and their fur is very shaggy. Their odor is from a musk that they exude from special glands, but they cannot spray as skunks can.

Their faces are patterned in black and white. Inexperienced people might confuse a badger with a raccoon or a skunk. The facial patterns are not alike—but if you come upon a snarling, hissing animal in your toolshed along about twilight, you might not hang around long enough to pick up the fine points of the field marks.

Accurate badger sightings are the concern of Richard Warner of the Center for Wildlife Ecology of the Illinois Natural History Survey. At the request of the Illinois Department of Conservation, he is directing a survey of the badgers of Illinois: How many of them are there? Where do they live? And how do they live?

American badgers are grassland animals. Their natural range extends only as far east as Ohio, and the center of their abundance—now as in the past—is west of the Mississippi. Badgers are thoroughly fossorial animals, which means that they dig. They live in holes in the ground, and they hunt mainly by digging into the burrows of ground squirrels, gophers, and the other small burrowing animals that make up most of their diet.

Badgers are nicely shaped for this kind of life. Their heads and bodies are broad and flattened. The look from head-on is elliptical. This elliptical shape is one of the field marks that set a badger burrow apart from holes dug by other burrowing animals.

Badgers have short, powerful, bowed front legs and enormous front feet tipped by stout claws that average about two inches long. This combination is their digging apparatus. In actual field tests—which I would have loved to see—badgers were able to dig faster than a man with a shovel. There is one recorded case of a badger digging an exit to its burrow and coming up through an asphalt highway.

One investigator tried to keep a badger in her basement, but the animal was able to dig through the concrete floor. Its technique for doing this was carefully worked out and not just the application of brute force. The badger found a small crack in the floor and carefully dug at it until small bits of concrete began to flake off. It widened and deepened the crack one small piece at a time until it was able to get its front claws through the crack and under the concrete. Then it pulled up, breaking off piece after piece until the hole was big enough to squeeze into.

Hunting badgers search for the holes of gophers, ground squirrels, and such, and then rapidly dig to enlarge the burrow to a size they can get into. If the gophers have a back door on their burrows, they may get out before a digging badger can get to them. According to various old stories, coyotes sometimes follow badgers around and snatch up escaping gophers for their own dinners. This led to stories that coyotes and badgers hunt together cooperatively, but the truth seems to be that the badgers cooperate with the coyotes but the coyotes do not cooperate with the badgers.

There are lots of stories about the pugnacity of badgers. A farmer in Illinois' Vermillion County recently spotted a couple of badger burrows along a roadside. He went home and got his kids to show them this wonder of nature. When they got back to the burrows, he knelt down to look in one and was suddenly face to face with a growling, hissing, grunting badger seemingly intent on biting his nose off.

In Mason County, which is along the Illinois River south of Peoria, the local sheriff told Warner of a badger that had successfully stopped traffic in both directions on a state highway. The animal was in the middle of the road, and anytime a car tried to go around him in either direction, he would charge right at it.

A lot of this ferocity seems to be bluffing, although most people don't stay around long enough to find out if a charge is for real. Warner raised a young badger this past summer. Its mother and all its littermates had been run over on the highway, so he took it in. From a very early age it reacted to people with growls and hisses, but Warner's children stuck their fingers into its cage and never got bit.

Badgers were probably common animals in presettlement Illinois. The prairie is their home, and it is unlikely that you would ever see one in the woods. Most likely they were common until after World War II. The prairies were gone by then, but there were a lot of cow pastures and hay fields that would have been good places for them.

In the late '40s and through the '50s most of our man-made grasslands were converted to corn and soybean fields, and badger numbers began to decline. This was also a bad time for our grassland birds.

There was a year-round open season on badgers for a time. People who raised cattle and horses hated them because their animals sometimes broke a leg stepping in a badger burrow. Trappers took a certain number, although there was not much demand for badger fur. Badger hair is used to make high-quality paintbrushes, but otherwise the pelts are not especially valuable.

An apparent decline in badger numbers led to regulations outlawing trapping or hunting them, but the evidence for the decline was largely anecdotal. The Department of Conservation recently decided that harder evidence was needed on the status of badgers in Illinois, so they hired Warner to check into it.

He and his assistant Barbara Broussard have been collecting information for a little more than a year now. They have reliable reports of badger sightings in 80 of Illinois' 102 counties. The sightings range from the southern tip of the state to the Wisconsin border, with the biggest numbers in the west-central and northwest counties. (I should explain here that Wisconsin is the Badger State not because of the animal but because of some early settlers. Cornish miners came in to work lead mines in the southwestern corner of the state. Not only did they spend their days digging in the mines, but they also dug their houses into the sides of the hills.)

Mason County is a particularly good spot in Illinois for badgers. It has very sandy soil—which makes for good digging—and it also has more prairie and savanna landscape than any other Illinois county. The DOC owns a 1,500-acre scrub-oak and prairie preserve there where badgers can be found regularly. There are also badgers at the Nachusa Grasslands, the large preserve near Dixon that is owned by the Nature Conservancy. The animals are strictly nocturnal and are therefore rarely seen, but their burrows are distinctive. In addition to the elliptical shape, you can look for bones and fur of their prey scattered near the entrance.

In northeastern Illinois, in addition to the Villa Park animal, there have been sighting in the Mount Auburn Cemetery in Stickney (at Oak Park Avenue and 42nd Street) and in Lake County near Lincolnshire. There is also a population in Chain O'Lakes State Park.

Illinois badgers move around a lot. Warner has tracked—by radio— one animal that moved ten miles from the location where it had originally been found. Warner thinks that mobility is typical of badgers, but circumstances in Illinois have probably made movement more necessary than ever. With their habitat fragmented into scattered islands, badgers have to move often in order to find enough food to sustain themselves. Badgers would be among the animals that would be well served by larger preserves.

They also make great use of corridors of seminatural land, such as railroad rights-of-way, hedgerows, and stream banks. These corridors are their first choice as ways to move from one feeding ground to another. The house in Villa Park had a railroad embankment right behind it, and the day after the animal was driven from the toolshed, a German shepherd had a brief run-in with a badger a few miles farther down the embankment. Corridors connecting natural areas have long been recognized as important for conservation.

Chorus Frogs
The Most Urban Amphibian

March 27, 1998

Chorus frogs are singing. Even after cold nights that leave a skin of ice on the breeding ponds you can hear this lovely sound of spring as the sun begins to do its warming work. The songs of chorus frogs—to be precise, our local animals are *western* chorus frogs—are like the rasping noise made by somebody dragging a fingernail across the teeth of a comb. This is a generalized description. According to Conant and Collins's *A Field Guide to Reptiles and Amphibians*, the "sound may be roughly imitated by running a finger over approximately the last 20 of the *small* teeth of a good-quality pocket comb, rubbing the shortest teeth last." Your cheap pocket combs are not going to fool anybody.

Chorus frogs could not produce the sound in that fashion because they have neither nails nor claws. The absence of claws or nails is one of the defining characteristics of amphibians in general. Chorus frogs belong to the tree-frog family, and like other members of that group, their toes end in adhesive pads, which are useful for hanging on to the trunks and branches of trees and shrubs. These pads are not very well developed in chorus frogs, which fits their habits well. They do climb some, but they generally stay on or very near the ground.

Their principal habitat in ages past was undoubtedly the prairie, a place that offers few opportunities for climbing, but they have been able to move into farm fields and even suburban neighborhoods where pesticides are not used too heavily. You can hear chorus frogs in the city at North Park Village and in various parks and cemeteries. They're the most likely frogs to hang on in an urban environment, though how potential mates can hear the songs of the males over all the traffic noise is beyond me.

The classic image of the singing frog has it sitting on a lily pad, and indeed chorus frogs will do just that. They also sit on other kinds of floating vegetation or stay hidden in clumps of grass or sedge in very shallow water. I have spent a lot of time standing absolutely still listening to chorus frogs singing just a few feet away. But I have almost never seen one, unless I flushed it and caused it to hop into deeper water. They are cryptically colored—dull grays and browns variously striped and spotted with darker shades—and a big one is only about 1.5 inches long, so they are easy to miss. They usually respond to disturbances such as the approach of heavily booted humans by shutting up. A whole pond full of them can fall silent in an instant. If is as if their chorus had a conductor giving them signals.

Male frogs sing to attract females, and females seem to respond strongly to large choruses. A single chorus frog in a tiny pond may get no response at all. A massed chorus of a large number of males apparently signals listening females that the pond is a really great place to have a family. The massed chorus also makes it impossible to tell where one frog's song leaves off and another's begins. Imagine 50 people with good-quality pocket combs all simultaneously scraping their thumbnails along the last 20 teeth.

The image of a frog on a lily pad leads many people to believe that frogs live in and around water all the time. But only some do that. Bullfrogs, for example, live in permanent bodies of water. Many frogs—and all toads—come to the water only to breed. They may favor moist habitats at other times, but they don't require standing water. Some frogs have adapted to desert conditions. In the southwest, desert frogs breed during the brief period of summer rain. When things get too dry they burrow into the ground and estivate. Estivation is like hibernation, but the animals do it in the summer instead of the winter.

Vernal ponds are vital to the success of chorus frogs. Low spots that fill with water in late fall and early winter and stay wet until midsummer give amphibians enough time to mate and lay eggs and give the eggs enough time to hatch and the tadpoles enough time to grow legs, lose their tails, and move out into the larger world. The frogs could use permanent bodies of water as breeding sites, but permanent bodies of water tend to have fish in them, and fish are very fond of frog eggs and tadpoles.

Last Sunday I was hearing chorus frogs in three vernal ponds at Somme Woods in Northbrook. All of these ponds are likely to be dry by the Fourth of July. I also saw a couple of great blue herons passing over. Their arrival from the south is nicely timed to coincide with the emergence of frogs—and they hunt quite happily in vernal ponds.

Primeval Chicago must have been a paradise for frogs. It was practically nothing but vernal ponds. People probably couldn't sleep for all the frog noise. Of course as settlers began to pour in, pond after pond was drained. With the development of field tile in the late 19th century, every landowner could become his own hydraulic engineer, converting wet prairies, sedge meadows, and pothole marshes into cornfields—and wiping out population after population of frogs and toads.

You often hear complaints these days about how the government is forcing landowners to preserve tiny wetlands, the implication being that vernal ponds that cover only a couple of acres can't be of much use. But the frogs I heard last Sunday were singing in ponds of less than an acre. One was only a few thousand square feet. The value of these tiny wetlands is considerable, and it increases if the small wetlands are part of a complex of scattered wetlands. Frogs are mobile enough to get from one of these wetlands to another, and so are turtles. A couple of years ago a female Blanding's turtle with a small radio transmitter attached to her carapace was tracked wandering north from Bluff Spring Preserve, a Lake County forest preserve north of Zion, into the Chiwaukee Prairie in Wisconsin. The animal covered about half a mile from one marshy pond to another, and in the process became a threatened species. Blanding's turtle is considered "threatened" in Wisconsin but not in Illinois.

I was most pleased to hear chorus frogs singing in Oak Pond at Somme Woods. The first time I visited Somme, nearly 20 years ago, trees were growing right out of the middle of the pond. Their shade was so dense that nothing grew under them. The pond was a mud hole practically devoid of life. There were no frogs in those days.

The restoration work that has been going on at Somme since that first visit has made a dramatic difference. The trees were girdled. That killed them, but it let sunshine reach the water. Now the pond is covered with greenery throughout the summer. Smartweeds and pickerelweeds, bulrushes and wild irises, and many other wetland plants live in the shallow water. Dragonflies hunt for insects. Mallards and wood ducks rest on the waters in spring, and on some of my visits I have scared up a green-backed heron, which was probably hunting for chorus frogs. Oak Pond is nowhere near large enough to support a green-backed heron, but as part of a cluster of small wetlands it can make its contribution.

Those ducks may be responsible for bringing in some of the wetland vegetation. Seeds can cling to mud on a duck's foot and hitch a ride from one pond to another. Plants and animals adapted to life in scattered habitats often develop methods of getting around. At a time when most stories about amphibians tell of declines and disappearances, one can take some comfort in the arrival of frogs at a pond where they could not previously live.

Coyotes in the City

Staging a Comeback

February 2, 1996

Coyotes are turning up everywhere these days. A report from the northwest suburbs blames a coyote for breaking the neck of a shih tzu. Not long ago Don Coyote turned up in an editorial in the *Tribune,* where he was incorrectly identified as *canine latrans* rather than *Canis latrans*. But the tone of the editorial was welcoming, seeing this addition to the local fauna as a contribution to the variety of the metropolis rather than a menace to our way of life.

We might as well accept coyotes, since centuries of attempts to destroy them have been absolute—and expensive—failures. Many states are still paying bounties for coyote corpses.

The practice of encouraging citizens to kill animals considered destructive goes way back. As Americans moved out of the eastern forests and onto the prairies, their attention shifted from the timber wolves of the east to the smaller "brush wolves" of the plains. Iowa had a $2 bounty on coyotes as early as 1795—long before there was an Iowa. To collect you had to find a territorial judge and give him the head of the animal you'd killed. Over the years bounties have been so successful at encouraging the slaughter of annoying animals that local governments have often had to suspend them because they were emptying the treasury.

Coyotes have been shot by hunters on foot, on horses, in Jeeps, in helicopters. They have been trapped in countless ingenious and painful ways, poisoned, even dynamited out of their dens. And they have responded to this persecution by remaining plentiful everywhere, even expanding their range by several hundred thousand square miles. Once they were uncommon east of the Mississippi. Now they roam the forests of Maine.

It is instructive to think about why our anticoyote efforts were a total failure while our antiwolf campaign was so effective. Wolves were eliminated from the entire lower 48 with the exception of northern Minnesota,

Isle Royale, and a few locations in Wisconsin. We even exterminated them in wilderness areas such as Yellowstone National Park. Relevant differences between the two species are physical—a significant size difference—and behavioral. Wolves are highly social. Coyotes tend to be solitary. Wolves require very large territories; a pack may roam across 100 square miles. Coyotes can get by on a few thousand acres, at times even less. One study in Los Angeles suggested that a lone coyote could get by on as little as 200 acres. Wolves concentrate on large mammals—deer, elk, moose, bison. Coyotes eat mostly rabbits. It seems likely that coyotes could be both more abundant and less obtrusive than their larger cousins.

When a new predator arrives on the scene the effects of its presence are likely to be felt throughout the ecosystem. To learn what those effects are likely to be we need to study the animal's habits, starting with what it eats. The Coyote Project is addressing just what question in the Chicago area. The project was started by a man named Wiley Buck, who's working on a master's degree in wildlife conservation from the University of Minnesota. His thesis topic is the diet of coyotes in the metropolitan area.

There are essentially two ways to study the eating habits of any wild animal. One is to shoot large numbers of them and examine the contents of their stomachs. The other is to collect their droppings. Buck is using the latter method, with the help of a group of volunteer collectors who are checking selected natural areas every couple of weeks. Coyotes use their droppings as territorial markers, so they tend to leave them in conspicuous places. Trails are the places to look, especially high places along trails. Presumably scent carries better from such places than from lower ground.

The usual practice is to take only a part of the scat. Coyotes might get nervous and move on if someone were consistently stealing their boundary markers. You pick it up with a plastic bag, take it home, and put it in the freezer. Eventually you pass it along to Buck, who stores it in his freezer until he is ready to analyze it.

At this point you may be asking yourself how somebody would go about gathering a group of volunteers to collect coyote doo-doo. Here in Chicagoland we have a ready answer to that question. The Volunteer Stewardship Network is an organization that involves thousands of people in the metropolitan area in the work of ecological restoration and management in county forest preserves and other natural lands. It is jointly sponsored by the Nature Conservancy, the county forest-preserve districts, and the state Department of Natural Resources. People in the VSN are connected by newsletters, workdays, meetings, and other activities, so any call for help will reach a large number of potential assistants. VSN members are also people who spend a lot of time in forest preserves and have a large interest in what is happening in our natural areas.

So Buck sent out the call through the various tendrils of the VSN and found himself directing scat collectors from all over the metropolitan area. One of these volunteers, Phyllis Shulte of Mokena in Will County, spends most of her time working for an auto dealer. But off the job she is costeward of a place called the Hickory Creek Barrens. At this point she is the champion scat collector of the Coyote Project, having delivered samples of more than 50 *Canis latrans* bowel movements. Hickory Creek gets heavy (illegal) use by off-road vehicles and snowmobiles, and she credits her success to the way the heavy traffic keeps down the vegetation.

After a year of collecting she still has not seen any coyotes at Hickory Creek. Her only sighting came recently when she was driving to work very early one morning. She saw two animals crossing U.S. 45 near 145th Street. "I think they were going to the Orland Square Mall," she says. Maybe they were hunting mall rats.

Rose Golembieski works for Allstate Insurance in Northbrook between expeditions to Somme Woods to survey for coyote droppings. A few weeks ago, after a year of collecting samples, she saw her first live animal. "I was walking through the woods, and I looked behind me—and there it was. I guess it saw me at the same time I saw it. We both froze for a moment. I tried to raise my camera to my eye, and the coyote took off."

Analyzing coyote droppings is a complex, time-consuming, and not altogether pleasant business. Buck begins by weighing the samples. Then he puts each sample in a separate porous nylon bag and puts the bags into a washing machine. Twice through on the gentle cycle removes most—but not all—of the smelly stuff. What is left is mainly hair, feathers, and bones. The bones are usually parts of small animals—vole skulls and such—that can be identified. Hair shafts have distinctive scale patterns that can be seen under a microscope and identified.

He measures two aspects of food preference: volume and occurrence. Occurrence tells you how many coyotes are eating the animal in question and how often they eat it. Volume tells how much of their diet consists of that animal. The two numbers may differ widely. For example, many coyotes eat insects in summer, so grasshopper remains and beetle carapaces turn up in lots of scat, but they make up a very small amount of the total food intake of individual coyotes.

No matter how you measure it, our local coyotes are eating more rabbits than anything else. Cottontail remains account for about two-thirds of the volume of the scat, and they occur in about the same proportion of samples. A survey of coyote stomachs done in Iowa two decades ago also found cottontails to be the most prevalent food item. The Iowa coyotes ate lots of domestic animals—including sheep, cattle, pigs, and chickens—and these formed the second largest category of their diet. Scientists tend to think that much of the domestic-animal intake is carrion. Farmers tend to disagree. Still, the Iowa study found that wild dogs accounted for more livestock losses in the state than coyotes.

Metropolitan coyotes don't have access to many farm animals. Buck's results show deer to be the second most popular item around here. Deer remains amounted to about 15 percent by volume and about 28 percent by occurrence. Thus far Buck has not analyzed his data sufficiently to see if there is seasonal variation in deer eating. Golembieski found a half-eaten fawn at Somme Woods, and it may be that young or injured animals are the main targets of the coyotes. However, there is evidence that coyotes have learned to trap deer in fence corners. It would probably take more than one coyote to bring down a healthy whitetail. Coyotes don't average much more than 30 pounds each, though they look a lot bigger when you see them in the woods. The hunters could have been a mother and her nearly grown pups. Raccoons, voles, birds, and

squirrels—in that order—account for most of the rest of the diet of local coyotes.

The effect of this new predator won't be known for decades. Ecological time operates in longer rhythms than human time. But thanks to Wiley Buck and his volunteers we are getting in on the beginning of the story.

Yellow Jackets

A Most Social Insect

September 11, 1987

Everybody in our family—even the dog—has been stung by a yellow jacket in the past few weeks. They are everywhere, not just in parks and backyards but on busy streets as well. You stop for a light on, say, Lincoln Avenue, and a yellow jacket flies through the window of your car and starts buzzing around the front seat.

Yellow jackets are always common in September, but this year they seem to have enjoyed a real population explosion. However unpleasant our subtropical summer may have been for people, it was obviously just right for wasps.

My wife got stung on the Ravenswood el. I got it in the middle of my back from a wasp that was apparently sitting on the car seat and got upset when I leaned against her. The dog got it on the foot, and my daughter was stung on the arm.

Only my daughter could trace her sting to the nest of yellow jackets on the back porch, a nest that I have been waffling on for three months: should I destroy it or leave it alone?

It does give a certain edge to hanging out on the porch. You step out the back door more or less into a cloud of hovering wasps. You have to learn to retain your cool while dangerous insects inspect your body. It is a valuable educational experience, a way to prepare yourself for encounters with the Hell's Angels or the Insane Unknowns. Don't get hysterical; don't make any sudden movements. Maybe they will just go away.

It is also the sort of thing you need to have around if you are a nature columnist. You have to be willing to endure nature if you are going to write about it.

Yellow jackets, as I said above, are wasps, members of the order Hymenoptera—a group that also includes bees and ants—family Vespidae, subfamily Vespidinae, genus *Vespula*. They are easily recognized. They are large insects, a half-inch long or more, marked by a pattern of black and yellow transverse stripes. They hold their bodies horizontally as they fly, and they often hover in one place, especially if the place is right in front of your face.

They are among the most social of wasps. Eusocial, Edward O. Wilson calls them in his book *The Insect Societies,* meaning that they possess three distinctive traits. First, they cooperate in caring for their young. Second, they display a division of labor in reproduction, with sterile individuals assisting fertile individuals engaged in reproduction. And third, at least two generations assist in the operations of the colony.

The life cycle of the colony on our back porch began sometime early this summer—I did not note the exact date—when a single insect, the queen, discovered a small opening in our porch railing, an opening that seems to lead to a large open space in a hollow pillar, a space that is ideal for a yellow jacket nest.

I noticed her slipping in and out and I gave some thought at the time to closing up the entrance at night and sealing her in. I hate to do thing like that. It seems so suburban. I have only impressions to back this up, nothing like what scientists would consider hard data, but I think that we have far more insects in the city than they do in the suburbs.

Suburbanites are much more into poisons that we are, and their obsession with guarding the ethnic purity of their lawns leaves them with an impoverished selection of arthropods. Suburbanites are people who saturate their property with a mixture of Agent Orange and dieldrin and then say things like, "I couldn't live in the city, I like nature too much." Or, "I don't know how you can live in the city. I wouldn't feel safe there."

So I watched through the summer as the queen, the lone wasp who established our back porch colony, was joined by a growing horde of workers slipping in and out of that hole in the porch railing.

Queens are the only yellow jackets that live through the winter. They have been fertilized the previous fall. When they find a suitable nest site, they gather bits of wood and other plant fibers, chew them up, and saturate them with saliva to make paper. They shape the paper into a cluster of cells and deposit an egg in each cell. When the eggs hatch, the queen begins to bring food to the developing larvae. Adult wasps live on plant nectar, but the babies have a richer diet consisting mostly of insects prechewed by an adult. The adult will also carry off bits of food from your picnic table or your garbage can to feed their young.

The young from the first batch of eggs grow up to be sterile female workers. As soon as they emerge from the pupa stage, they begin to assist the queen in the job of expanding and maintaining the nest and gathering food for the young. As their numbers grow, they take over these jobs completely. The queen stays inside and lays eggs. She does not leave the nest at all.

As a group, wasps display several levels of social development. Some species are solitary; a single female digs a burrow and rears her young in it with no help from anybody. Some are semisocial. Among paper wasps, for example, several fertile females build a common nest.

Vespula wasps like our yellow jackets have well-developed castes that seem to be controlled largely by nutrition. Colonies produce workers in early and midsummer when the population is small and only a few individuals are out foraging. By late summer, the colony has grown. There are more hunters out so there is more food. Nurse workers in the nest build larger chambers for eggs and then start stuffing food into the larvae in those chambers. Hawaiians used to do the same thing to members of their royal family. The powerful ought to look powerful.

These late-summer, well-fed larvae will become queens. They will mate with males—also produced only in late summer—and then go into hibernation. Next spring, they will found their own colonies.

Nutritional control of reproduction is regarded as a sophisticated method of keeping the lower orders in line. Among the more primitive, semisocial wasps, the queens use aggressive behavior, including eating the eggs of rivals, to maintain their monopoly on the production of the next generation.

I had always thought that feeding was a one-way street in a colony of social insects. Adults went out and got food, brought it back, and gave it to the larvae. But I have discovered that the process is actually reciprocal. The term entomologists use to describe this phenomenon is "trophallaxis," which is Greek for "to exchange nutriment." We could call it "food exchange," but things always sound more scientific in Greek.

Vespid larvae produce a salivary fluid that is close to 10 percent sugar. When an adult brings in, say, a prechewed fly for a larva, the larva spits out a bit of this juice and the adult licks it up.

This sweet saliva seems to function as a sort of food reserve for the colony. It has been calculated that the amount released in one typical feeding is enough to keep a worker going for half a day. It would also seem to serve as an additional incentive to the workers to keep feeding the young.

The level of interdependence that can be achieved through this mutual feeding was revealed in a study done in Israel of a wasp called *Vespa orientalis*. The study showed that adults of the species cannot convert protein to carbohydrates. Only the larvae produce the enzymes—chymotrypsin and carboxypeptidase A and B—that create this chemical change. So the adults feed the young on protein-rich insects, which the adults cannot digest, and the young convert some of the protein into growth and some into glucose, fructose, and sucrose that they feed to the adults.

The *Vespula* wasps that live around here are not as limited as the Israeli insects. Adult yellow jackets feed mainly on nectar and larval secretions, but they can eat meat if it is available. In fact, as winter approaches, they will begin to eat each other.

As the season advances, the population mix in the colony changes. Nonproductive males and queens begin to outnumber workers. Finally, the burden of supporting the ruling class gets to be too much, and the adults start to eat any remaining eggs and larvae in the nest. The colony has served its purpose. It has produced a new generation of reproducers who will carry on the species next year. October larvae are irrelevant and useless, so you might as well eat them.

By the way, this year's huge crop of yellow jackets means that there will be large numbers of queens hibernating and, therefore, large numbers of colonies founded next spring. So barring a really bad summer for wasps next year, we will probably have another superabundance in the fall.

Reading Animal Tracks
Snow Makes it Easier

January 25, 1991

I have always envied dogs their noses. Imagine being able to walk into a room and instantly know not only who was there but who just left.

When I was a kid reading stories about mountain men and cowboys and Indians, the expert trackers were the people I admired most. The stories usually had at least one guy who could look at a patch of bare rock and tell you that six men had walked across it less than an hour ago, that two of the men were left-handed, and that one had a slight astigmatism. To be able to observe and interpret subtle signs seemed a wonderful gift. Other kids wanted to be the fastest gun alive; I just wanted to follow a trail.

Tracking wasn't a very real ambition for somebody growing up in the Chicago suburbs. Generations had trod over every square inch of land around my neighborhood. In the books I read, expert trackers from the Cheyenne or the Comanche would notice a broken blade of grass and instantly know that whatever, or whomever, they were after had just passed by. Around my house broken blades of grass were all over the place, and they might record nothing more than the passing of a Com Ed maintenance truck.

So I grew up with very little tracking ability. I do notice the hoofprints of deer in muddy paths or the webbed prints of gull feet on Montrose Beach, but that's about it.

Except when it snows. In freshly fallen snow, snow that has not yet been subjected to thawing and refreezing, snow that has not yet been blown about by the wind, even unskilled trackers can learn a lot about the movements of animals we seldom see.

Deer tracks are the best place to start. The tracks are big and obvious, and since the white-tailed deer is the only wild hoofed animal in northeastern Illinois, it is impossible to confuse deer tracks with anything else.

In dry, powdery snow you'll probably see only the heart-shaped outline of the hoof. Wet snow holds an impression better, so you should see separate marks for each toe. (I should be more accurate here. The hooves of a deer are not toes, but toenails.)

On average the hooves of adult deer range from two to three inches long. The larger hoofprints probably belong to bucks, the smaller ones to does. Very tiny prints would be fawns, but there won't be any of those around until this year's cohort is born in late winter or early spring.

Tracks can also tell you how fast an animal was moving. A bounding deer has a stride of six feet or more. Each set of legs moves as a unit, so the two front hoofprints will be more or less side by side, and the rear hoofprints will register in a similar way. The rear prints are ahead of the fore. Like many four-legged animals—dogs and cats among them—running deer put their forelegs down and then swing their hind legs past them at each stride. Walking deer tend to drag their feet. You will notice a trough in the snow behind each hoofprint. The trough is dug by the foot as it swings forward with the stride.

Deer beds are easy to find in snow. They are circular or oval depressions where the snow is packed hard by the weight of the animal's body. If the snow cooperates, you can follow a deer from the moment it arises from its bed. Keep your eyes open as you track it and you should be able to see what it is eating.

Deer are browsers rather than grazers. In winter they eat mainly the twigs and dormant buds of woody plants. Rabbits go after similar food, but rabbits snip the tips off twigs very neatly. Deer do not have upper incisors, so the tips of twigs they have eaten are raggedy. From the look of them, you would say the deer bit about halfway through the twig with its lower incisors and then pulled upward, leaving a stub an inch or two long above the point where the lower incisors cut.

Deer find food from ground level up to a height of four or five feet. In woods with heavy deer populations a browse line can form at that height, an easily visible mark below which every bit of deer food has been eaten.

It occurs to me that I ought to explain a little about how mammals get around. As I mentioned, the prints of deer are made by their toenails, not by their toes. The hooves of all hoofed animals are really enormously enlarged and thickened nails. This is why a good blacksmith can shoe a horse while causing the animal no more distress than you and I feel when we clip our fingernails. Animals that walk on their nails are called unguligrade.

Dogs, cats, and many other carnivores are digitigrade; they walk on the tips of their toes. Humans, bears, raccoons, and other comparatively slow-footed creatures are plantigrade; we walk on the bottoms of our feet.

Tracking gets complicated when you try to identify some of our local digitigrade animals. For example, we have three species of wild canids in northeastern Illinois. Red foxes are widespread and common, gray foxes are scattered and rare, and, as you know if you have been reading the papers, coyotes are around in growing numbers.

The footprints of all three animals are quite similar. They show four toes, each with a pad, forming an arc around the front of a single, large central pad. In a clear print the blunt claws are likely to register. Red fox and coyote feet are about two and a half inches long, while gray fox feet are close to one and a half inches. In a clear print you may see a distinctive ridge crossing the central pad of a red fox.

The problem with identifying these tracks is dogs. We have dogs in all sizes, from smaller than a gray fox to bigger than a wolf. There are ways to tell coyote and fox tracks from dog tracks, but I am not a good enough tracker to do it—and I probably couldn't explain the process in the space of this column even if I were.

The secrets have to do not only with the precise shape of the foot but also with the characteristic gaits. Watch a dog walking or trotting toward you and you will see that it walks sideways. Foxes move somewhat more straight ahead.

There are also behavioral clues that you can use. A dog out for a walk with its owner is interested mainly in having a good time. It will run for no reason at all. It will charge directly into snowbanks. Wild animals don't act like that. They proceed cautiously. They run only when they have to. They don't waste energy plowing through snow if they can find a way to avoid the deep places. Of course stray dogs, dogs on their own, will adopt the ways of the wild if they live long enough to learn them.

The other digitigrade animal tracks you may encounter on a walk through a forest preserve belong to the family called mustelids: weasels, minks, otters, and others. Weasel and mink tracks can be told immediately from those of any canid because they have five toes instead of four. Skunks, which are also mustelids, put their whole hind foot down with each step, but they are digitigrade with their front paws. However, skunks spend the winter asleep in a den, so you won't often find their little footprints in the snow.

Squirrels bound along putting their large five-toed hind feet down flat somewhat ahead of their smaller four-toed front feet. Of course, the fact that the tracks always start and end at the base of a tree is a further clue.

Cottontail rabbits are easy. The footprints of a bounding rabbit are roughly Y-shaped. The small front feet are put down one in front of the other. One is at the bottom of the Y, the other is at the fork. The large rear feet are at the tips of the fork. Twigs eaten by cottontails are nibbled by many tiny bites into a blunt point.

Raccoons leave prints that look almost like the palm print of a very small person, with five long toes extending out of a flat foot. Opossums have five toes too, but on their hind feet three of the toes point forward, the baby toe points outward, and a large thumblike big toe points inward or even backward. No other local mammal has a foot like that.

Sometimes when the snow is just right, you can follow the tiny tracks of a deer mouse or a vole. These little creatures don't spend any more time than is absolutely necessary out on top of the snow. Once in a great while, if you get really lucky, you can see why. You might find the spot where a mouse's tracks have met the tracks of a weasel or fox. Or you might see the broad disturbance in the snow created by the wings of a great horned owl as it settled over a hapless mouse. Reading signs of what happened before you arrived is like having a nose as good as a dog's.

4 › Birds and More Birds

The Bird Hunter

Nature Is Everywhere

May 10, 1985

This time of year, it is hard to think of anything but birds. Birding is a year-round game, and each season has its peculiar pleasures. November mornings, standing on a jetty at Gillson Park in Wilmette, icy Lake Michigan waves lapping at my feet, hoping that a surf scoter or black-legged kittiwake would materialize out of the mist, I have had fun. It is even a pleasure to spend a muggy June morning fighting off mosquitoes in hopes of discovering a nesting prothonotary warbler.

But nothing beats the middle two weeks of May. If you like birds, you want to see a lot of birds, and there are more of them passing through Chicago now than at any other time of year.

This is the season when birders plan Big Days, campaigns as tightly organized as D day, precisely plotted assaults on the local bird life whose only goal is to see or hear as many species as possible in 24 hours. This is the time when even Illinoisans can hope for 150 species in a day. The state record is 170, set by a party working out of Springfield on May 11, 1974. This year, another group is trying to get hold of an airplane so that they can bird the whole state in a day and rack up 200 species.

If you aren't into the game, you may ask what all this proves, and the answer may be nothing, except to other people in the game, but to them, it is wonderful.

Birding is, before everything else, a hunt, a chance to search and stalk, a chase that rewards skill and patience and experience.

When I was a lad, I used to hunt with a shotgun. I loved getting out at dawn, tromping through woods and fields in the crisp fall air. I loved the camaraderie of the chase, the running gags that developed among the partners in this pleasureful enterprise.

But as time went on, I began to get good enough to hit most of the animals I shot at, and the fun went out it. Watching a rabbit with a shattered spine trying to drag itself into the bushes with its front legs is not my idea of a good time.

153

When I discovered birding, I realized I had found the ideal substitute. It had everything I liked about hunting and none of the gore. And I could do it year-round and almost anywhere. I didn't even have to drive to the country. In fact, I could play the game in a small way in my backyard. Memories are my only trophies, but they seem to be the only ones I need.

The ancient cliché holds that the typical birder is a little old lady in tweed underwear gushing about how cute the little dicky birds are. Certainly such people exist, and some of them are pretty good birders, but in truth birding has always been a young man's game. Some kids get hooked in the third grade, and the real fanatics are teenagers and lads in their 20s. For whatever reason, at that age the game, like the game of collecting recordings of obscure 1950s doo-wop groups or amassing a complete set of EC comics, is mostly played by males. The best women birders tend to be older than these teen hotshots.

Young men set the styles in the game. The Big Day itself, 24 hours of more or less nonstop birding, a frantic rush from one hot spot to another, breakfasting on Twinkies in the backseat of a moving car, is pure American youth. A few years ago, a rare Mexican warbler showed up at Big Bend National Park in southwest Texas. A bunch of college students in Tampa decided that they had to see that bird. So they rented a car on a special weekend deal, Friday night to Monday morning, unlimited mileage and low, low discount prices. They drove nonstop to west Texas, found the bird, swung south to Brownsville to pick up a Mexican crow at the city dump, and nonstopped back to Tampa to turn in the car on time. Six people in an Avis Impala, sleeping, scratching, sweating across the south, living with even weirder smells and a steadily deepening pile of junk-food wrappers, lead-footing it toward Terlingua, Texas, where it's 110 in the shade and there is no shade. I wasn't a birder in college, but I made trips in that style under the joint inspiration of Jack Kerouac and Woody Guthrie, so I am familiar with the form.

In 1973, a young high school dropout named Kenn Kaufman decided to take on a North American Big Year, birding's equivalent of the Iron Man. The idea is to see as many birds as possible in North America in a calendar year. Kaufman figured that three things were necessary to success in a Big Year: time, money, and experience. He had two out of the three, so he decided to try. Since money was the one he lacked—his total budget for the year was $1,000—he did most of his traveling with his thumb, racking up to 70,000 miles, spending a couple days in jail for hitchhiking on an interstate, briefly getting kidnapped by a crazy lady. On a few occasions he dined on Gravy Train.

By the end of summer, he was totally burned out on the project, but he realized that he couldn't quit. He was carrying the hopes of every birder who had helped him out with guide service, a free meal, and a place to sleep. So he stayed at it until the end of December, collecting a list of 671 species and the breaking the old Big Year record by 45 species.

Two Big Years have been undertaken since Kaufman, and the record is now up to 714, but the style is changing. Even birding has begun to enter the world of corporate sponsorship and book contracts. These days, the quest is carried on by jet at staggering cost, and only the well-to-do need apply.

All right, you may ask, some people do it by thumb and some people do it by jet, but why does anybody do it at all? Why chase all over the continent just to look at birds? I'm tempted to answer that it is because they are there. Or to suggest that if you have to ask that question, you won't be able to understand the answer. But seriously, friends, for me, becoming a birder was like being cured of color blindness. Imagine seeing red and green after a lifetime of viewing the world in shades of gray. Through birding, I discovered that the natural world exists not just in special parks and preserves but all around us.

The brown thrasher phenomenon, a friend called it. He had never seen one of these common birds before I took him on a bird walk through Lincoln Park, but once he had seen one, he started to see them everywhere. The previously nonexistent was suddenly ubiquitous. The shades of gray had turned to red and green.

It's not easy when you start out. What people call the natural order seems like the natural chaos. The birds do not help you. Watch a small songbird in a treetop. It appears and vanishes again and again, slipping through the leaves, flashing a glimpse of wing, then a bit of the head, a small patch of the breast. When you are a novice standing under the tree getting in crick in your back from looking straight up for 15 solid minutes, this elusiveness induces a profound despair. You wonder what this flickering apparition has to do with the formal portraits in the field guides. The world seems full of strange birds that were unaccountably left out of the books.

But in time, with experience and study, these sightings begin to sort themselves out. Mystery birds become rarer. Order reasserts itself.

Roger Tory Peterson has been called the "father of the environmental movement." The title is an overstatement, since the movement has had several fathers, but he is certainly one of them. His field guides made birding accessible, helped millions of people start seeing brown thrashers. Once their eyes were opened, the advancing destruction of the natural world became a very personal question. We read of millions of acres of tropical forests being destroyed every year, and it seems like a distant event that has little to do with us. But serious birders all across North America are reporting noticeable declines in numbers of migrating warblers, vireos, tanagers, and flycatchers. Birds that winter in the tropics are dying because their habitat is being destroyed, and we birders don't need David Attenborough or Jacques Cousteau to tell us about it. We can see it right now in Lincoln Park.

Birding also lets you get inside a special subculture, an egalitarian place where there is room for precocious ten-year-olds and great-grandmothers, the only place in American society, so far as I know, where a pubescent kid can be taken seriously by adults, and where doctors in Mercedes listen to retired steelworkers.

Once you are in the network, you can go almost anywhere and find kindred spirits. If you belong to the American Birding Association, you can look up local members, get some advice, and, in some cases, acquire a free guide to the local action. Even with jet planes and corporate sponsors, a successful Big Year depends on the network, on people who will help you out because they know if you like birds, you must be OK.

Woodpeckers

How They Fly, Feed, and Breed

January 16, 1987

You hear it sometimes on quiet streets, a light irregular tapping from somewhere up in the trees that at first seems like the random swinging of a loose branch in the wind. Listen for a minute, and you may sense some pattern. Listen longer, and you may hear a sharp, single call note that might be rendered orthographically as something like *tchip*.

If you hear that, start searching the branches above you. Somewhere up there is a downy woodpecker. Downy woodpeckers are the smallest of the five species of woodpecker known to breed in the Chicago area. A sixth, the pileated, may also nest somewhere around here.

Downies are not only the smallest, they are also the most urban of our local woodpeckers. You can usually find some along tree-lined streets, in any of our larger parks, in the bigger cemeteries, and in almost any forest preserve. They are residents, birds that are more or less equally abundant year-round.

As a group, woodpeckers are so distinctive anybody should be able to identify one. They don't look like anything else, and they don't act like anything else.

Consider their manner of flight. They fly not in a direct line, like a starling or pigeon, but in swooping arcs, beating their wings in a few quick flaps to rise and then coasting, wings folded, down to the bottom of the arc. This style makes great sense when you see woodpeckers land. Their typical landing is a feet-first crash into a vertical tree trunk. It is a very sudden stop, so it doesn't pay to be going too fast. The downward glide helps slow the birds, and at the last moment, they use their wings and tails like ailerons to turn up, exhausting the last of their velocity just as their feet swing forward and the claws hook the bark.

In flight, woodpeckers look slender bodied and thick necked. The latter is a condition required of animals that derive both food and shelter from their ability to bang their heads very hard against tree trunks.

Those thick neck muscles drive beaks that are long, straight, and sturdy. Woodpeckers use their beaks like chisels, chipping away at the wood, changing the angle of attack to fit the needs of the job.

Their skulls are thick and well cushioned against shock, but the most remarkable feature of their heads is the hyoid bone. The hyoid is a small bone in the lower jaw that serves to anchor the muscles of the tongue. In most birds, the hyoid is attached to the lower part of the skull, but in woodpeckers the base of the bone is extraordinarily elongated. The two halves of the base pass down the front of the throat and then loop around the back of the skull and over the crown. They join near where they are both anchored—in the right nostril.

This whole elaborate mechanism can swing forward to allow the bird to extend its tongue as much as four times the length of the beak. The

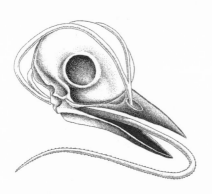

extensive musculature gives the bird a high degree of control. A woodpecker can slip its tongue into a hole dug by the larvae of a wood-boring beetle and find the bug that did the job. Once it finds it, barbs on the tongue help it remove the insect from the hole.

Downy woodpeckers were favorites of the ornithologists of the Victorian era. Audubon commented admiringly on their industry, perseverance, and sober demeanor. Downies work a tree with great care. They hitch their way up the trunk, hanging on with clawed feet that have two toes pointing forward and two pointing back. The shafts of their central tail feathers are quite stiff, and they help brace the birds against tree trunks. On horizontal branches, downies will search both upper and lower surfaces. If they find something, they start that soft tapping. They may continue for a minute or more until the food is exposed.

The Victorians must have loved the downies' color scheme. Males have a small red spot on their napes, but otherwise, both sexes are entirely done up in black and white. Their faces are boldly patterned, their wings and tail feathers are either black spotted with white or white spotted with black. Their breasts and backs are pure white.

The only other woodpeckers around here with white backs are hairy woodpeckers, close cousins of the downies. The two species have virtually identical plumage, but hairy woodpeckers are almost half again as large as downies, and they have relatively larger and heavier beaks.

The two species are separated to some extend by their habitat choices. Downies favor more open woods, which is why they can get along amid the scattered trees of parks and cemeteries. Hairies can usually be found only in dense woodlands.

The difference in size and strength between the two species directs them toward different food sources. With their stronger beaks, hairies rely heavily on the larvae of wood-boring beetles for food. These worm-like creatures live in tunnels in the wood, and hairies are strong enough to dig them out. The beetles form a full third of the annual food supply of an average hairy woodpecker, and when such larvae are abundant, the hairies will live on them almost exclusively.

Wood-boring beetle larvae form only about 14 percent of the diet of an average downy woodpecker. With their smaller, weaker bills, they concentrate more on eggs, cocoons, and overwintering insects in or immediately under the bark.

The annual cycle of life for downy woodpeckers begins in spring when pairs form for nesting. Males will call at this time, and both sexes do some drumming, apparently to advertise their territorial boundaries. Drumming is a hard, fast, staccato banging of the beak against some resonant object. Originally, the resonant object was probably always a hollow tree, but the birds have discovered that tin roofs, drainpipes, and empty barrels will serve quite well.

Birds create all sorts of noises with their ordinary vocal apparatus. Some birds also produce whistling noises with specialized feathers that catch the air just right. Ruffed grouse make their drumming noise by beating their wings against their breasts. But only woodpeckers are instrumentalists, producing their "music" with the help of hollow logs.

Both birds of a pair work to dig the nest hole. They excavate it in a tree trunk anywhere from 3 to 50 feet above the ground. The entrance is always a perfectly round hole about an inch and a half in diameter. The hole extends into the trunk a short distance and then widens out into an egg chamber that may be ten inches deep. Downies dig in either live or dead wood, although they use dead—and therefore weak—wood more often than the stronger hairies.

Birds that nest in holes are more successful at fledging young than open nesters. The eggs and nestlings are protected from bad weather and predators, and the young can remain safely in the nest until they are well grown. The young of open-nesting birds of about the same size as downies usually leave the nest when they are 12 days to two weeks old. Downy woodpecker young may remain safely inside the nesting hole until they are 24 days old.

As sedentary birds, downies don't have to worry about long, hazardous flights, but they do have to worry about their winter food supply. All they have to eat is what grew last summer. No new beetle larvae will hatch this month.

To preserve this limited food supply, families split up. The adults drive off the young, and pairs that have bred together separate. The birds become quite antagonistic to others of their kind. There are even records of one downy woodpecker killing another during this period of hostility.

The birds live through the winter as hermits, each individual guarding a feeding territory. To survive cold winter nights, each bird digs itself a roosting hole in a likely tree trunk. Many of these are taken over by other birds or small mammals, so downies often have to dig two or more holes over the course of the winter.

All this excavation of nesting and roosting holes is vitally important to woodland ecology. Looking through *A Field Guide to Birds' Nests* by Hal Harrison, a book that covers only the eastern U.S., I find 2 owls and 17 songbirds listed as nesting in old woodpecker holes. The list includes the great crested flycatcher, the tree swallow, the tufted titmouse, three species of chickadees, three species of nuthatch, three species of wrens, and the eastern bluebird. Many of these hole-nesting birds are incapable of doing their own excavating, so without woodpeckers they would be extremely short of places to live.

The importance of woodpeckers was demonstrated in European forests where experimenters increased breeding populations of various hole-nesting species simply by putting out nesting boxes—birdhouses— for them. The experiments showed that a lack of nesting sites limited populations even when food was superabundant. The whole forest has an interest in the prosperity of woodpeckers.

Looking for a Gyrfalcon

Rare in Illinois

February 8, 1991

I decided to go in search of the gyrfalcons last Friday. I wrote a column about them in January. Two of them have been hanging around the cooling lake at Commonwealth Edison's LaSalle nuclear power station since Christmas. The obvious attraction is the waterfowl that spend the winter on the lake.

Gyrfalcons are a big deal in Illinois. We have had only 17 previous sightings in the state, and some of those are not terribly well documented. The possibility of seeing two gyrfalcons in one day is a literal once-in-a-lifetime opportunity. As a bonus, there was the chance to see a prairie falcon. This western falcon should be classified "rare but regular" in the winter in Illinois. We get them almost every year, but usually only one or two birds are reported.

We can be sure there are two gyrfalcons because gyrfalcons are a variable species with three color phases: dark, gray, and white. One of the birds at LaSalle is a dark phase; the other is a gray phase.

As a further bonus, the Chicago Audubon Society's Rare Bird Alert reported that a merlin had been seen near the cooling lake. It occurred to me that I could drive to LaSalle County and see the merlin, the prairie falcon, and the gyrfalcons. Then I could drive back to Chicago and find the peregrine falcon that lives along the lake near Montrose Harbor. Add a kestrel or two—you can find them almost anywhere—and I would have seen all but one of North America's native falcons in a single day. The only one I would be missing would be the Aplomado falcon, which is really a Mexican and Central American bird that shows up very rarely in south Texas and southern Arizona. I would also be picking up no fewer than three life birds. I have never seen a prairie falcon, a gyrfalcon, or a merlin. And if I did pick up those three species, my North American life list would reach 400 species.

The one thing that made me reluctant to undertake the trip was the fact that I never find any of the rare birds I go searching for. The Rare

Bird Alert keeps announcing the presence of extraordinary species and provides very precise directions for finding them. I go out and tromp around all day through snow or mud and see nothing but crows, starlings, and the occasional junco. People who show up the day before me or the day after come back with stories about how the bird landed on a tree branch within 20 feet of them and posed for half an hour.

There are two possible explanations for this. One is that I'm really not very good at this game. The other is that the whole edifice of organized bird-watching, with its guidebooks and magazines, its national organizations and local clubs, is an enormous hoax, a huge practical joke being played on me. While I'm shivering on some windswept cornfield or slogging through ankle-deep mud in search of imaginary rarities, the jokesters who concocted this jape are sitting around laughing until their sides ache.

Or maybe the birds are real, but the stories they tell on the hotlines about where the birds are located are fictions. Last spring I decided not to drive all the way to Lake Calumet to see a brown pelican that had been reported there. Instead, I took the very short drive to Montrose Harbor, and there on the beach was the brown pelican. I felt for a moment like I had outsmarted the puppet masters who have been jerking me around all these years.

So I set out for LaSalle County with a general feeling of hopelessness. But it was a beautiful sunny day, and I could enjoy the scenery even I didn't see any birds.

The LaSalle nuclear generator is just south of the town of Seneca, which is on the Illinois River about 30 miles southwest of Joliet. The countryside is typical Illinois farmland: flat, few trees, bare fields now covered with a thin layer of snow.

I drove down into the narrow Illinois River valley, where there were deeply cut ravines thick with trees and my first raptor of the morning: a red-tailed hawk sitting on a utility pole right next to the road. I stopped and looked him over and then drove on into Seneca.

Downtown Seneca is all north of the river. There are vacant stores and even some vacant lots on Main Street, but there is also a nice new public library and a bank building of recent vintage. Across the river the road climbs up out of the valley and returns the traveler to the sort of Illinois landscape I love: no hills, few trees. I feel at home in this kind of setting. Hills always seem unnecessary and inconvenient to me, and they also block the view. In Illinois the sky is a major component of the landscape, and the horizon is miles away.

The earthen berm that contains Com Ed's lake is just west of the road. Apparently, the warmth of the water in the lake has penetrated the soil enough to melt the snow on the berm. It is the only place in sight where the brown earth shows through the white.

Clouds of vapor rise from the water and hang over the top of the berm. In cold weather blowing vapors can produce localized fogs that affect visibility on adjoining roads.

The grid of roads that follow the section lines south and west of the lake is numbered, and the Rare Bird Alert supplied the numbers of intersections where the falcons have been seen. I spent the entire morning driving slowly over those township roads, checking a corncrib at 22 North and 25 East and utility poles around 18 North and 22 East. Along 23 East between 18 and 19 North a plantation of red pines borders the road for about a quarter mile. Central Illinois is not exactly prime country for red pines, and all the trees have a rather scruffy look, but the birds had been seen perched in the trees. Gyrfalcons are birds of open country—their nesting ground is the arctic tundra—and they are as likely to perch on the ground as on something tall, so I scanned the fields as I drove.

Early in the search I made out the distant shape of a large bird hovering over one spot. Gyrfalcons do hover, but that sort of behavior is more typical of rough-legged hawks, another tundra hunter that comes south in the winter. When I got close enough to see the wing shape, I could tell it was rough-leg. A rough-legged hawk is a good bird, but one you can see every winter if you get out birding much.

At the pine plantation I ran into three birders from Fort Wayne who were making the same fruitless search I was. They had been looking since the previous afternoon with no luck.

I scared up lots of kestrels. Each brought me a thrill of possibility that lasted a fraction of a second, just long enough for me to notice that the bird was far too small to be a gyrfalcon or prairie falcon and had all the wrong colors to be a merlin. And I was attended everywhere I went by horned larks. America's only native lark regards a windswept plowed field as an ideal spot to spend the winter. They are preeminent open-country birds. Even tall grass is too much ground cover for them.

Watching the small songbirds flying off into the fields as my car approached, I was looking for Lapland longspurs and snow buntings. Both species had been seen by birders in search of falcons, but I could not pick any out.

I began to realize that I shouldn't have come alone. I was moving slowly, and there was no traffic, but I still had to pay some attention to the road. I could have used another pair of eyes to help scan the fields.

Every time I saw something large flying in the distance—and in this kind of landscape you can see large flying birds a long way off—it resolved itself into a crow. Large birds out standing in the fields resolved themselves into pheasants.

At some point on a trip like this you have to decide how much longer you are going to search. For me the point came after nearly four hours. I had driven about 60 miles over the township roads and found none of the birds I was seeking. But it was a nice day, and it is good to get out in the country once in a while. I drove into Seneca for cheeseburger and beer and ate while listening to another customer tell the bartender—at great length and at great volume—about a custody battle he and his ex-wife were having over their son.

As I drove out of Seneca and up the hill to the north of town I looked up and saw that same red-tailed hawk. It was still sitting on the utility pole, just as it had been almost five hours ago when I entered the valley. My suspicion is that it is a sort of sentinel. Its job is to warn the rarities that birders are coming.

Sparrows
Small Brown Birds

April 6, 1984

A wise man of my acquaintance once said that there are only three kinds of birds in the world: small brown birds, big white birds, and owls. April is the month for small brown birds.

The most cosmopolitan of small brown birds is the house sparrow, a.k.a. English sparrow or, in the days before the automobile, horseshit sparrow. Natives of Eurasia, these adaptable creatures have followed Europeans all over the globe.

The early settlers in North America found no house sparrows (they later imported them), but they did find lots of SBBs that reminded them of the sparrows of home, and eventually they gave the name sparrow to no fewer than 32 species of North American birds.

These American sparrows are variously streaked and patterned, mostly in shades of brown, tan, rust, yellow, and ochre. Nearly all of them are smaller than the house sparrow, but they share the short, stout, seedeater's bill.

As a group, these New World sparrows are furtive little beasts. They tend to favor open places, grasslands, savannas, or recently cut-over ground just beginning to return to forest. They feed—and usually nest—on the ground, and many of them are very reluctant to take to the air. Grasshopper sparrows, prairie nesters, slink away like field mice through the grass stems if you get too close to them.

Many species sing "songs" that sound more like insects trills, so even if you heard one of them, you might not know you were hearing a bird. Henslow's sparrow, a prairie species that nests around Chicago, "sings" a hiccuping, two-note rasp so primitive that Roger Tory Peterson, describing it in his *Field Guide to the Birds,* departed from his usual evenhanded tone to declare it "one of the poorest vocal efforts of any bird."

Their names suggest the near invisibility of many of these sparrows. Ornithologists who discover new species tend to act like politicians with expressways to christen: they name them after each other. The honor usually shows up in the scientific name, but when *Melospiza lincolnii* becomes Lincoln's sparrow in the vernacular, you know you are dealing with an obscure bird, a species that was so little noticed by unspecialized humanity that it never acquired a common name. Almost a third of our native sparrows carry this badge of obscurity.

But in April, the shadows lift a bit. Migrating birds can't always find the tangled vegetation they prefer to lurk in. They appear in backyards and vacant lots and especially in our lakefront parks. On a good day in April, a day with a south wind to stimulate movement by the migrants, it is almost impossible to visit Lincoln or Jackson Park without seeing sparrows. They forage over the lawns and in the shrubbery and make themselves quite conspicuous. In a typical spring, 21 different species of native sparrows will be seen along the lakefront, and there is always the chance of some rarities to swell the total. A couple years ago, a Cassin's sparrow, a Texas species never before seen in Illinois, spent several days in Olive Park near Navy Pier while eager birders came from all over to see it.

The white-throated sparrow is the most conspicuous and abundant of these lakefront migrants. This is one of the few woodland sparrows, a bird that nests in young second-growth forests in the north woods. Unlike many of its relatives, it has a long list of common names, most of them based on its distinctive song. White-throats sing in a high, clear whistle, a pure tone without overtones. New Englanders listening to the rhythm of this whistle decided that the bird was calling "Hey, Old Sam Peabody, Peabody, Peabody," so they called the bird Sam Peabody. In Ontario, they decided the bird was a nationalist and its song was translated as "Oh, Canada, Canada, Canada," and the singer was dubbed the Canada bird.

White-throated sparrows sing during migration, and Sam Peabody can be heard all over the place during the next few weeks. There will be thousands of them in the parks, and I even hear them near my apartment on Malden Street in the middle of Uptown.

Visually, they are also quite distinctive. They have white throat patches as the name suggests. Their crowns are decorated with black and white stripes, and they show a small spot of bright yellow just over the bill. You really can't miss them.

One species in this tribe of secretive skulkers has paradoxically become one of the best known animals in the world. The song sparrow is a streak-breasted bird that ranges over North America from Key West to Alaska and from Mexico to Hudson Bay. Its preferred habitat is open ground with scattered small trees and shrubs. This preference can be satisfied in many backyards, and song sparrows are among the birds that adapt quite easily to humans.

Our intimate knowledge of *Melospiza melodia* comes from the work of one person, Margaret Morse Nice. In 1928, Mrs. Nice was living in a house on Patterson Street in Columbus, Ohio. Her backyard overlooked a piece of the floodplain of the Olentangy River, an area of weeds and scattered trees and shrubs that was ideal song sparrow territory.

Mrs. Nice was married to a professor at Ohio State and most of her time was taken up with raising children and keeping house. She lacked the full course of professional training that respectable ornithologists are supposed to have, but she had a deep interest in birds. Since her housewifely duties kept her at home, she decided to study the song sparrows along the Olentangy.

She began by observing a single nesting pair, but she quickly decided that what was needed was a study of the whole population, and over the next eight years she did the study.

Her first requirement was that she be able to recognize individual birds in the field, so she began trapping and banding birds on the 40 acres of floodplain that she named "Interpont" since it lay between bridges. She attached a standard Fish and Wildlife Service aluminum band to one leg and variously colored celluloid bands—she made the first ones from some of her children's toys—to the other leg. Over the eight years of the study, she banded nearly 900 birds.

With the identification problem solved, she could study every aspect of the lives of this population of song sparrows. She could learn the songs of individual males. Each of them had a repertoire of several, each distinctive within the general pattern of the species. She could determine—because she knew who was related to whom—that males learned their songs by listening to other birds and did not inherit them from their fathers.

She could study mate selection and learn that in general female song sparrows chose males rather haphazardly and that they showed more attachment to a territory than they did to any particular mate. She could learn that some of her birds spent the whole year in Interpont while some migrated each fall and returned in the spring. She learned that females were more likely to migrate than males and that the tendency to migrate was apparently not inherited. Sedentary birds had migrant children, and vice versa, and some birds changed their minds, migrating in some winters and not in others.

Monitoring nests continuously, she discovered how heavy song sparrow eggs were (average, 2.28 grams), how much newly hatched birds weighed, and how much weight they gained each day until they left the nest.

Her first publications on the study attracted the attention of the heavies in the new science of ethology, the study of animal behavior, and she made a trip to Europe to meet Konrad Lorenz and Niko Tinbergen and share her results with them.

Eventually, she published *Studies in the Life History of the Song Sparrow*, a two-volume work that is a classic of ornithological literature.

The most fascinating aspect of this huge mass of facts is the degree of individuality shown by those small songbirds. They are definitely not automatons living out the species program. Consider 57M, a nonmacho male who nonetheless did quite well with the ladies. Of him Mrs. Nice says, "57M is a particularly interesting bird, because he has always been retiring, almost never singing, yet he survived to be almost six years old, obtaining mates during each of the five seasons, and raising young at least once."

4M was his polar opposite, a pugnacious bird who sang loudly and aggressively drove off challengers to his territory. He was the longest-lived bird in the study. Already living on Interpont in 1928, he survived until December 1935, a life span more than three times the average for the species. Mrs. Nice's early publications made him famous. Ornithologists on two continents followed his saga. He was arguably the most famous wild songbird that ever lived, an international celebrity whose annual matings attracted almost as much attention as Burt Reynolds's. He, at least, was not your typical obscure sparrow.

[*Studies in the Life History of the Song Sparrow* by Margaret Morse Nice is out of print.]

Red-Tailed Hawks

Lessons from an Expert Flyer

March 13, 1987

Last Saturday afternoon, my friend David Standish and I were sitting in the living room of his house watching a basketball game on television. It's the sort of thing we nature lovers like to do when the temperature hits 70 degrees on a weekend in early March.

Suddenly through his front window we both caught the flickering swirl of what looked like every pigeon in the neighborhood in frantic flight. David was out of his chair first. "There's something out there," he said. Standing near the window, he pointed up. "Hawk," he said.

I followed him to the window, and looking high into the pale blue sky, saw the bird. Its wings and tail were long and broad. "Could be a red-tail," I said. David confirmed it. He had seen a flash of burnt orange in the tail as the bird passed over us.

The pigeons' wild excitement was an innate reaction. Baby birds of many species are born with a sort of imprint of the shape of a bird of prey in their little brains. Flightless infants will hunker down in the nest at the passing of a silhouette that suggests hawk. Older birds are more likely to react like the pigeons and try to present a moving target.

The passing red-tail showed a shape that pigeons living near the lake probably haven't seen much of. Although the red-tailed hawk is the only large bird of prey that is common year-round in the Chicago area, for some reason the species is seldom seen along the lakeshore.

Red-tailed hawks live almost everywhere in North America. Their range extends from Alaska to Panama, and they are completely absent only from the treeless tundra and from very dense woodlands. They prefer a landscape with a mixture of woods and open fields, since they nest in trees and hunt over open land. We can surmise that they were common in Illinois before settlement, when prairie and savanna were the dominant plant communities in most of the state. Farms with scattered woodlots are prime red-tail habitat.

Like most animals with a huge range, red-tails vary in their appearance from place to place. The typical red-tail that we see here is a sort of chocolate brown on the head, back, and upper wings. The underparts are white with some mottling and an irregular brown band across the belly. From the underside, the wings show a dark bar along the leading edge and alternating brown and white transverse stripes. Wingspan varies from just under four feet to just under five feet. The adults' reddish-orange tails show a narrow dark bar about an inch from the tip, and the feather tips themselves are almost white.

Out on the Great Plains, an extremely pale form is more usual, and in parts of Canada and Alaska there is a dark form that is deep brown almost all over. This latter form, called Harlan's hawk, used to be considered a separate species.

Red-tails are a partially migratory species. Northern birds come south, but most of our Illinois birds probably stick around all year. Red-tails are early migrants, so numbers of them pass through in March, making early spring a particularly good time to see them.

Their scientific name is *Buteo jamaicensis*. The genus name comes from a Latin term for hawk. The species name derives from the fact that the first specimens known to science were collected in Jamaica. There are about 25 species of the genus *Buteo* worldwide. They are found everywhere but Australia and parts of India.

Buteos are soaring birds. With their long, broad wings and tails they look like scaled-down eagles. The structure of their wings allows them to stay aloft for hours with practically no effort, riding thermals and other updrafts while they survey the country below.

The shape and size of a bird's wings can tell you a lot about how it gets along in the world. Underlying all these differences is a basic skeletal structure that is essentially the same for all birds.

The next time you have occasion to eat a chicken wing, look it over while you chew. The first thing you will notice is that it doesn't have much meat on it. The muscles that power flight are in the breast. Long tendons connect them to the wing bones. If the weight were out on the wing, the bird would have to work much harder as it flew because the extra weight would have to be moved up and down.

Next, notice the bones. The single bone nearest the body is the humerus. It is directly analogous to the bone of our upper arm. Next are a pair of bones, the radius and ulna, which are directly comparable to the bones of our forearms.

But out at the tip, the third segment of the wing is a pointy little thing with almost no meat at all. Here is where birds have really gone in for weight reduction. Instead of the complex arrangements in the feet of four-legged animals or the even more elaborate structure of our wrists and hands, birds have only two tiny wrist bones, three palm bones—and two of those are fused together—and three small finger bones, two of which are very small.

Airplanes have wings to provide lift and propellers to provide power, but a bird's wings perform both functions. Most of the lift comes from the inner two sections, where the humerus and radius and ulna bones provide the support for the feathers called the secondaries, which form the trailing edge of the wing. The third segment, those tiny wrist, palm, and finger bones, is the point of attachment for the primary flight feathers, the propellers of bird flight.

Small birds get their power on the downstroke. The primary feathers are then oriented to cut the air like a propeller blade and pull the bird through the air. On the upstroke, the primaries open like venetian blinds, offering a minimum of resistance to the air.

Larger birds can't afford to idle on the upstroke. Their wings move in a complex pattern that gives them propeller action on both strokes.

The cross-section of a wing shows a streamlined, teardrop shape, with a blunt but rounded leading edge tapering to a narrow trailing edge. As this shape moves through the air, it splits the airstream. Half the air flows over the upper surface, half under the lower.

Lift, the force that makes flight possible, is created when the air flowing over the upper surface exerts less pressure than the air flowing under the lower surface. Bird wings create this pressure difference in two ways, first by being cambered and second by being held at a slight angle so that the leading edge is slightly higher than the trailing edge. A camber is a curve in the cross-section of the wing that makes the concave lower surface shorter than the convex upper surface, which has a greater area. The air over the upper surface is, in effect, spread out over a greater area and thus exerts less pressure than the denser air below the wing.

Holding the leading edge of the wing higher creates more lift only up to a point. If the angle of attack becomes too great, the smooth flow of air over the upper wing breaks up into swirling turbulence and lift vanishes. This is called going into a stall, and both birds and airplanes do it. Watch birds coming in for a landing, and you will see that they deliberately tilt their wings to create stall conditions, which they use to lose speed and altitude. Long, slender wings are much less subject to stalling than broad wings.

If you see a red-tail soaring, notice that the primary feathers, those out at the tip of the wing, are spread apart. There is space between them. This is an aerodynamic necessity for a bird that soars over the land.

The thermals, the rising currents of warm air the birds ride, are often quite small. To stay within them, the bird has to turn in very tight spirals. Tight turns require slow speeds, so the problem for a red-tail is to fly slowly and still get enough lift to avoid sinking. It needs a very high angle of attack, but a high angle of attack combined with low speed and broad wings produces a stall.

Those separated—the correct term is slotted—primaries are the solution. Each feather becomes a separate, slender wing that can be turned sharply to create a high angle of attack without stalling.

So it is that the bird David and I saw could drift slowly over Byron Street, terrifying every pigeon in the neighborhood, and never once move its wings.

Birding in North Channel
A Memorable Canoe Trip

July 17, 1992

Our suspicion is that black-crowned night herons have been nesting along the North Shore Channel. This bird is on the endangered list in Illinois. We have three known colonies around Chicago: Lake Calumet, Lake Renwick near Plainfield, and Baker's Lake in Barrington. There are two other colonies along the Illinois River south of Peoria and another near two East Saint Louis. And that is it for the whole state.

The North Shore Channel brings water from Lake Michigan into the North Branch of the Chicago River. It is part of the system that turned the river around, directing its flow to the Illinois River rather than to Lake Michigan. The lake end of the channel is in Gillson Park in Wilmette, just down the hill from the Baha'i temple. From there it runs southwest to Emerson Street in Evanston, where it turns south, paralleling McCormick Boulevard and Kedzie Avenue in Chicago until it hooks up with the river just south of Foster.

Birders have seen the herons regularly along the channel throughout the breeding season, so on July 1 Alan Anderson, Allen Feldman, and I loaded my canoe on top of my car and set off to paddle the channel in search of them.

Alan suggested that we start at the lake and paddle all the way to Devon Avenue, since this would cover the area where most of the sightings took place. So we drove into the Sheridan Shore Yacht Club in Wilmette Harbor, unloaded the canoe, and put it in the water. We weren't sure we would be allowed to do this, since the yacht club is a private place. But we followed the golden rule of gate-crashers—always act like you know what you are doing—and got under way without incident.

Unfortunately, things took a rather bad turn almost immediately. We paddled around the clubhouse and discovered that an enormous building sat athwart the channel dead ahead. The building houses the machinery that controls the flow of water out of—or into—the lake, and it also contains the controls for the lock that would allow boats to pass

into the channel. Our problem was that this lock is no longer in operation. So, doing our best to act like none of this was a surprise, we hauled the canoe out of the water and portaged around the building.

Now, I should have known this building was there. I've seen it before, and I've even written stories about the structures that control our river. I need to start reading my own stuff more carefully.

The portage turned out to be rather long. Sheer concrete walls bracketed the channel beyond the lock, so we couldn't put in there. We climbed some steps up out of the deep cut that holds the channel and found ourselves carrying the canoe through a golf course. Golfers gave us bemused stares. I said, "You haven't seen a river around here anywhere, have you?" But I was thinking, "I may look ridiculous, but at least I'm not playing golf."

The water level in the channel is a good 15 to 20 feet below ground level, but we eventually discovered a narrow path down the steep slope and slid the canoe down to the water. But even before we got launched, we knew we were too late. We saw two immature black-crowned night herons sitting on a steel railing on top of the sheer concrete walls just beyond the locks. They had already left their nests. Which suggested we wouldn't find any active nests. We would see no young birds screaming to be fed and no trees spattered with the whitewash of several months' accumulated dropping. We would, in short, not be able to verify nesting by black-crowned night herons. But it was a lovely day for a paddle, so why not enjoy ourselves?

There was a very slight but steady current in our direction, so we didn't have to work all that hard at paddling. I was in the stern, Alan took the bow, and Allen sat in the middle and kept the bird list up-to-date. When the two of them were looking through binoculars to check out birds along the banks, all I had to do was use my paddle as a rudder and keep us pointing in the right direction.

We were far enough below street level to escape traffic noise, and the line of trees on each side of the channel hid all the obvious signs of civilization. The occasional bridges were the only intrusions, and their impact was softened by the barn-swallow nests that studded the beams on their undersides.

We compiled a list of 32 species of birds. All but two of those could be nesting along the channel. The two exceptions were great blue heron and ring-billed gull. We saw very young green-backed herons, obviously just out of the nest. We counted a half dozen belted kingfishers, and Alan pointed out two burrows in the bank that were likely nesting sites for that species.

The water toward the lake end of the channel had a slightly milky look, but seemed otherwise inoffensive. As we got near the Howard Street sewage-treatment plant, water quality seemed to take a sharp dive. Some weird smells began to rise, and instead of slightly milky, the water began to look nearly opaque. The outfalls at Howard Street were spewing a sudsy effluent, and when I accidentally splashed some water on my pant leg, I began to wonder if my jeans would dissolve.

Allen was our fish expert, though it didn't take much expertise to identify the carp we saw along the way. They were thrashing around in the shallows near shore, laying eggs in the mud. Carp are yet another example of an alien species bringing nothing but harm to a new environment. Their constant thrashing and their bottom-feeding habits destroy the eggs of a number of native fish, and they also stir up so much bottom mud that they keep the water constantly cloudy. There is experimental evidence that even a muddy ditch like the Des Plaines River would run clear if there were no carp in it.

Allen also noticed a muskrat swimming along the bank near the lake end of the channel, and he identified the three turtles we saw. One was a red-eared slider, a nonnative species that could just as well be called Woolworth's turtle. Presumably somebody got tired of having this one around the house and let it loose in the channel.

The painted turtle basking on a downed log is a genuine native species, and so is the snapping turtle we saw catching some rays on the bank. This may have been the most impressive sight of the whole trip. Allen said it was probably a female, because the females are generally larger than the males—and this beast was very large. Its shell looked as big as a garbage can lid, and its thick tail must have been a foot long. We saw it just downstream from the Howard Street plant, and its size set us all thinking about weird mutant strains of reptiles feeding on toxics pouring out of our sewers.

As we drifted south of Howard toward Touhy, we disturbed a bird in the water near the bank where overhanging branches partially hid it from our eyes. It may have been a pied-billed grebe, but we couldn't be sure. It didn't fly; it pattered over the water ahead of us. It could have been a young bird. If it was a young pied-billed grebe, bred on the channel, that would be a second endangered species for this waterway.

South of Howard Street we also started to see trees at the water's edge with large pieces of their bark stripped away. Here and there we saw small trees felled by something that had cut them down by chewing through them. Yes, indeed. Beavers. These industrious rodents, once nearly extirpated from this region by overtrapping, have made a major comeback. We have thousands of miles of drainage ditches in the farm regions of Illinois, and these have served as both homes and travel routes for the beavers that have recolonized the state. And now we have them living in Chicago waterways. They won't try to dam the North Shore Channel. They will dig burrows in the banks, the entrances placed underwater for safety, and live on the trees that line the channel.

We saw 30 to 40 black-crowned night herons on our trip, but it was too late in the year to verify nesting for the species. Next year we will schedule our trip for late April or early May, before the leaves emerge. At that time of year we should be able to see the night herons building their nests.

Kestrels

Urban Predators

January 18, 1985

My friend David Standish once saw a kestrel snatch a house sparrow from the backyard next door. It was about this time of year, and the sparrow was one of a horde that gathers each winter for a little alfresco dining on the rich assortment of avian comestibles David stocks in the four bird feeders in his yard.

The largest free lunch in Lakeview draws tree sparrows, juncos, chickadees, blue jays, cardinals, and all those alien house sparrows, so it isn't surprising that it also draws the occasional kestrel, North America's smallest falcon and the only real city dweller among American birds of prey.

David's bird dropped out of the sky, paused for a second on a tree limb, and then swooped down on the hapless sparrow and pinned it to the ground with its powerful talons. The sharply hooked upper beaks of all falcons are equipped with special notches that fit neatly around the neck bones of small birds and mammals. A quick snap, the neck is broken, and the kestrel flies off, the sparrow dangling from one taloned foot.

Falco sparverius, the American kestrel, to give the bird its full title, is one of six members of the genus *Falco* in North America. Falcons have the distinctive silhouette of birds built for speed. Their wings are long, slender, and pointed, their tails moderately long and slim. They perch in an upright stance, and sitting birds have a bullet-headed, barrel-chested look, the latter presumably created by the large breast muscles that move those long wings.

Kestrels are not much longer than robins from tip of beak to tip of tail. A typical male might measure nine inches; a female could be a foot long. (By the way, this pattern—smaller males, larger, more aggressive females—is typical of all the birds of prey.) By comparison, robins range from 9 to 11 inches, blue jays up to 12.5 inches.

But an 11-inch robin has a wingspan of about 16 inches, and a big blue jay only reaches 17 inches, while a large female kestrel sports wings that measure two feet from tip to tip.

I would guess that you could see kestrels in any Chicago neighborhood at any time of year. Certainly they have been around any neighborhood I have ever lived in. Their plumage is beautifully distinctive. Look for two dark vertical stripes under and behind the eye—presumably natural versions of the gunk quarterbacks apply to their cheekbones to cut glare—a breast of brown spots on a field of pale cinnamon, back and tail a rich rusty red. The males' wings are a gunmetal gray, the females' the same rusty hue as the back and tail.

Look for kestrels perched high in a tall tree or on a rooftoop antenna. If you ride the el around midday, you may see one on a trackside building or tree. However, the best place to look for kestrels in winter is along the expressways. Don't look near downtown where everything is concrete. Look along the Edens or on the Kennedy west of the junction or along the western two-thirds of the Stevenson. Any place where there is a grassy median strip and a grassy border is likely to be a hunting ground for a kestrel.

Kestrels eat almost anything small enough to kill, but presumably the expressway birds are looking mainly for mice. And they search in a style so uniquely their own that they are easily recognizable—even if you are going by at 60 miles an hour. Winsor Marrett Tyler, writing in A. C. Bent's *Life Histories of North American Birds of Prey*, describes it thus: "The bird, arresting its flight through the air, hovers, facing the wind, its body tilted upward to a slight angle with the ground, its wings beating lightly and easily. Then, sometimes, with a precise adjustment to the force of the wind, it stops the beating of its wings and hangs as if suspended in complete repose and equilibrium, seeming to move not a hair's breadth from its position." No other local bird acts like that.

Readers with a literary education will be aware that Gerard Manley Hopkins's famous poem "The Windhover: To Christ Our Lord" draws its central image from the identical habits of the closely related Eurasian kestrel. Accountants in their BMWs commuting on the Edens can, just as much as Irish Jesuits, catch morning's minion, the dapple-dawn-drawn falcon, and have their hearts stirred by the achievement and mastery of the bird.

Of course, a hunting falcon may remind them more of T. Boone Pickens than Jesus Christ, but they can go to their church and Gerard can go to his.

Kestrels are the only North American birds of prey that have been able to establish themselves fully in cities. Their larger cousins, the peregrine falcons, do occasionally take up residence at the upper levels of skyscrapers, but even in the days before DDT nearly wiped out the species, city peregrines were rare and special—and confined to downtown where the tall buildings are. Kestrels live among the two-flats just like real people.

The kestrel's ability to adapt probably starts with the fact that its preferred habitats—woodland edges and savannas—are passably re-created in the scattered trees and open lawns of every city park and cemetery. Add to that its habit of nesting in holes, and you have a formula for success in the city.

Birds that nest in holes in trees generally enjoy a higher ratio of success in rearing young than birds that build open nests. Eggs and young tucked safely away inside a tree trunk are more protected from both bad weather and predators than they would be in an open nest. This extra protection is especially important to a bird like the kestrel that takes a full two months to run the cycle from laying eggs to the departure of the young. By comparison, most small songbirds take about half that time to do the same job.

The downside of hole nesting lies in the difficulty of finding a good hole. Only woodpeckers are equipped to excavate their own. Other species have to wait for a woodpecker hole to become vacant or for nature to rot a hole in a dead trunk. Experiments in European forests have shown that hanging bird houses on trees can more than double the populations of many common hole-nesting species.

Fortunately, cities are full of holes. Check the eaves of any slightly unkempt building and you will find the odd missing brick here, the crack in the molding there, the small imperfections that open the way for the enterprising kestrel.

When I lived on Berteau Street near Clark, a pair of kestrels nested in the eaves of the small apartment building on the corner. The pair used to perch at the top of a big ash tree a few doors from my apartment, and I could hear their calls, slightly hysterical staccato cries usually rendered as *ki-ki-ki-ki* etc., from my office. When they took off on one of their courtship flights, they often passed right over my roof, and I could look out the window in time to see every sparrow on the block hitting the dirt. Baby birds are apparently born with the ability to recognize birds of prey flying overhead, and this get-down-and-lay-low response is automatic, even when the falcons have their minds more on sex than dinner.

Like most city dwellers, kestrels have very eclectic palates. In the winter, they will take sparrows, and even the occasional starling, along with mice. Summers, they add grasshoppers and other insects to the menu, along with frogs, lizards, and small snakes. Unlike the larger peregrines, they look for food on the ground, rather than snatching it out of the air, and in addition to hovering, they hunt by flying low or by perching high in a tree and scanning the ground below. Sometimes they soar.

In flight they show a combination of speed and grace that is positively DiMaggian, soaring, diving, hovering as if they own the air.

As far as I know, nobody has ever really systematically investigated urban kestrels. It would be fascinating to know just how many birds live in Chicago and how many square blocks of territory it takes to support a pair.

Unfortunately, wildlife biologists tend to be country folk who think that squirrels, pigeons, and cockroaches are the only nonhuman wild things capable of surviving in the city. If we produced more big-city biologists, we might know more about big-city falcons.

Savanna Birds

What Were They?

February 19, 1993

For the past few weeks I've been spending as much time as I can afford studying the birds of the oak savannas of the Midwest. This is a bookish enterprise. All but a few tiny, degraded remnants of our native savannas vanished before the end of the 19th century, so there is no place I can go to actually see a savanna and the birds that live in it.

So I'm looking at historical accounts written by people who were around when savannas still existed. And I'm studying the habits of various species of birds to figure out which ones have a way of life that would fit into one of the environments on a savanna. It's a matter of inference and surmise, of deductive reasoning from premises that are sometimes strong and sometimes not so strong.

My goal is to create a list of species we can call, with a fair degree of confidence, savanna birds. My deadline for the list is February 20. That is the day I have to give a talk on savanna birds at a conference on Midwest oak savannas being held at Northeastern Illinois University and sponsored by the university, the Nature Conservancy, the EPA, and the University of Wisconsin at Stevens Point.

Ecology, like every other human endeavor, has its fashions, and right now the oak savanna, the mixture of grassland and trees that covered a large part of presettlement Illinois, is a fashionable ecosystem. It also represents a second stage in our rediscovery of the native vegetation of the Midwest. You could say that stage one began about 60 years ago, when botanists at the University of Wisconsin started trying to create a native tallgrass prairie in the university's arboretum. It accelerated 30 years ago when Robert Betz of Northeastern Illinois University, working with Floyd Swink and Ray Shulenberg of the Morton Arboretum, began to study prairie remnants in the Chicago area.

In the early 1970s, Betz persuaded the Nature Conservancy to buy the Gensburg-Markham Prairie, the largest remnant in the area, and his efforts had a lot to do with making public conservation agencies aware of the need to acquire prairie lands for preservation. Betz, Shulenberg, and Swink also played key roles in initiating the now-flourishing work of prairie restoration around Chicago. Some of that work helped arouse interest in the oak savanna.

Early accounts of the Illinois landscape all mention the groves of trees that were scattered around the prairie. Drawing on memories of Europe, travelers likened the land to the parks on English estates. The landscapes of our city parks are still nothing more than manicured savannas.

Early settlers were drawn to the oak groves on the prairie for sternly practical reasons as well as aesthetic appreciation. Groves provided shade on hot summer days, protection from winter winds, and wood for lumber and fuel. Downers Grove, Elk Grove, Buffalo Grove, and all the communities with he word "park" in their names are reminders of the attraction those oak groves exerted.

Ecologically, one of two things happened to the groves after settlers arrived. Where farmers turned their cattle loose in the groves, the old oaks remained as a canopy but the plants of the understory were nibbled to extinction. Where the groves became ungrazed woodlots, protection from fire allowed trees like the sugar maple and basswood to invade, converting the groves into dense forests. By the time botanists began the serious cataloging of native plant communities they couldn't find a good example of a savanna to survey.

We have learned a bit since then. A recently discovered plant list compiled in the 1840s has given us a small glimpse of some oak groves before much damage took place. And we have discovered a few remnants that escaped the notice of earlier investigators.

There is a temptation to focus on the oak groves when we think about savannas, since they seem like the most distinctive feature of the landscape. But the essence of a savanna is variation. There were indeed shady groves of tall oaks whose broad crowns formed a nearly continuous canopy of leaves. There were also large patches of prairie dotted with scattered single trees. There were groves that covered a single acre and groves that extended over hundreds of acres. There were groves of big old trees and groves of small young trees. And there were places called brush prairies where low shrubs of dogwood and blackberry and hawthorn where the dominant plants. Each of these varied landscape types would have had its own distinctive group of birds, so the list of savanna birds has to include them all.

Despite the lack of savannas to study and the complexity of the savanna landscape, I have found that it is possible to construct a list that is about 90 percent sure things and 10 percent species that reasonable people can disagree about.

The obvious candidates are birds whose ways of life require both trees and open areas. The red-tailed hawk is a good example, and so are robins and grackles, eastern bluebirds, and flickers. Red-tails nest in trees but soar high over open lands in their search for prey. Robins and grackles build their nests in trees but feed on the ground both under the trees and out in the open. Flickers and eastern bluebirds are both hole nesters, so they need trees, usually dead ones, for nest sites. Flickers are woodpeckers, but they often feed on the ground both in woods and in the open. Eastern bluebirds typically feed in open areas.

Robins and grackles are both perfect examples of savanna birds that have become birds of city parks, golf courses, and suburban neighborhoods. Flickers do well in those places too if the area is unkempt enough to have some dead trees—or at least dead branches—to provide nest holes. When farmers still used wooden fence posts, bluebirds commonly nested in them.

There is a whole group of species we usually think of as edge birds because we typically find them along the borders between woods and open ground. But most of these should really be thought of as brush birds. Song sparrows are a good example, along with yellow warblers and catbirds. In today's landscapes we typically find these birds at woodland edges, but that may be simply because woodland edges are a good place to find shrubs and brushy tangles. At Somme Woods, where I have been helping with a nesting survey for the past few years, we find these birds nesting in dogwood thickets well away from any trees.

There are other brush birds with a greater need for trees. House wrens need at least one dead tree to provide a nest hole, and indigo bunting males like to sing from the tops of the highest trees around. We can imagine them at edges where grove met prairie.

The greatest mysteries are the birds now on the endangered, threatened, or extirpated lists. Most creatures who qualify for the very dubious honor of inclusion on these lists are rare or extinct because their habitat has become rare or extinct. The Illinois lists are dominated by wetland species. Prairie birds are the next most numerous category. And then there are a number of species we would have to consider savanna species.

Bachman's sparrow is one of those. This is a southern bird whose range extended only as far north as the central part of our state. In Texas, Bachman's sparrows live in pine groves. In the Georgia piedmont they live in brushy fields with young pines. Based on historical records and what few recent sightings we have, the Illinois birds prefer old fields with brush and scattered small trees. This was a savanna bird.

We used to have two kites in Illinois. Kites are a very aerial group of birds of prey. They feed on a mixture of large insects and small reptiles, amphibians, and mammals. They often snatch flying insects right out of the air and then eat them in flight, holding the luckless arthropod in one talon while pulling it apart with their beaks. The swallow-tailed kite, a bird that can take your breath away, has a wingspan of four feet and a deeply forked tail more than a foot long. You could imagine it living totally in the air, never touching ground at all. It is officially extirpated from Illinois. Its smaller relative, the Mississippi kite, is on the endangered list. These were savanna birds in Illinois. They nest in tall trees and hunt over both wooded areas and open prairies and marshes.

The long-eared owl is another likely savanna bird. This species also nests in trees and hunts over open areas.

As complicated as my job of historical construction is, I am supported by two thoughts. One is that despite the destruction of our native savannas, nearly all the birds that once inhabited it are still around. Their numbers and their geographic ranges may be much reduced, but they have not disappeared. Restoration efforts, combined with better management of lands where significant portions of savanna ecosystems remain, could bring them back.

My other comfort is that in the absence of healthy savanna ecosystems to study, no matter what birds I put on my savanna list, nobody can prove I'm wrong.

Feathers

How They Work

April 10, 1987

The oldest known bird fossil was dug out of a limestone quarry in Bavaria in 1861. It was given the genus name *Archaeopteryx,* ancient winged, and since the quarry was a source of the fine-grained limestone used for lithographic printing, the species name became *lithographica.*

We know from the age of the rocks where it was found that archaeopteryx lived about 150 million years ago during the Jurassic period of the Mesozoic era. Its contemporaries included a variety of dinosaurs, among them the first pterosaurs, the flying reptiles, as well as primitive mammals and the first frogs.

Archaeopteryx was about the size of a crow. It was beautifully preserved in the stone. You can see every bone in its body, and if that was all you could see, you would suspect that you were looking at the remains of a reptile. The ancient winged one had large, heavy jawbones armed with teeth set in sockets. Its wing bones end in large, heavy claws, and its long, sinuous tail contains no fewer than 20 vertebrae.

Modern birds have lightweight beaks rather than big jawbones, and no living bird has any teeth. There is a South American bird called the hoatzin that retains a wing claw, which it uses mainly for climbing, but all other birds have clawless wings. And of course the tails of modern birds have been reduced to a tiny stump that scientists call the pygostyle and the rest of us refer to as the pope's nose.

But surrounding the skeleton of archaeopteryx, perfectly preserved in the stone, are the unmistakable impressions of feathers, the only evidence we really need to declare this creature a bird. There are other winged animals and other flying animals, and for that matter, some birds can't fly and some don't even have wings, but all birds have feathers and only birds have feathers. Feathers are the evolutionary invention that made birds what they are today.

The reptilian scale was almost certainly the starting point for the evolution of the feather. Birds still retain scales, especially on their legs and

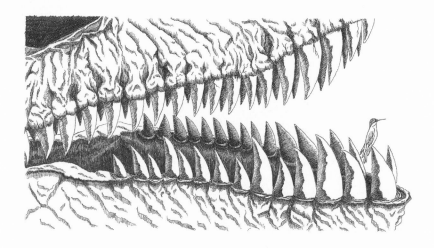

feet, and these scales are just like those on a snake. They grow from follicles set into the inner dermal layers, which makes them quite different from the loosely attached scales of fish. You could not scale a lizard by scraping a knife over its hide.

Our best guess is that at some point in the Mesozoic, some reptiles began to grow longer and more finely divided scales. Insulation was probably the major function of these proto-feathers. Their use for flight came later. In fact, it seems likely that archaeopteryx was a glider rather than a flier. Perhaps it was an arboreal animal whose feathers allowed it to glide from tree to tree the way flying squirrels do now. The advance to true flight would come only after some further skeletal modifications, such as the loss of those heavy jaws and the long tail and the addition of a keel bone at the center of the breast to serve as an anchor for the massive muscles that power a bird's flight.

Feathers grow in five different basic styles: vaned feathers, down, semiplumes, filoplumes, and powder down. The most visible on a living bird are the vaned feathers. As contour feathers, these give the bird its streamlined shape, and as flight feathers on the wings and tail, they keep it in the air.

Vaned feathers have a central shaft with a flat vane attached to each side. These vanes are the most complex epidermal structures known in the animal kingdom. Next time you see a pigeon feather on the sidewalk, pick it up and take a look at it. At first glance, you can see that each vane is made of hundreds of hairlike filaments called barbs. Near the base of the feather, these barbs are loose and fluffy, but over most of the length of the shaft, they are stiff and straight.

Take a closer look with a magnifying glass, and you can see that each barb is fringed with even tinier filaments called barbules. There are hundreds of these barbules on each barb, which means there are as many as a million on a large feather of a large bird.

Subject your pigeon feather to a magnification of 75 to 100 times and you can see that these barbules come in two different shapes. Those on the distal side of the barb, the side away from the bird, have tiny hooks on their undersides. Those on the proximal side, the side nearer the bird, have tiny flanges on their upper sides.

The barbules meet at right angles, and the hooks on the distal barbules grab the flanges on the proximal barbules and knit the vane of the feather into a single, solid sheet.

It's a system that is better than Velcro. It will hold the feather together while the pigeon is flying at 70 miles an hour, and if something does pull it apart, the bird can rezip it just by drawing the barbs through its beak.

Down feathers have no central shaft, just a cluster of fluffy filaments arising from the base of the feather. The barbules on down feathers don't hook together, but they do help trap an enormous amount of air. That ability gives them their value as insulation and explains why a bulky down coat can keep you warm all winter even though it weighs far less than a fur coat. It also explains how a mallard duck can paddle happily around in water that is only a degree or so away from turning to ice.

Semiplume feathers are a sort of intermediate between down and vaned feathers. They have central shafts but no barbules. Filoplumes are hairlike feathers of obscure function. My grandmother called them pin feathers, and when she dressed a chicken, she used to singe them off by holding the carcass over a flame.

Powder down feathers are unique in that they grow continuously. Their tips are constantly breaking down into a water-resistant powder rather like talc. The powder seems to help waterproof the plumage.

You may wonder how many feathers a bird has. Thanks to our system of graduate education, a system that provides ornithological labs with a constant supply of intelligent, highly motivated young people willing to work for wages well below the legal minimum, I can answer that question. The answer is: it varies.

As you might expect, big birds have more feathers than small birds. One investigator found that a whistling swan had 25,216 feathers (I think the suffering grad student who counted that one should have been given a Ph.D. on the spot). Sparrow-sized birds are likely to carry 2,000 to 3,000 feathers. A ruby-throated hummingbird had 940.

Some of the variation is harder to explain. There is a tendency for birds to carry more feathers in the winter than in the summer, but some counters have found substantial variations between birds of the same species, age, and sex taken at the same time of year. For example, two female song sparrows taken on March 5 in the same location had 2,208 and 2,093 feathers respectively.

To really appreciate the wonder of feathers, you need to compare birds to bats, the only other flying vertebrates. A bat's wing is skin stretched on a framework of bone. It is living tissue that has to be maintained at body temperature, so it radiates a huge amount of heat. Bats cannot live where it is cold. Bats of the temperate zone must either migrate or hibernate to make it through the winter.

The feathers of a bird's wing are dead, just like our hair. They insulate the wing while requiring no heat themselves. So ivory gulls can make a living in the winter scavenging polar bear kills on the pack ice in the Arctic Ocean, and tiny chickadees can maintain a body temperature of over 100 degrees through a winter in northern Minnesota.

If a bat gets blown against a tree branch and pokes a hole in a wing, the wing needs to heal. The animal may get an infection in the wound or the two sides of the tear may not grow back together.

A bird in the same situation may need to do nothing but draw a feather through its bill to refasten the barbules. At worst, it might lose a feather or two, and if it does, it will immediately start growing new ones. Archaeopteryx was onto something good.

Winter Flocks

Chickadees Lead the Way

December 1, 1989

Our winter woods are usually as still as death. The trees are bare; the ground is blanketed with dead leaves or snow; the dominant colors are gray, black, and white. The silence is broken only by the moaning of the wind through naked branches.

And then you hear the chickadees. Their buzzing *chicka-dee-dee-dee* call announces their arrival long before you see them flitting through the lower branches of the taller trees or in the crowns of the tall shrubs. Behind them, most of the time, trails a mixed group of nuthatches—especially white-breasted nuthatches—brown creepers, golden-crowned kinglets, and downy woodpeckers, all the birds of the winter woods gathered together in a single flock, noisily foraging on the bare limbs of dormant trees.

Mixed flocks like these are a common feature of bird life. In the tropics, you can find them year-round. Here in the misnamed temperate zone, they are a phenomenon of winter, forming each autumn and breaking up in spring.

The birds in these flocks are predominantly insect eaters, although they also eat seeds and fruits. Chickadees, in fact, are among the most common visitors to backyard bird feeders. Feeding on insects in the winter means searching for those in dormant stages—eggs, pupae, or hibernating adults—and that is principally what they are doing as they bounce from branch to branch through the forest.

Ornithologists use the word "aggregation" to describe a group of birds that have simply gathered in one place. Gulls at garbage dumps are aggregations. They are there because they can find food there, but the individual birds have very little to do with each other.

Flocks are social organizations with an internal structure, a set of relations that defines the positions of individuals in the group. At the center of each of our winter flocks are members of the genus *Parus*, the group of birds that includes chickadees and titmice. In the Chicago area, the tufted titmouse is usually confined to southern and eastern sectors. You find them commonly at the Indiana Dunes and in extreme southeastern Cook County but not north or west of these areas. So the black-capped chickadee is the usual leader in these parts. From southern Illinois to the Gulf of Mexico, the Carolina chickadee replaces the black-capped.

Black-capped chickadees are sedentary birds that typically spend their whole adult lives in one small area. An ornithologist named Susan Smith studied the lives of black-capped chickadees around Mount Holyoke College in South Hadley, Massachusetts. Using colored leg bands that enabled her to follow the movements of individual birds, she was able to construct a complete picture of the lives of her study population.

Winter flocks actually form at the end of summer. The birds have spent the breeding season living in pairs, each pair on its own breeding territory. At summer's end, the young of the year began to wander. Each year, she found that these young birds completely abandoned her study area. They were replaced each year by young wanderers from elsewhere. She had no way of knowing how far these wanderers had come.

Smith's study area held about a dozen breeding territories. In fall, these territories would be consolidated into four winter flock territories, each sustaining three breeding pairs—which remained together all year—and varying numbers of young that had wandered in from elsewhere.

The birds create a dominance hierarchy with each rung in the status ladder occupied by a pair of birds. The bottom rungs of the ladder belong to the newly arrived young birds. Some young birds—Smith called them floaters—do not pair up. Instead they drift from flock to flock through the winter. Smith discovered that these floaters were essentially opportunists. Instead of pairing up as low birds on the totem pole, they would wait for mortality to eliminate a higher-status bird and then they would move in on the widow or widower and take over the position in the flock vacated by the deceased.

Parus birds are the essential nucleus of every flock. The nuthatches, creepers, kinglets, and downy woodpeckers cluster around them. If there are no *Parus* birds present, there are no flocks. The *Parus* birds lead the flock through the woods. The other birds watch them and follow after.

If you are approached by a moving flock, you will see chickadees in the lead and at the center and the other birds ranged in a sort of horseshoe shape around them. The birds are all searching for the same sort of foods, but they tend to concentrate on different parts of trees and to use different hunting methods.

Chickadees usually glean their foods from the smaller twigs out at the tips of branches. They often hang upside down to search the undersides of the twigs. Kinglets often hover near the tips of twigs. Nuthatches and creepers work the trunks and larger limbs. Creepers start near the ground and hitch themselves up the trunks. Nuthatches move down the trunks, their heads pointed toward the ground, their tails in the air. Woodpeckers use their beaks as chisels, digging food out of cracks the other birds cannot penetrate.

There is substantial overlapping in this search for food, but there is also change in response to the presence of other species. Chickadees tend to forage higher when titmice are present, and kinglets do more hovering when chickadees are present.

Douglas Morse studied mixed flocks in woodlands in Maine, Maryland, and Louisiana. He found that the dominance hierarchy was mainly within each species. Attacks, chases, and actual fights flared up between two chickadees or two kinglets far more often than they did between members of different species.

The speed of a flock's movement through the woods was directly related to the size of the flock. Flocks with fewer than 10 birds moved at an average rate of about 100 meters an hour; flocks with 30 or more birds moved about four times that speed.

The birds are feeding as they move. The kind of quick once-over they give the trees as they pass is apparently a sound feeding strategy. We tend to think of winter woods as totally dormant and unchanging, but there is actually a lot going on. Even in January, unusually warm, sunny days can stimulate insects to get out and move around. Storms blow down trees and strip dead bark from standing snags, exposing eggs and pupae that had been hidden. The birds in these flocks don't often feed on the ground, but they will search through pieces of bark blown from trees. Their winter strategy is to make repeated visits to all corners of their territory—which in a deciduous woods might cover about 25 acres—searching for newly exposed food.

But why make these visits in flocks? These birds are not cooperative hunters like wolves. They each hunt separately, and their chances of finding a cluster of insect eggs on a dormant bud would be just as good if they were alone. Indeed they might lose meals to other members of the flock.

The answer seems to be that traveling in groups provides some protection from predators, especially airborne predators: hawks, owls, and shrikes. The chickadees take a leading role in the defense of the flock. They are very alert to any threat, and experiments have proved that the other species in the flocks respond to chickadee alarm calls. These calls—and many other species make similar noises—are very high-pitched. They are concentrated on a narrow frequency with few overtones, and they have no sharp onset or ending. They just fade in and fade out, making it very difficult to locate the birds that are making the noise.

The birds respond to these calls by freezing where they are, or by diving into cover and then freezing. They remain still until they hear an all-clear signal that signifies that the hawk has flown. The dominant male chickadee is most likely to be the bird that sounds the all clear.

More eyes provide greater safety, and greater safety means more time to feed. A Rutgers graduate student named Kim Sullivan conducted a very elegant experiment on downy woodpeckers at the Great Swamp National Wildlife Refuge in New Jersey that nicely proved the latter point.

Downies feeding on a tree trunk stop from time to time to scan the skies in a characteristic head-cocking movement, alternately looking left and right, searching for approaching hawks. Sullivan counted and timed these movements and compared the numbers for lone birds with those for birds in flocks. She found that lone birds averaged 20 head cocks a minute. Birds with one or two companions averaged 13 head cocks a minute, and birds in flocks of three or more averaged only 6 head cocks a minute. In other words, lone birds spent more than three times as much time looking for predators as birds in the larger flocks.

The time spent on defense had a direct effect on feeding. Lone birds took an average of more than two minutes to find a food item. Birds in large flocks averaged about one and a quarter food items a minute.

So the birds that follow the chickadees through the winter woods benefit very directly from being part of a flock. They can spend more time eating and less time scanning the sky. They can rely on the vigilance of many eyes, and especially on the extreme vigilance of the chickadees.

But what do the chickadees get out of this? The likely answer is cannon fodder. They move through the woods protected on at least three sides by skirmishers from other species whose position at the edge of the flock makes them far more vulnerable to the attacking sharp-shinned hawk or northern shrike. Like human generals, they observe the wars from a safe position behind the lines.

Christmas Bird Count

The Annual Census

January 8, 1988

Coal miners used to take canaries into the shafts to warn them of gas. The birds were much more sensitive to the lethal vapors than people, so the miners kept an eye on the bird while they worked, and if the canary fell off its perch, the miners skedaddled.

This is one of the first of many recorded instances of humans using birds as environmental monitors. Birds can fly. Some think they *gotta* fly. They move easily from place to place. If they aren't locked up in cages, they can leave a bad place and go in search of a good place, flying 20 or 30 miles an hour safely above the traffic that might doom a red fox or a star-nosed mole trying a similar migration.

Clear-cut a woodland and some of the mammals will remain simply for lack of the ability to get out quickly. But the woodland birds will be gone immediately, instantly replaced by a whole new set of species that *prefer* clear-cut woodlands. New mammals will invade much more slowly.

Birds are also visible. You can monitor environmental changes by measuring population shifts in assorted species of mice and voles, but it's a real project, requiring time, patience, and a sizable research grant. By contrast, a birder with skilled, experienced eyes and ears can make a single slow pass through a patch of woods and come out feeling certain that he has noted a large majority of the birds present—not just species, but individuals as well.

The biggest environmental monitoring scheme going is the National Audubon Society's Christmas Bird Count project. Every year during the holiday season, birders all over the U.S., Canada, and about 17 other countries conduct one-day bird censuses. Over 1,500 census tracts are now being surveyed—each is a circle 15 miles in diameter—and on many tracts the accumulated data cover several decades.

It takes many years for information like this to reveal its full value. A single count can be skewed in all sorts of directions by variables like weather, but over time these differences ought to even out.

Dave Johnson of the Evanston-North Shore Bird Club has compiled a summary of 24 years of results for the North Shore Christmas Count. The North Shore count covers an area bounded by Evanston and Lake Forest on the south and north and Lake Michigan and the Des Plaines River on the east and west. His summary is a formidable looking document. Three pages of very tiny print, each page consisting of a column of bird names on the left followed by 28 columns of figures that record the shifting numbers of North Shore birds between 1963 and 1986.

It's amazing what you can learn by following the ups and downs of an assortment of birds. In 1963, the North Shore count area was developed—mostly in houses and small commercial districts—near the lake. To the west, there were still lots of cornfields and vacant weedy grasslands. Today, the vacant lands and the croplands are almost gone and the count results reflect the change.

In the first five years of the count, '63 through '67, an average of 86 ring-necked pheasants per year were reported. In the past five years, '82 through '86, the average was 9. Eastern meadowlarks, common birds of the Illinois prairies, were reported on each of the first five counts, but they have been seen only three times since, and the last sighting was in 1979. Marsh hawks, or harriers, also open-country birds, were seen seven times in the first 15 years of the count and not at all since. And horned larks declined from an annual average of 33 in the first five years to an average of 4 per year in the last five.

All this sounds quite bleak, and in fact it is, but some birds are managing to prosper through the changes. Consider, for example, the mallard duck and the Canada goose.

During the first five years of the count, the counters reported an average of 200 mallards per year. They saw no Canada geese at all until 1966, when they found one bird. They got ten a year later, and the explosion was on.

In the four years from 1983 through 1986, the average annual mallard count was 1,943. The average for Canada geese was 4,435! Two sets of events caused the explosion. The first was the introduction of the giant Canada goose into northeastern Illinois. In the '60s, geese passed through here in spring and fall. Now the giant Canada goose nests and winters here. The second trigger for the population surge was the arrival of the corporate pond.

The North Shore count area is filled with corporate headquarters and research labs set on fashionably campuslike grounds, and these grounds would not be complete without an ornamental duck pond, usually equipped with a bubbler to keep it ice-free in the winter. The ducks and geese live in and around these ponds, and when winter closes down their other options, they are so thick on the water that if you could step from one to another you could cross the pond without getting your feet wet. Huge geese waddle about the grassy banks, apparently traveling in family groups.

The North Shore is not all corporate ponds, of course. Much of it is covered with houses, many of them big houses on big lots, some set in woodlands by developers with enough sense of the landscape to leave the bigger trees standing between the buildings.

These suburban neighborhoods are now the winter home of a very large number of birds, most of whom are supported by backyard feeders. Thanks to an upsurge of interest in things natural and environmental over the past couple of decades, a substantial percentage of the people who live in upscale subdivisions have bird feeders in their backyards, and not surprisingly, that's where the birds hang out.

Walking through a winter woods, you're lucky to see 15 birds in an hour, but you can find twice as many all at once in many backyards.

The spread of winter bird feeding shows up plainly in the North Shore count results. Species that typically come to feeders are enjoying boom times. The black-capped chickadee, the ultimate feeder bird, expresses the trend most strongly. An annual average of 191 chickadees was reported in the first five years of the count. The last four years produced an average of 729 birds a year.

The pattern holds for goldfinches (92 to 316), cardinals (121 to 388), downy woodpeckers (100 to 157), and white-breasted nuthatches (33 to 102).

Years ago Roger Tory Peterson predicted that the prevalence of bird feeders would change the distribution of winter birds. On the North Shore, it certainly seems to be increasing the populations of feeder species, at least during the winter. Next spring, this larger population will be competing for nest sites in the same old woods, woods that probably are near their carrying capacity already. We may be sustaining generations of maiden aunts and bachelor uncles, grouchy celibates who will spend their summers waiting for the holders of nesting territories to die.

Overall the pattern on the North Shore is the sort of thing you would expect in a newly urbanized environment. Cities typically support large numbers of individual birds—far more per square foot than the richest natural environments—but small numbers of species. City birds are often semidomestic, depending on humans to provide food and habitat. Both the mallard in the corporate pond and the chickadee at the backyard feeder fit that pattern.

But what is disappearing, on the North Shore and in most of the rest of the world as well, is the truly wild, the creatures whose presence is an expression of the essence of a particular place, the birds who would be there even if we weren't.

How to Find Nests

Let the Birds Show You

June 14, 1991

Give birds enough time, and they will show you their nests. In years past I couldn't fully appreciate this truth because I didn't know how to approach the birds, how to persuade them to reveal their secrets. Looking back I realize that what I thought of as nest hunting was really mostly random wandering and aimless staring. I may have thought I was searching diligently, but mostly I was standing around hoping a bird would walk by carrying a nest. My results showed it. When I tried to survey nesting birds at Somme Woods in Northbrook last year, the few nests I did find were pure accidents. Mostly I confirmed nesting by sighting awkward little stubby-tailed fledglings. Since they obviously couldn't fly very far, I could conclude that their former nests must be somewhere nearby.

My inability to find nests fed my deepest anxiety: that I am an impostor. Certainly a big-time environmental/nature columnist shouldn't need a week to find a miserable robin's nest. I affected an air of confidence, but I knew nest finding was like whistling with your fingers in your mouth or computer programming, a skill you either picked up in childhood or never got at all.

But that was before the day I found the frame of an Acadian flycatcher's nest slung between the tines of a tree fork and watched the female adding stems to a foundation that looked as flimsy as a spider web. And that was before the day the Carolina wren with a grass stem in her beak crawled into a hole in the side of a hummock of moss and revealed where her nest would be.

I saw these things in the Shawnee National Forest near Jonesboro in deepest southern Illinois. The birds lived in Trail O'Tears State Forest and the LaRue—Pine Hills Ecological Area, both within the boundaries of the Shawnee and both among the largest remaining blocks of forest in Illinois.

I was there to learn about Scott Robinson's studies of the nesting success of neotropical migrant forest-interior birds. That string of adjectives specifies that we are talking about birds that nest in southern Illinois, spend their winters in the tropics, and live not along the edges but in the deep shade in the heart of the forest. Prominent species include wood thrushes, hooded warblers, cerulean warblers, scarlet and summer tanagers, and Kentucky warblers.

Dr. Robinson has a small army of graduate students—along with a few undergraduates—scouring the woods every day. They search for nests, and many of them are very good at it. Robinson sent me out three different days with three different guides. Doug Robinson, Lonny Morse, and Rob Olendorf are all graduate students at Champaign who did learn to find nests when they were kids, and their work was wonderfully enlightening.

Forests are especially hard places to do nesting studies. The birds are spread out. You can't see far. Some of the most important species nest high in the canopy. But Robinson's army is piling up the data in spite of these obstacles, collecting information on cowbird parasitism, predation, year-to-year population levels, habitat choice, and the numbers of fledged young that return to their native woods the following spring.

All this starts with finding nests, a job that isn't easy, even for the experts. The average rate for nest finding among Robinson's skilled workers is one nest every two hours in the field. It's a job that takes a fairly advanced level of patience. You have to sit for long periods waiting for something to happen, and you have no guarantee that anything will.

In most cases the male is the starting point in the search. He is singing, often from an exposed perch, so he is easy to find. But once you find him, you may think that you haven't really found much. Males sing on their territory, but in most species they stay about as far from their nests as they can manage.

If you find a male, watch him. He will move around his territory, singing from different song perches. Noting the location of those perches, you can get a rough idea of the shape of the territory. Somewhere in that territory is a female and a nest—unless the male hasn't found a mate and is singing to attract one.

Once you have figured out the approximate shape and location of the territory, the real waiting begins. If the bird's territory is uniform habitat, all woods or all grassland, you can start a very slow stroll through it looking for some sign of the female. If it is a mixture, if it includes both woods and prairie, you look only in the parts where your particular quarry is likely to be. Most birds with a mixture of woods and prairie in their territory are edge species, and you can find them gathered within a few yards either way of the boundary where forest meets prairie.

When you have figured these things out, you find a likely observation post and sit down to wait. You are waiting for some kind of break, for a clue that will help you get closer to the nest. The clue may be the female with a grass stem in her beak. It may be the male with a caterpillar in his beak taking food to the female on the nest. It may be both parents carrying food to young in the nest. It may be the female taking a break from incubating eggs and moving around the territory feeding. In many species the males accompany the females on these outings.

Working on this year's edition of my Somme Woods breeding bird survey, I have tried to apply what I learned in the Shawnee—and to my surprise, it has worked. After eight visits spread over two weeks I have found 35 nests belonging to 17 different species.

This sudden leap into competence is totally amazing. The veil has been lifted. The most secret aspects of these birds' lives have been suddenly revealed to me. In this one small corner of the world I know more or less what is going on. And that is a claim I cannot make about any other part of my life.

My first find was a northern oriole. This one was a gimme. I looked up into a treetop and saw a male northern oriole. I glanced into the tree next to his, and there was the nest hanging on a branch about 20 feet up.

And then a hard one. Close to an hour spent mostly on hands and knees studying a thicket that eventually got me my first song sparrow nest. My first catbird nest came while I was searching for a second song sparrow nest. I've found five red-winged blackbird nests. These are easy. The males are so eager and noisy in their defense of the nest that they lead you right to it. I found my first yellow warbler nest after watching a pair of the birds flying together around their territory for about 20 minutes. She mainly led the way, and every time she flew to a new branch, he would follow. I lost sight of them briefly, but by and by he appeared on a bare branch in a tall snag. He seemed to have a caterpillar, or something like it, in his beak. He dropped straight down into the dense thicket of shrubs at the base of the snag. When I went to that place, I found the nest. It had three yellow warbler eggs and one brown-headed cowbird egg left for the warblers to care for.

Sitting down and shutting up turns out to be the secret of nest finding. It's a learnable skill. You don't need to remain motionless for an hour at a time, but you shouldn't move without good reason, and you should move slowly and quietly. Stay reasonably quiet and still for an hour, and nature will start to show you things. I was sitting watching a blue-winged warbler, hoping to locate its nest, when a pair of bluebirds began inspecting an old woodpecker hole in a tree stub 30 yards away. A house wren flew up singing, contesting their control of this nesting hole. He stormed about the place for several minutes, while the bluebirds sat, silent and unmoving, between him and the hole, showing what animals that are really good at holding still can accomplish. Out of the corner of my eye I saw a chickadee slipping through a tiny hole into a nesting cavity in a tree stub no more than a foot tall.

While watching a pair of yellow warblers feeding together, I saw a northern oriole perched in a tree above me and in the next tree his mate about to enter her nest. Watching an indigo bunting, I saw a field sparrow carrying blades of grass to a tangle of low shrubs.

The blue-winged warbler was the best so far. I spent over two hours hanging around one little patch of ground watching and listening to the male, but I knew that my chances of finding the nest were slim. Blue-wings nest down in the brush where things are dense, and their nests are only three or four inches across.

But I watched and listened and sat still until the male landed on one of his singing perches with a caterpillar in his beak. This was the break I needed. I watched him fly into a narrow strip of trees and brush and then walked to a place about 20 yards from the strip and sat down to watch. Presently he flew up from the base of a tall tree. I figured he had just fed the female on the nest, and since I didn't have a very clear idea of where he had been down in the brush around the tree, I waited. After about 15 minutes he was back. I saw him emerge from the brush a few yards from the trees. I walked over and started to search. The vegetation was re-sprouts of buckthorn and other shrubs that had been cut by work crews from the North Branch Prairie Project. The resprouts were only about knee-high, but they were quite dense. I saw a flash of movement in the brush. It was the female leaving the nest. Just under the crown of leaves of a buckthorn sprout, I saw a few brown dead leaves. I remembered that the field guides said that blue-winged warblers use dead leaves as a foundation for their nests. I parted the crown of live leaves, and there was the nest. Three tiny eggs no more than three-fourths of an inch long were inside. I took a good look at them and then got the hell out so the birds could get back to their parental duties. I danced down the trail back to my car.

Mourning Doves
Family Values

March 24, 1995

A mourning dove has been living on my block since we moved in in early February, often perching in a tree on the corner or doing its head-bobbing pigeon walk around the courtyard of our building searching for food. It—only another mourning dove can tell whether it is a he or a she—may have found a mate.

I was pleased to see it, because in our highly urban Edgewater neighborhood the only other birds around were the alien triumvirate: starlings, house sparrows, and pigeons. Our lonesome mourning dove was the sole representative of North America in either the flora or the fauna of our community. It was the only living thing here now that would have been here 200 years ago. I developed a rooting interest in its well-being, so I am happy to see it has found a companion.

Rigorous honesty forces me to admit that the pair I am seeing now may be birds that just arrived in the neighborhood. The bird I was seeing last month may have flown headlong into a window and squashed its skull like a grape. But I prefer to believe that this is the same bird, and since pairing up is a normal springtime phenomenon, I'll go on believing that one of the birds in this pair is our resident dove.

There are other mourning doves in the neighborhood. I even see them in the shadows along Sheridan Road, where the solid wall of high rises shows what a dynamic free enterprise system can do to a lakeshore.

Most mourning doves spend the winter in small flocks, which break into pairs in early spring. Long-term studies suggest that these pairs are permanent, that the birds stay together for life. Of course the mortality rate is very high—about 55 percent per year for adult birds—so a lifetime commitment for most individuals lasts no more than a year.

Yesterday I heard doves singing for the first time this spring. One singer was perched on a wire in the alley behind my apartment. It could have been the bird I have been seeing for the past month, but I can't assume that without being sexist. The resident bird could have been a female that has now been a joined by a male. The other singer was a block west on Winthrop Avenue. It would be interesting to know how many pairs a highly urban neighborhood could support. I should probably take some early morning walks and count singing birds—at least those I can hear above the traffic.

The singing—the soft, mournful cooing that gave the bird its name—means that the birds are setting up territories, laying claim to a piece of land they hope will be big enough and rich enough to support a family.

Once they start nesting they will keep it up until September, raising as many as five broods. As far as I can discover, mourning doves raise more broods of young in a typical nesting season that any other North American bird. However, those broods are very small. Two is the usual number of eggs in each clutch. By comparison, robins nest two or three times a season, but the female typically lays five or six eggs in each clutch.

If the marital fidelity of mourning doves suggests support for family values, their child-rearing practices are a feminist's delight. The female builds the nest, which is a platform of interwoven sticks so flimsy that you can stand underneath it and actually see the eggs through gaps in the weave, but the male finds the sticks and brings them to her.

Once the eggs are laid incubation is divided precisely between the sexes, with the male sitting on the nest by day and the female at night. Once the young hatch, after about two weeks, both parents feed them for the next two weeks, the time it take them to mature to the point that they can leave the nest.

Birds of the family Columbidae, pigeons and doves, produce a highly nutritious substance called pigeon milk, which is used to feed the young until they are old enough to take solid food. The "milk" is produced in the crops of both males and females.

A bird's crop is an enlargement in the esophagus. In some birds it's just a slight swelling, in others it's a well-developed sac, and in pigeons and doves it's a two-chambered sac.

Many birds, especially insect eaters, don't have crops. They feed more or less continuously throughout the day, taking in lots of small meals that they can digest as they go. Most birds with crops get only occasional shots at a really big meal. Vultures, for example, may go days between carcasses. The crop allows them to take in a very large amount of aged steak and store it until their stomachs are ready to digest it.

Seed-eating birds use their crops in much the same way. If a turkey finds acorns littering the ground under a particular oak, it can really pig out, stuffing as much as a pound of nuts in its crop to be digested at leisure. Finches of the northern forests store seeds in their crops during the day and digest them at night, providing themselves with a continuous fuel source during cold winter nights.

But only pigeons and doves produce milk in their crops. During the breeding season the walls of the crops of both males and females thicken by as much as 20 times. The milk comes from cells that are continuously sloughed off the insides of the walls. It is a cheesy substance, rather like ricotta. About 25 percent of it is fat, and another 10 percent is protein. The blind, helpless chicks stick their heads down their parents' throats to suck up the milk, which is their sole food during the first ten days to two weeks of life. As they get older they begin to swallow partly digested seeds mixed with the milk. When they leave the nest they are ready for the nearly all seed diet of their parents.

Much of what we know about the details of the lives of mourning doves comes from research paid for by hunting licenses. In more than 30 states, including Illinois, doves are considered game birds. We have regular seasons and bag limits on them. They are fast and maneuverable fliers, and you would need to shoot very well to hit one—so you can see the attraction for the sportsperson. However, the average mourning dove weighs about four and a half ounces—feathers, feet, and all—so you would have to kill a lot of them to put together a dinner. Plucking and gutting a bird is a major effort, and it's hard to see much sense in doing all that work if all you get is a mouthful of meat.

Mourning doves are the most widespread of the 17 species of Columbidae native to North America. Their nesting range covers the continent from Alaska to Panama and the islands of the Caribbean. They can get along in all sorts of habitats. The mourning doves in the Edgewater of 200 years ago would have been feeding across open dunes and nesting in pines and cedars, and you can find them now in mesquite in the southwest or in cottonwood windbreaks on the Great Plains. They like open ground to feed on and scattered trees to nest in, but in a pinch they can nest on the ground.

It is hard to write about mourning doves without mentioning the other pigeon that was around these parts 200 years ago. The passenger pigeon, America's most famous extinct bird, might have been the most common bird in eastern North America in 1795. It favored dense forests rather than open woods, but like the mourning dove it was a seedeater, a builder of flimsy nests, a fast and powerful flier, and a devoted parent.

The main difference between the two species was the way they bred. Mourning doves scatter their nests. Pairs quietly install themselves in the thin trees of a Chicago parkway, raising their young while very few humans even notice their presence.

Passenger pigeons nested in huge colonies. Thousands of pairs of birds would gather where the chestnut and beechnut and acorn crops were especially rich and raise more thousands of young. In the North America of 200 years ago this was an excellent strategy. It took the utmost advantage of local and temporary abundances of food, and it simply overwhelmed the local predators. Cooper's hawks or raccoons, whose populations were held in check by the much lower numbers of resident prey, could stuff themselves silly and still not make a dent in the passenger pigeon colonies.

Unfortunately the strategy could not withstand large numbers of men with shotguns who had boxcars standing by to haul away as many pigeon carcasses as their marksmanship could create. And it couldn't withstand the loss of habitat created by the greatest clear-cut in history. The sadness in the coo of the mourning dove reminds us that we have something to be sad about.

Goldfinches
Wild Canaries

September 28, 1990

When I was a little kid, I didn't know many birds. I could recognize a robin or a house sparrow. When I was about eight years old and staying on my grandparents' farm, I knew what pigeons looked like. I was even allowed to shoot them with a .410 shotgun. They were very good to eat, as I recall. These were grain-fed farm pigeons, not city pigeons raised on pizza scraps and leftover French fries.

I even shot a few starlings on the farm. My grandfather believed that if you shot it, you ate it—so I actually plucked and gutted several starlings. As I recall, they had a much heavier coat of down than chickens. Grandma would singe them over the coal stove in the kitchen to remove the down and then roast them whole. I have no clear memory of what they tasted like. But I do remember that I ate them without complaint, so they couldn't have been too awful.

When I wasn't on the farm, I lived in an isolated subdivision within the corporate limits of Des Plaines. We were well out from town and totally surrounded by open fields. Trees were scarce, but we did have two patches of willows and cottonwoods. They grew in narrow strips on steep slopes between the railroad tracks and Weller Creek. We called one of these strips the Jungle and the other the Bird Jungle.

I do not know who decided on these names, but I do remember that in the Bird Jungle we used to see the gloriously beautiful birds we called wild canaries. Wild canaries had bright yellow bodies, black skullcaps, black wings crossed with white stripes, and black tails.

Now I know them as American goldfinches, and I'm supposed to think of them as nothing special. They are common birds. They nest in the city and in most every forest preserve and in any patch of trees in rural Illinois. They are more common in summer, though you can find them year-round.

But for me, they still carry the emotional freight of those wild canaries. When I was eight years old, those canaries flitting though the trees turned a strip of land along the railroad tracks into a tropical rainforest. I was used to dark, somber birds, and these bright yellow beauties made me realize that actual nature existed not just in books or in places such as Brazil and Alaska, but in Des Plaines as well.

What I didn't know then was that those goldfinches in the Bird Jungle connected with birds all over the world. The American goldfinch is scientifically named *Carduelis tristis*. The genus name comes from the Latin *carduus*, which means thistle. Thistle seeds are a favorite food of goldfinches. People who are seriously into backyard bird feeding put out thistle seed—which, by the way, is very expensive—if they want to attract goldfinches. *Tristis* means sad. It comes from one of the call notes of the species, which has a rather plaintive tone.

Carduelis tristis breeds across southern Canada as far west as Alberta, and its winter range extends a short way into northern Mexico, but it is mainly a bird of the good old USA. It nests and/or winters in every one of the lower 48 states.

Goldfinches are easy to recognize, even in flight. As they fly, they rise and then fall in a looping arc. At the bottom of each fall they bound up so rapidly it looks like they are bouncing off some invisible trampoline in the sky.

The short, conical beak marks the American goldfinch as a seedeater, although they are known to eat small insects and especially insect larvae and eggs. Like many other seedeaters, they are gregarious. They live in flocks all year except for the breeding season, and even then their territorial behavior is limited. Males will drive other males away from their nests, and females will treat other females the same way. But once the nest has been built and the eggs laid, their aggressiveness declines rapidly.

Where food is abundant, the birds will build nests quite close together. One investigator found 66 nests in a 19-acre woodlot in southern Michigan.

Goldfinches are noted for delaying breeding until midsummer. At Somme Woods this year I was still seeing birds in flocks as late as the beginning of July. This delay seems to be related to the importance of seeds in their diet. By July many plants have gone to seed, so there is a lot more food around than there is in May or June.

After laying her eggs, the female goldfinch spends about 95 percent of her time incubating them. Goldfinches are frequent victims of cowbirds, since their edge habitat is also prime cowbird territory, but this habit of close sitting probably provides a degree of protection. Cowbird females need to find unattended nest to lay their eggs in, and goldfinch eggs are rarely unattended.

The female can spend all that time on the nest because the male feeds her. He arrives periodically with a crop full of partially digested seeds that he regurgitates into her beak. She welcomes him by fluttering her wings and tipping her head back and opening her beak wide. This is the same posture that the nestlings will adopt when they are looking for a meal.

There are six finches of the genus *Carduelis* in North America. The pine siskin is mainly a North Woods bird that we see here in winter. Common and hoary redpolls nest up on the tundra but move south in winter. We see the common here most every winter, but the hoary gets this far south only rarely.

In the southwest there is the lesser goldfinch, and California has Lawrence's goldfinch, a species that nests only in that state and winters in Arizona.

But the genus *Carduelis* is almost cosmopolitan. The wild canaries of my childhood have relatives on every continent save Antarctica and Australia. Actually, there are now *Carduelis* finches displaying their bouncing flight in Australia as well. The European goldfinch and the green finch were both introduced there in the 19th century, and both are comfortably established now.

There are a dozen *Carduelis* finches in South America, and among them they cover most of the continent. The southernmost is the black-chinned siskin, which lives in Tierra del Fuego and on the Falkland Islands.

Carduelis birds have always been big favorites with people who enjoy imprisoning small wild birds in tiny cells in their living rooms. These finches are wonderful singers. Our goldfinches make singing a major part of their courtship behavior. Sometimes several males will gather in one tree and sing like crazy. Some observers have suggested, only slightly fancifully, that the males are having a song contest, and that the females, like groupies, will choose their mates according to who sings best.

Native American songbirds can no longer be legally kept as cage birds, but *Carduelis* finches from elsewhere in the world are major articles of trade in the pet business. Some of them are suffering for their singing ability. In Costa Rica the yellow-bellied siskin and the lesser goldfinch have both been seriously reduced by trappers for the pet trade.

Trade in finches is largely unregulated. The pet business successfully lobbied for exemptions for this group in laws governing importation of exotic animals.

The species that may be suffering most from this trade is the red siskin, a native of Venezuela and Colombia. Bird dealers want red siskins because they can be crossbred with the closely related canary—the all-time favorite cage bird. The cross produces canaries with a bit of the siskin's red coloring. These apparently fetch a premium price from fanciers of imprisoned birds.

The situation of the red siskin has grown so desperate that the recently published field guide *A Guide to the Birds of Venezuela* by Rodolphe Meyer de Schauensee and William H. Phelps Jr. provides the following entry to describe the range of the bird in Venezuela: "Upper tropical zone. The northern Cordillera region (no exact localities are given as the bird is much persecuted by bird catchers because of its popularity as a cage bird)."

My suspicion is that if people would open their eyes to the wild canaries that live all around them, they would have less need for captive birds stolen from the tropics.

The Passenger Pigeon
Once There Were Billions

April 4, 1986

When the Pilgrim fathers were shooting birds for their supper, two kinds of doves lived in eastern North America. One came to be called the mourning dove for its soft, moaning call. The other, a vagrant that could cruise at 60 miles per hour, was named the passenger pigeon.

They were both seedeaters. The slightly larger passenger pigeon specialized in big seeds, eating acorns and the nuts of hickories, beeches, and chestnuts. The mourning dove ate the seeds of dozens of kinds of plants.

Mourning doves lived in thickets. They invaded land cleared of trees by fire, windstorm, or farmers, nesting in the brush or trees at the borders of the clearing and feeding on the open ground and at the edge of the woods. They probably moved into the farmyard early in our history. They now nest in parks, cemeteries, suburban yards, and the quieter neighborhoods in the city. In the beginning, they were around, but not especially abundant.

The passenger pigeon may have been the most abundant bird since archaeopteryx fluttered its first feather back in the late Jurassic. John James Audubon rode the 55 miles from Henderson, Kentucky, to Louisville one day in autumn 1813, and through the whole long day, he rode under a sky darkened from horizon to horizon by a cloud of passenger pigeons. He estimated that more than a billion birds had passed over him. In 1866, a cloud of birds passed into southern Ontario. It was a mile wide, 300 miles long, and took 14 hours to pass a single point. Latter-day estimates suggest something in excess of 3.5 billion birds in that flock. The continental population may have been as high as 6 billion, a number that could represent anywhere from 25 to 40 percent of all the birds in North America 350 years ago.

The passenger pigeon became extinct in the wild by 1900 at the latest, and the last known individual, a female named Martha, died in the Cincinnati Zoo in 1914. The mourning dove is probably more common now than it was in 1620. The continental population is estimated at 400 million, that despite the fact that it is a game bird and hunters bag about 30 million birds a year.

The demise of the passenger pigeon has drawn a lot of scientific attention. How do you go from the most ever to zero in less than a century? The current consensus is that the passenger pigeon was done in by its way of life. Accustomed to a high-speed life on a continental scale, the pigeons couldn't survive the invasion of humans who measured the world with transits and plotted section lines and property boundaries to the fraction of an inch.

Primeval North America was mostly wooded east of the Plains, and the huge flocks of pigeons toured the entire region in search of food and roosts. They spent the winter at the southern end of the forest—the gulf states, Tennessee, and Arkansas—and the summer around the Great Lakes, in New England or upstate New York, or in Ontario.

And throughout the year, all those billions of birds lived mostly together. The population consisted mainly of a small number of very large flocks, groups of a billion or more that roosted together in winter, migrated together in spring, and nested together in summer. There has never been anything like them. There are other nomadic birds, northern seedeaters like crossbills that follow the good tree-seed crops from place to place, but no species ever wandered through such a rich environment, a half million square miles of woods where warm summers and abundant rainfall produced huge food surpluses for the birds.

Wherever they went, they must have hit like the plague. Imagine if you were a turkey living on acorns in a Georgia woodland. Life is good, until one day a billion passenger pigeons move in down the block. They all plan to eat acorns too.

And the trees. The birds roost in piles, one atop the other, weighing down limbs so heavily that they snap. The dung rains down, burying the trunks in tons of droppings. When the flock leaves in spring, the roost is mostly dead trees.

To feed their hordes, the pigeons needed a large area of forest that was enjoying a great year, a year when every oak produced an abundance of acorns. A nesting colony might take over 50 square miles, and inside that area, every branch was loaded with nests. As many as 500 birds might nest in a single tree.

Imagine the scene. Birds several deep on the branches, a constant roar of wings as birds take off and land, the smell of droppings and of the pigeons themselves—people say you could smell the passing flocks—the crack of branches. So many birds that a man in Ohio could remember firing a 12-gauge pistol into a bush in the dark and bringing down 18 pigeons with the shot. And every hawk, owl, crow, raven, vulture, fox, raccoon, and weasel within miles getting fat feeding on eggs, unfortunate nestlings, and awkward squabs fresh from the nest.

They stayed only a month, just long enough to throw together a nest, incubate one egg—the usual number—and feed the nestling until it was two weeks old. Then the adults left, abandoning the squabs, who lived on their fat for a few days until they learned to feed themselves. And then they took off. The huge nesting grounds would be deserted. The birds might not return to this spot for decades.

Passenger pigeons show what mobility can do for you. If you can fly 60 miles an hour for a solid day and night, you can turn half a continent into your feeding ground: breakfast in Tennessee, dinner in Michigan.

And those enormous numbers just overwhelmed anything else. All the predators who gathered around nesting sites ate until they couldn't hold any more, but they couldn't make a dent in the big flocks. The local predators faced local population controls that kept their numbers in some sort of balance with their prey. Suddenly add a billion or so prey animals to the scene, and the carnivores just don't have enough fangs and claws to take advantage of their windfall.

Passenger pigeons did a sort of avian version of slash-and-burn agriculture. Tropical people slash the trees and brush from a patch of land, burn everything they cut, and then farm the land. When yields begin to fall, they move on, and the wild plants return. It is a benign way to use the land as long as you have enough space, and as North America became settled, the passenger pigeon began to lose its space.

And we hunted it unmercifully. As many as a thousand men worked as professional pigeon hunters in the late 19th century. They traveled around the country on the new railroads, searching for nesting grounds. When they found one, they killed all they could. When the birds moved to a new roost, the hunter followed them. The market was enormous.

New York City could absorb 100 barrels of pigeons a day. Each barrel held 500 to 600 birds. Remember that this was a bird with a very low reproductive potential. Laying just one lone egg every year, it could not keep up its numbers in the face of hunting pressure and habitat loss.

And finally, it could not change its ways. Colonies of 100 to 500 or even 5,000 birds might have been able to survive. But the birds couldn't seem to reproduce successfully in such small groups. A passenger pigeon was too stressed to function unless it had millions of its fellows right in its face. And so the passenger pigeon passed.

Meanwhile, the mourning dove was laying low. The one habitat it shunned was the deep woods, and as the settlers advanced they cut those and replaced them with pastures, orchards, woodlots, and ornamental shrubs, and the mourning dove could slip quite happily into any of those situations. It could place its flimsy looking stick nest in any tree or shrub, and it could nest as often as five times a summer.

You can see them almost all over town right now. The males are cooing their territorial announcement. In the air, they fly fast, as most pigeons do, and their wings are pointed. Their tails are long and bordered with white. On the ground, they are brown, smaller and slimmer than a street pigeon, with a single dark spot on the side of the neck.

In the stable environment of primeval America, the passenger pigeons could live in their billions. They had learned to exploit the forest like no other animal. But animals that require a continent to live their lives are likely to die in these times. The bison herds that used to migrate from Alberta to Texas are long gone. Only the African wildebeest and the barren ground caribou still operate on the epic scale. Animals today live in reserves, little islands of wildness, and those that do well stay put. If you need 50 square miles of fresh new forest every year, if the only reserve that could hold you would have to stretch from the Gulf of Mexico to Lake Superior, if you can't get along in groups of less than a few million, you might as well hang it up.

5 › Plants

Healthy Communities

Biodiversity Is the Key

February 27, 1998

The phrase "presettlement conditions" has been bouncing around in the *Sun-Times* in recent days as the paper weighs in on the issue of what our forests preserves are and what they should be. It makes the claim that recreating presettlement conditions would mean the destruction of forests. This is not what people involved in the work believe. The phrase has been commonly used by professionals in the ecology biz for many years. If you ask people who study or manage natural lands for a precise definition, you will get some variation in the answers, but the variations differ more in emphasis that in conception. However, the phrase seems to produce confusion among people who are not in the business, and that confusion adds heat to the controversy over how we should manage our preserves and gets in the way of reasonable discussion of the issues.

Full disclosure requires that I state at this point that I work for the Forest Preserve District of Cook County. However, I do not believe that my employment there has altered my point of view (other people may have biases; I have a point of view). Everything that follows in this essay is my own opinion. I don't think my colleagues at the Forest Preserve District will have any major disagreements with it, but in no sense does it represent any sort of official Forest Preserve District opinion.

The problem with phrases such as "presettlement conditions" or "presettlement vegetation" starts with the words themselves. They are generally understood to refer to the period prior to the massive influx of people into northeastern Illinois that began about 1820. But people settled this region shortly after the glaciers left, so don't they count as settlers? Some writers try to get around this one by calling the recent immigration "European settlement," but that leads to the charge that they are overlooking the undeniable fact that not all the new settlers were Europeans or the descendants of Europeans.

I prefer using an expression like "large-scale settlement." The number of Native American populations had been drastically lowered by the plagues that swept across the continent in the wake of their first contact with Europeans explorers, so populations in northeastern Illinois in 1820 were probably lower than they had been. However, there is no reason to think that native populations ever reached anything like the levels we have achieved in the past 175 years.

Of at least equal importance is the alteration in the relationship of the people to the land. Those who arrived after 1820 plowed thousands of square miles of prairie to support an agriculture based not on local needs but on the bottomless demand of a growing market. We removed bison and elk, the native grazing animals, and replaced them with cattle and horses, a change with major implications for native plant communities. We imported hundreds of new species of plants, some of which have gone wild, with devastating consequences for the native vegetation. We altered the hydrology of the region, turning former wetlands into uplands and upsetting the flood regime along the rivers. We removed such major ecological processes as fire from the landscape. And we remade a landscape where areas of human occupation had been islands in a sea of natural land into one in which the natural areas were isolated islands.

However, we also created forest preserve districts, first in Cook County and subsequently in the collar counties. We set aside state parks and created the nation's first system of nature preserves. Illinois nature preserves are granted the highest level of protection under state law. According to the Illinois Nature Preserves Commission, they are supposed to be places that retain "a high degree of their presettlement character." The enabling act that created Cook County's Forest Preserve District is quite specific in declaring that the purpose of the district is to save the "native flora and fauna." Many of the current difficulties arise from figuring out just what this obligation means in the context of a contemporary metropolis occupied by a people who have lost any historical memory of the native landscape.

The landscape of northeastern Illinois in 1820 was extraordinarily diverse. Several different kinds of forests grew here: sugar maple-basswood forests on glacial terraces along the rivers, American elm and silver maple forests on the floodplain, and oak-hickory forests—we now call them "woodlands"—on the slopes of the moraines. There were also savannas, grassland communities with some trees—more trees than could be found on the prairies but fewer than in the woods. Prairies covered great expanses. On the lake plain, where much of the city now stands, were wet prairies intergraded with marshes and sedge meadows—some of the most productive wetlands in North America.

Each of these natural communities had its characteristic species, and the juxtaposition of so many communities means that the Chicago region still has a very high level of biodiversity. According to *Plants of the Chicago Region*, by Floyd Swink and Gerould Wilhelm, 1,638 species of plants are native to this area, an amazing number for any location north of the tropics. We will never know how many native animals there were. In the past two years scientists from the Field Museum have found five species of beetles previously unknown to science in just one Cook County forest preserve.

Some of the biodiversity of 1820 is gone for good. Passenger pigeons are extinct. Black bears and bison are unlikely candidates for reintroduction to Cook County. Many species may have vanished before anyone had an opportunity to learn of their existence. But through a combination of foresight and dumb luck, we have managed to hold on to a very large number of species that have disappeared from much of their former range. You might say that rarities are commonplace here. Among the 102 counties in Illinois, Lake County has the most endangered and threatened species, and Cook County runs a close second.

We can be pleased that so many rare species survive here, but we also have to be worried that so many qualify as endangered or threatened. And our worries are compounded by the results of scientific investigations that clearly show species after species disappearing from preserves where they were once common. Woodland wildflowers go, taking with them the butterflies whose caterpillars once fed on their leaves. Mature oaks die by the thousands and leave no offspring to replace them. Prairies lose a plant species a year, and the accumulation of plant remains on the ground drives out the grasshopper sparrows that once nested there. Forests whose soils were held in place by a profusion of grasses and wildflowers have become wastelands where dense thickets of exotic shrubs shade bare, eroding earth.

Faced with clear evidence of ever steeper rates of decline, land management agencies throughout the Midwest—for that matter, throughout North America—have turned to ecological management and restoration as a way to keep what we still have. Protecting rare and endangered species—or rare and endangered communities—is a complex business, but at the broadest level of generalization you could say that the best way to protect species is to protect communities and that the best way to protect communities is to return to the land the processes that created and sustained those communities in the past. The artificial flood the Interior Department sent crashing through the Grand Canyon two years ago is an example of ecological management. So are the prescribed burns now being conducted from the Florida Everglades to the prairies, woodlands, and wetlands of Cook County.

If you survey the wild lands that still survive in Illinois, most of what you look at conforms to a pattern. A modest number of species will be present, and those species will be common. Look at ten woodlands or ten wetlands and you are likely to find that a high proportion of the species you see are present in all ten. You will probably also see a significant number of exotic species; in some cases they dominate the landscape.

But every once in a while you will come across land that doesn't conform to this pattern. This land will have few exotic species, and those in small numbers. It will have a larger than usual number of native species, and—most significantly—many of those species will be rare. Check into the history of this unusual place and you are likely to find that some lucky combination of circumstances protected it from many of the upheavals that have been visited on our landscape in the past 175 years.

These are the places that retain "a high degree of their presettlement character." They are the kinds of places that are selected for inclusion in the Illinois nature preserve system. They are also our best single source of information about the native landscape of northeastern Illinois. Sixteen such preserves—woodlands, wetlands, savannas, and prairies—are located in Cook County forest preserve system. You could reasonably define ecological management as an attempt to make the whole system as rich, diverse, and beautiful as these nature preserves.

When the surveyors from the Government Land Office were laying out section lines and township boundaries across northeastern Illinois 175 years ago, they were walking through a beautiful and endlessly varied landscape. Somehow through thousands of years all the animals and plants they saw had thriven in this place.

We could say that we will have achieved presettlement conditions when all the native species still with us are thriving. They can't all thrive in the same preserve, but somewhere there should be good sedge meadows for yellow rails, and somewhere there should be good woodlands for white oaks, and somewhere there should be good prairies for white fringed orchids and smooth green snakes.

Ecologists often talk of the health of natural communities. I think you can gauge the health of a community by asking three questions:

First, what species are present? Healthy communities support populations of a high proportion of the native animals and plants adapted to the conditions in that community.

Second, how are those species faring? Are they sustaining themselves or are they dying out?

Third, is the community as a whole perpetuating itself?

If the answer to these three questions is yes, then the community is healthy. Healthy, diverse natural communities were characteristic of pre-settlement times. They are the real goal of management now.

Oak Trees

Civilization Is Based on Them

December 16, 1994

For a long time the official state tree of Illinois was "the native oak." Purists have argued that there is no such tree, that we have many native oaks, and that if our state is going to honor one we ought to designate it properly by both genus and species. Realists have responded that getting the genus right is about as much as we can expect from the Illinois legislature.

Not long ago the legislature managed to get definite on the question by specifying the white oak, *Quercus alba,* as the true Illinois state tree. It's a good choice. White oaks are common throughout the state, and the species is the largest of our native oaks. Record heights are in the neighborhood of 30 meters—about 100 feet in American.

My own preference would be the bur oak, since this was the most common tree in the upland savannas that were once such a distinctive feature of the Illinois landscape. Bur oak, with its thick bark, is the most fireproof of our local oaks, a trait that gives it a competitive edge.

Both bur and white oaks are part of the white oak group, a cluster of closely related species that can be easily identified by the rounded lobes of their leaves. Leaves on trees of the black oak group have sharply pointed lobes.

All oaks belong to the genus *Quercus,* and all show a strong tendency to hybridize, making precise identification difficult. Through the years, books on the flora of Chicago have differed on just how many kinds of oaks we have here. The latest edition of Swink and Wilhelm's *Plants of the Chicago Region* lists nine full species and three hybrids.

Lately I have been leaning toward the idea that oaks are the basis of civilization as we know it. In part this thought arose from the experience of living in Seattle for a year. The Pacific Northwest has only one native oak, and the region is also very thin in the civilization department. Coincidence? I doubt it.

As partial proof of the intimate connection between oaks and civilization, consider the fact that we could use a tin pot to brew up some slop and drink it to the point of intoxication. But getting plastered in an elegant and civilized way is almost impossible without using oak. Oak barrels are absolutely essential to the creation of Chateau Latour, Nuits-St.-Georges, Maker's Mark, and *grande fine champagne.*

The excellence of oak—and particularly the wood of the white oak group—as a material for cooperage stems from the presence of tyloses in the conducting tissues of the wood. Tyloses are cells that scale off the walls of the vascular tubes, blocking them and effectively waterproofing the wood. Thanks to the tyloses, you can store cognac in an oak barrel for 20 years or more without losing a drop.

Tannic acid helps with the flavoring. Oak trees produce this acid—also called tannin—in substantial amounts. We have traditionally extracted it for tanning leather. It is bitter, astringent, and, in large doses, poisonous. But in small amounts it can add interest to the flavor of aged spirits. Tannic acid is also present in coffee beans. It takes temperatures in the 90 to 100 degree Celsius range to dissolve it, which is why coffee made with very hot water tastes like it has been strained through a shoe.

Tannic acid is a very effective fungicide. It is the main reason why oak is so durable and resistant to decay.

Acorns also contain tannin. Indians in California, for whom acorns were a staple food, ground the nuts into flour and then had to put the flour through an elaborate leaching process to make it palatable. Acorns of the white oak group are supposedly sweeter, and some sources say that bur oak acorns that have been through a frost can be ground, baked, and eaten without any leaching.

Of course any account of oaks and civilization could not leave out the cork oak, *Quercus suber,* the tree whose bark protects fine wines after they have been taken from the barrel and put into bottles. Bark is first stripped from cork oak trees at about age 20. Regeneration is rapid, and further stripping can be done every eight to ten years for the life of the tree. The bark is boiled, scraped, and dried, then cut into appropriate shapes.

Cork oak is native to areas near the western Mediterranean in both Europe and North Africa. These are places where summer drought is the usual condition, and it is a reasonable guess that the thick bark served mainly as fire protection. I wonder if anyone has ever tried to make bottle stoppers from bur oak bark?

French oak from species other than *Quercus suber* is the favored barrel wood of wine makers all over the world. Even California wine makers prefer imported wood over their abundant local oak.

About 20 percent of France is still covered with forest, and about 25 percent of that is oak woods. The French have been managing their oak woods since about 1000 A.D. They use a coppice system that involves making partial cuts that leave scattered trees to serve as seed sources. Oak stumps produce many sprouts that grow into trees, but trees grown from sprouts tend to develop heart rot at an earlier age than trees grown from acorns. So the French system alternates generations. After a cut, the relatively fast-growing sprouts provide a new crop in a relatively short time. Then the slower-growing trees produced by acorns become large enough to cut. Since this system has been successful in maintaining both the woods and a continuing yield of timber for about 1,000 years, it seems reasonable to believe that the French are on to something.

The ability of oaks to sprout from stumps or from the roots themselves played an important role in sustaining the genus in fire-prone areas such as the Midwest. In *Vegetation of Wisconsin,* John Curtis suggested that once oaks had become established in an area, fire could not remove them. Oak grubs—which is to say the root systems—could survive the mightiest fire and send up new sprouts the following spring.

The biggest, oldest oaks in the Chicago area almost all began growing at roughly the same time, about 1830. This is the time when settlers began to protect the land hereabouts from fire, so the sprouts produced in that decade were not incinerated. With well-established root systems to support them, the sprouts grew rapidly, and lands that were considered prairie in 1830 became oak woods in a very short time.

When glaciers covered Chicago the oaks retreated far to the south, but when the ice left the oaks started coming back. The speed of their northward advance, reconstructed from fossilized pollen and other evidence, averaged 350 meters or less per year.

Oaks are not the sorts of trees that can easily pioneer in new ground. Cottonwoods, which produce millions of very tiny seeds that can be blown miles by even a moderate breeze, are ideal for that sort of role. It would take a hurricane to blow an acorn any distance at all, so how did the oaks manage their inexorable march from the gulf coast to the Midwest?

The answer may well be blue jays. We know that blue jays cache

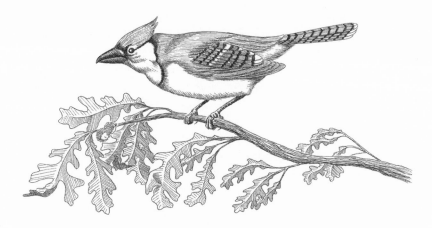

acorns, and that they often don't return to eat what they have cached. And that they may carry the nuts for up to a mile before caching them.

So upon the wings of blue jays the oaks advanced into the Midwest. Here they encountered the civilization of the Native Americans. And here was created one of the world's many symbioses between humans and oaks.

Our attitudes toward oak trees are an interesting piece of social/scientific history. Until recently scientists treated our oaks as just another tree of the forest, like maples and basswoods. Then prairie restoration began, and oaks assumed a somewhat villainous role. They were trees, and invading trees destroyed prairies by covering their sun-loving plants with shade.

But as prairie-restoration work proceeded, it became obvious that oaks belonged in re-creations of our native landscape. They were not just another tree in the forest, and they certainly weren't villains. They were, it seems, a major part of the landscape, dominants in a biome that ranged from treeless prairie to prairie with a few scattered oaks to open oak groves to true oak woodlands. Restoring the presettlement landscape meant restoring oaks as well as northern dropseed grass or lead plant.

Then we took our thinking a step further. Why were all these oaks here? We knew that fire favors oaks. That it drives out maples and basswoods and other fire-sensitive competitors. And we knew from early travelers and from tribal traditions that the native peoples deliberately set fires. And anyone who cared to look could see that tribes are still using fire as a deliberate management tool on reservation land.

We also know that oak woods are very productive when it comes to game animals. Deer, turkey, and quail are all very fond of acorns, and the open character of an oak woods favors these important game animals. And we know that contemporary Native Americans measure the value of an oak woods by the number of game animals it can support—just as medieval Frenchmen calculated the worth of a woods by the number of pigs it could feed.

But it took us a long time to make the logical inference: that the prairie/savanna landscape of Illinois was to a considerable extent a human creation. Its ecosystems had been continuously shaped by human intervention, perhaps for as long as people had existed in this place.

This is not a comfortable idea for many Americans. We like to imagine America as an empty continent, a primeval wilderness that we shaped into a home for ourselves. If the place was empty, then we don't have to think about what we did to the people who lived here. And if we do think about them, it is much more comforting to imagine them as ignorant savages than as sophisticated ecologists who knew centuries ago things we are only now beginning to learn.

But if we examine this idea it is full of hope for our expanding efforts to restore our native plant and animal communities. After all, if humans could shape this landscape once, perhaps we can do it again.

Sedges

Scaberulous or Scabridulous?

June 27, 1997

I have decided that this should be the year of the sedge. I have been bluffing my way through this family of plants for decades, nodding sagely when people told me that *Carex jamesii* or *Carex laxiculmis* was growing at this or that place, trying to cover the fact that I wouldn't know either one of these rare species if it turned up in my backyard. Trying to cover also the fact that without a quick consultation of the relevant books, I wouldn't know whether either of these species qualified as rare or special.

I am not alone in my lack of knowledge of sedges. I would hazard a guess that more than 95 percent of my fellow Americans have never heard the word "sedge." Weed out—pardon the expression—the people who have read the name in a crossword puzzle clue list but have never knowingly seen a living sedge and you are left with a minuscule fraction of the population. An even smaller fraction can not only look at a plant and say, that is a sedge, but can tell you what sedge it is.

John and Jane Balaban are prominent among the elect in the Chicago region. Neither of them is a biologist—John teaches high school physics and math, Jane is a pharmacist—but they have spent enough hours in the field and picked up enough mosquito bites to earn the respect of the most highly trained botanists.

Every year in June, John and Jane offer a one-day course in identifying sedges. Class convenes at 9 A.M. at Bunker Hill Woods at Devon and Caldwell. At noon, the class breaks for lunch at the Balaban residence in Skokie. This is a working lunch, since John and Jane have various notable sedges growing in flower beds around their house and students are encouraged to figure out their identities. Afternoon is more sedges at Harms Woods in Glenview.

At this point you may be asking yourself, is he ever going to tell us what sedges are? Indeed I will. Sedges are members of the family Cyperaceae. Along with the family Gramineae, the grasses, they form the order Poales. They are herbaceous plants, which means they have no woody tissue. Some are annuals; most are perennials that sprout each spring from long-lived roots. Grasses are economically the most important family of plants. Without such grasses as corn, wheat, rice, oats, barley, and millet, a substantial part of the human race would starve to death.

Sedges do not have that kind of direct importance to human life, though papyrus, the plant that provided the Egyptians with paper, is a sedge. But sedges are often major players in natural communities. In fact, one kind of local wetland community is called a sedge meadow. We have 13 genera of Cyperaceae in this region, but the big genus is *Carex*. Biologists refer to genera with many species as "speciose," and *Carex* is about as speciose as they come. Our local flora includes 147 species of *Carex*, and 136 are native. This represents 8 percent of the total number of native trees, shrubs, grasses, wildflowers, and ferns in the Chicago area.

And there you have the reason why would-be field botanists flee from sedges. One hundred and thirty-six species—almost exactly the number of breeding bird species in Cook County. You might think it difficult to learn to identify all those birds, but they are a wildly diverse group, ranging from great blue herons with six-foot wingspans to blue-winged warblers weighing eight grams. With the genus *Carex*, we have 136 variations on a very limited theme.

The details of the structure, shape, and location of the flowers are the essential traits used in most *Carex* identifications, although things like leaf width also are important for some species. Since most of the species flower in spring or early summer, by mid-July many of them are unidentifiable even by experts.

Sedges are wind pollinated, and the flowers are small and plain, with none of the bright colors or elaborate patterns usually seen in species pollinated by insects. The female flowers are small green pouches called perigynia. The seeds develop inside these pouches. The male flowers are usually just sets of scales that produce slender stamens that release pollen into the air. Within this general pattern the variations seem endless. The perigynia may grow in globular clusters or tightly packed together in long slender spikes. They may be triangular or flattened in cross section. They may be shaped like footballs or have long, skinny necks.

Plants of the Chicago Region by Floyd Swink and Gerould Wilhelm, the absolute authority on matters botanical in our area, contains a key to the plants of the genus *Carex* written by Wilhelm. It runs to nine large pages of very small type, and it is filled with pitfalls.

You might reasonably ask why anybody who doesn't need to pass a test would want to get into all these technicalities. I would respond that we are human. Floyd Swink is fond of pointing out that, as a taxonomist, he is a member of the world's oldest profession. God's first commandment to Adam was that he name everything in the garden. Adam obeyed that one, and in the process gained a measure of control over all the things he named. God carefully forbade Adam from naming Him. We feel most at home not where everybody knows our name, but where we know everybody's name.

When you step off the pavement and into a natural area, the depth of your experience is directly correlated to the number of things you can name. If you operate with preschool categories like "tree" and "bird" and "bug" you are going to miss a whole lot. If you can reliably distinguish a two-spotted skipper from a European skipper or a monarch from a viceroy, if you can tell a white oak from a swamp white oak or recognize the call of a willow flycatcher, you are in a position to pick up on a lot more subtleties.

Mastering the subtleties of the sedges begins with learning to separate them from grasses. The most obvious difference is the shape of the culm—the flower-bearing stem. Grass culms are round; sedge culms are roughly triangular. "Sedges have edges" is the usual mnemonic. Roll the culm back and forth between your thumb and forefinger and you can feel the angles. Once you have got that far, your next step is to turn to a key.

Botanists use dichotomous keys all the time. As the adjective implies, these keys work by placing before you a series of either-or choices. You select your choice from the pair, and the key then directs you to the next set of choices. Choose 1A and you are directed to the pair of choices numbered 2. Choose 1B and you may be directed to the pair numbered 46. Some of the sedges in the genus *Carex* require six or eight choices before you arrive at an identification. Of course if you make the wrong choice at some point you become like a man lost in the woods: the farther you go the more lost you get.

To get the true flavor of Wilhelm's key to the genus *Carex*, you have to read the actual words. Consider this pair of choices:

All or essentially all of the pistillate spikelets drooping on elongate, slender, flexuous peduncles.
All but occasionally the lowermost pistillate spikelets ascending or erect on usually short peduncles.

Fortunately, there is a glossary where you can look up words like "peduncle" and "cuspidate" and "obconic" and all the rest of the specialized terms botanists use. There you can learn the differences among "scaberulous," "scabrid," "scabridulous," and "scabrous."

But note all the weaselly words, like "essentially" and "occasionally." The key is full of "usually" and "rarely" and "normally." If you have only a single specimen, how do you know if it is normal?

Actually I did fairly well during the class. I successfully keyed out plants of several species. Since then, however, I have spent a lot of time wandering through the key without reaching a positive identification. I have provisionally identified what I call the BPF, the Balaban Proximity Factor, as the major reason. My hypothesis is that if either John or Jane Balaban is within 20 feet of me—and therefore available for consultation—I can key out anything. If they aren't around I get nowhere.

The Balabans have made some notable discoveries in the world of sedges. One species, *Carex formosa*, was not known in Illinois until they discovered it along the North Branch of the Chicago River. Their discovery at Bunker Hill of a number of woodland sedges in a meadow that the Forest Preserve District had kept open by regular mowing helped shape a management plan that is returning the area to the savanna character it once had. Until recently nearly treeless, the area now supports many young swamp white and pin oaks. As we take up the task of restoring to our wildlands the biodiversity they once had, sedges will be important guides to management.

Nightshade

Nasty, Not Deadly

June 13, 1986

The alley behind my house is crawling with deadly nightshade. This does not set my alley apart from the rest of Chicago's alleys, because deadly nightshade is a quite common plant in what the field guides always refer to as "waste places."

This time of year, *Solanum dulcamera* is very showy. The flowers, in bloom now, have purple or violet petals that curve back toward the stem and a central yellow beak that produces a pleasing aesthetic contrast. The flowers are replaced by small, green berries that turn red as they ripen.

The name deadly nightshade is both a misnomer and an overstatement. The true deadly nightshade is *Atropa belladonna,* the source of the drug of the same name and a genuinely deadly plant. Our alley denizen should really be called something like "rather nasty nightshade." The plant contains an alkaloid called solanin; it is only mildly poisonous, but you should still keep your kids away from it. Some people die from bee stings, and any consideration of the effects of a specific poison has to begin with an awareness of all the variables—which means everything from the intensity of an individual's allergic reaction to the amount consumed per pound of body weight to the amount of poison in the berries. The quantity of solanin declines as the berries ripen, so red berries are not as dangerous as green ones, but they are still to be avoided.

The scientific name of our alley plant translates as "bittersweet nightshade," a name given it by intrepid botanists who chewed the roots and found them first bitter and then sweet.

Birds seem to be able to eat the berries without ill effects, a fact that explains the peculiar distribution of the plant in our alleys and waste places. Nightshade almost always grows along fences. The birds eat the fruits, perch on the fences, and defecate the seeds. Talking to Floyd Swink, chief taxonomist at the Morton Arboretum, I asked him about the apparent immunity of birds. He pointed out that birds eat many things we would find dangerous or irritating, poison ivy berries for example, but he also said that we do not know for sure that the birds survive their ingestion of *S. dulcamera*. They might drop the seeds from their perch on the fence and then fly off and die. Birds do learn to avoid food that tastes foul, but nightshade berries don't really taste too bad.

In this they are like some of their famous and desirable relatives. The family Solanaceae, the group to which nightshade belongs, is second only to the grasses in economic importance. Potatoes are solanaceous, as are tomatoes, peppers, eggplant, tobacco, and a number of obscure edibles that have been locally domesticated in various parts of the world.

South America seems to have been the center of development for this remarkable family. There are more species on that continent than anywhere else in the world, and potatoes, tomatoes, and peppers all originated there, as did one of the two species of smokable tobacco.

For centuries after its importation into Europe, the tomato carried an unjust rap as a poisonous fruit. People grew it as an ornamental plant and called it the love apple, a name that supposedly originated in the belief that maids or swains disappointed in love could eat a tomato as a romantic way of doing away with themselves. They were, of course, in for another disappointment. They might get a little heartburn from the tomato's acidity, but as even chronic Rolaids gobblers know, heartburn is a long way from death.

Some of Captain John Smith's soldiers at Jamestown, in search not of release from unhappy love affairs but of a little salad with their dinners, did die when they ate *Datura stramonium*, a truly lethal member of the Solanaceae. From their unhappy experience, the plant acquired the common name of Jamestown weed, which eventually evolved into jimson weed.

Small doses of various species of *Datura* are used throughout the Americas—and in the Old World—as psychedelic plants. The folk use of these plants is always tied to religious ceremonies and not to rock and roll concerts, and the people who take them are more interested in seeing God, or something like him, than in having a good time, so getting sick is regarded as part of the price you pay to find the truth.

The Algonquin Indians of our eastern forests kept adolescent boys stoned to the gills on *Datura* for 20 days until they were said to forget all of their past lives and be ready for a new beginning as a man.

Among the southwestern Zuni, the rain priests chew *Datura* at night to help them commune with the spirits. Former hippies will remember that Don Juan Mateus, the hero of Carlos Castaneda's books, employed

Datura as a bridge to the spirits. Similar uses of various members of the genus have been recorded from Mexico, Central America, South America, India, and Africa.

Other solanaceous plants believed to have magical properties include mandrake. According to German legend, mandrakes grew below gallows, sprouting from the sperm of a hanged man's last convulsive ejaculation. Even our bittersweet nightshade was used as a charm against witchcraft.

The source of both the death and destruction and the divine insight is a group of diverse chemical compounds called alkaloids, which are produced by many plants and even a few animals, including the beaver. Over 30 of the 85 genera of solanaceous plants produce alkaloids.

Alkaloids are mostly built up from amino acids, and as a group, they are distinguished by the intense physiological activity they inspire. Morphine is an alkaloid, and so are cocaine, psilocybin, mescaline, nicotine, caffeine, and quinine. The major active ingredient in *Datura* is scopolamine, a psychoactive chemical that for a time was called truth serum because people given the drug were supposed to be unable to tell a lie. They may have been just too stoned to think of one.

Botanists have looked into the question of why plants synthesize alkaloids and determined that alkaloids provide no noticeable protection from bacteria and viruses, but they do function pretty effectively against both insects and vertebrates. In other words, what we have here is chemical warfare. Eat these leaves and die.

The animals do not take this aggression lying down. They can evolve defenses as well as the plants do. Insects, with their short life cycles and enormous reproductive potential, can quickly transform the fortuitous immunity of a few individuals into a characteristic of a whole population—witness our recent experience with DDT and the bugs it was suppose to kill.

Potato plants contain solanin—which is why you should cut all green portions from the outer layer of a potato before cooking it—but the Colorado potato beetle can laugh—figuratively speaking—at the plant's deadliest venom. It has even been suggested that the artiodactyla, the group of grazing animals that includes deer, cattle, and antelopes, have replaced the older perissodactyla—horses and rhinos—as the world's dominant grazing animals because of immunities that allow cows to eat more kinds of plants than horses.

In support of the general theory of chemical warfare, I offer a bit of what is known in the science business as anecdotal evidence. The leaves of almost everything that grows in my backyard have the nibbled look that life eventually brings to us all. But a quick check of the nightshade growing along the back fence reveals almost no signs of nibbling. The leaves are as pristine as the day they unfolded from the bud. Only one leaf showed signs of nibbling, and it was missing just two tiny chunks along one edge, as if some hapless beetle or caterpillar managed two bites before suffering a fatal collapse. Chemical warfare works.

Purple Loosestrife

Progress against a Wetland Invader

September 5, 1997

Biological invasions are slow-motion disasters. They start small: a few insects hitchhiking on some imported nursery stock, a few seeds escaping from somebody's backyard and taking root in a ditch, a field, or a woodlot. The spread is slow at first. Small populations, even if they are very fecund, can produce only small numbers of seeds or young. Sometimes the invading species spends decades as a small, inoffensive part of the biota before suddenly becoming a major pest. It could be that the shift to pest status is the consequence of a genetic mutation that alters the behavior or ecological tolerances of a species, enabling it to push aside competitors and spread quickly onto new ground.

Purple loosestrife may have made that kind of genetic shift. This European wetland plant has been in North America for nearly 200 years and perhaps longer. It was well represented in botanical collections in the eastern United States by 1830, but it showed no sign of becoming troublesome until a century later. The first hint of difficulty was in southern Canada, where loosestrife began to invade pastures, forming dense monotypic stands. It had spread to the Midwest by the '40s, and by the mid-80s only three states in the lower 48—Arizona, New Mexico, and Montana—were free of the plant.

Lythrum salicaria is a wetland species. It can reach a height of six feet on favored sites. Each tall, slender plant is topped by a long spike of brilliant purple flowers that is quite beautiful if you don't know what it signifies. To the knowing eye the spikes look like the floral displays around a coffin. Their beauty makes them creepier than they would be if they were gross and ugly.

The seeds of *L. salicaria* can be carried by water, by wind, or in mud clinging to the feet of waterfowl. Purple loosestrife stems that break off from a parent plant can take root and grow into vigorous new individuals. Once established in a marsh, purple loosestrife grows so densely that it is difficult for large birds such as ducks to move through a stand.

The native vegetation retreats before the invader. The cattails whose roots support muskrats, the smartweeds whose seeds feed rails, all the bulrushes, arrowheads, cordgrass, wild rice, and other plants of a healthy wetland, die out. All the leaf beetles and weevils and butterflies and leafhoppers that depend on those plants disappear too, leaving less food for marsh wrens and leopard frogs. The yellow-headed blackbirds find that loosestrife stems are not strong enough to support their nests, so they leave.

Loosestrife seems to do best in disturbed areas: The Lake Calumet region is a major center of infection in this region. From that base the plant can spread into pristine nature preserves and kill off all sorts of native rarities.

Until quite recently there were only two methods available for fending off purple loosestrife: using herbicides and manipulating water levels. The main herbicide was Rodeo, a chemical approved for application to wetlands. Treatment was difficult and expensive. Each individual plant had to be sprayed, which meant that a person wearing a tank of herbicide on a backpack had to wade through a marsh dousing each stem. If the applicator missed any—and it is a virtual certainty that a few would be missed—the effect of the spraying would be to clear the ground for next year's crop. Altering water depth and the duration of flooding in marshes achieved some success, but it was possible only on sites equipped with water-control structures.

The need for a biological control method was clear, but it was not clear whether such a control existed and not at all clear if anyone had the resources to look for it. Then in 1987 the total budget earmarked for alien plant control by the U.S. Fish and Wildlife Service ($100,000) was granted to the New York Cooperative Wildlife Research Unit at Cornell University for research into purple loosestrife control. We can claim some local credit for this. Local Sierra Club activists led by Donna Hriljac called Congressman Sidney Yates's attention to the problem, and Yates, then chairman of the appropriations subcommittee that oversaw the budget for the Department of the Interior, saw to it that the funds were put in the budget.

The search for biological controls involves looking for an organism—often an insect, but other possibilities range from nematodes to fungi—that eats the invading plant but doesn't eat anything else. You start by looking at the plant's native ground, where it has a long evolutionary history—ample time to develop some enemies.

A preliminary survey of European purple loosestrife populations turned up about 100 species of insects that could feed on it. Of these, about a dozen were found only on purple loosestrife plants. Five of these, all beetles, were regarded as sufficiently specialized to undergo further testing. One insect was a weevil whose larva lives in—and eats—the roots of loosestrife. Two were closely related leaf-eating beetles, and the other two were extremely tiny weevils that live in the flowering heads of the plants.

The big question was whether these bugs would continue to specialize in purple loosestrife if they were transported to a new environment. This question was answered at the International Institute for Biological Control in Europe. The idea was to bring North American plants to the beetles rather than risk the release of European beetles in this country. In all, 49 species of plants were tested, using two different kinds of tests. In one test the bugs were given a choice. Caged with a purple loosestrife plant and a plant of another species, they 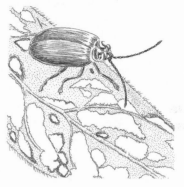 were observed to see if they stayed with the loosestrife or started nibbling on the test plant. In the second test the bugs were locked in with just the test plant. Here the choice was eat this or starve. The successful beetle chose starvation.

The most critical test involved plants that are closely related to the target species. Here in Illinois, *Lythrum alatum,* winged loosestrife, is a common wetland species. Would the beetles turn to *alatum* if they got the chance?

The two leaf-eating beetles of the genus *Galerucella* did nibble lightly on the winged loosestrife. Larvae can develop into adults on the plant, but adults reared on *alatum* produce only about 5 percent as many eggs as adults reared on *salicaria,* and few of those eggs survive to adulthood. *Galerucella* is not likely to be a threat to winged loosestrife.

In 1994 John Schwegman of the Illinois Department of Natural Resources bought some *Galerucella* insects from Cornell. He organized a cooperative venture with the forest preserve districts of Cook, Lake, Will, Kane, and Du Page counties and the conservation district in McHenry County and began releasing the leaf-eating beetles at selected sites in the summer of 1994. In Cook County the first releases were at Powderhorn Lake, a forest preserve east of Lake Calumet.

There was no evidence of overwintering by those first beetles, so Schwegman approached the Illinois Natural History Survey for help. The survey has the facilities needed to grow large numbers of *Galerucella* beetles, and large numbers would obviously be needed. In 1995 beetles from the survey were released at Powderhorn. They were placed on purple loosestrife plants, which were then covered for a week with netting to keep the insects on the plants. Again no beetles lived through the winter.

The 1996 strategy called for multiple releases at several sites, a strategy that was possible only because the Natural History Survey was by then able to raise large numbers of beetles. In Cook County releases took place at Powderhorn Lake, LaBagh Woods, Sand Ridge Prairie Nature Preserve, and Beaubien Woods, and in a marsh at Lemont and Bluff Roads in the Palos preserves. The cold spring and high water levels made things difficult, but the beetles persisted, and this spring all five sites showed signs that some beetles had made it through the winter.

By July damage to loosestrife plants was visible at all the sites except LaBagh. Some plants were damaged to the extent that they were not flowering. According to John Wiedenmann of the Natural History Survey, the insects have begun to show signs of their presence at several sites. At Hosah Prairie, near Illinois Beach in Lake County, a survey of 300 plants in 1996 found about one-third not flowering, another one-third with limited flowering, and one-third untouched. A similar survey this year found about 70 percent of the plants did not flower and another 25 percent had only limited flowering. Only 3 percent of the plants were undamaged. An Illinois DNR site near Savanna is showing spectacular changes, with many dead and damaged plants and few flowering individuals.

The Natural History Survey has received a grant from Chicago Wilderness, the consortium of organizations working to preserve biodiversity in this region, to develop a school curriculum about biological control. Students will grow their own beetles and conduct their own experiments on whether they'll eat only loosestrife. The student will work with the counties to assign their beetles to particular release sites. The plan is to introduce the curriculum in 20 schools during the coming school year and expand to 60 next year.

For at least the last 20 years people concerned about wetlands have been watching the advance of purple loosestrife with a mixture of anxiety and despair. Things were getting rapidly worse, and there seemed to be nothing we could do about it. Now we have some hope. In at least a few small sites things seem to be getting better. And we have a practical way to continue the improvement. The chatter of marsh wrens and the whinnying calls of soras may still resound in our marshes.

[These programs have expanded and are still controlling purple loose-strife.]

Jewelweed

Also Called Touch-Me-Not

October 3, 1986

Jewelweed flowers look like they were designed for hummingbirds. They are long, funnel-shaped tubes surrounded by flaring petals at the wide end and curving into a sort of spur at the narrow end. The stamens, which hold the pollen, and the pistils, which hold the ovaries where the seeds will develop, are at the wide end.

The nectar, the sweet reward the bird claims for its pollinating services, is tucked away at the narrow end of the tube. Sticking its long bill way back there, the bird can't help but dust both head and bill with pollen. Any pollen it happens to be carrying will get rubbed off onto the pistil.

Bumblebees sometimes rob jewelweed flowers by biting a hole at the back of the tube and slurping out the nectar without touching either stamen or pistil.

Despite this thievery, jewelweeds have managed to become common to abundant over much of eastern North America. We have two species in the Chicago area—*Impatiens capensis,* spotted jewelweed, and *Impatiens pallida,* yellow jewelweed—and both of them can be found in flower in autumn. A few plants of spotted jewelweed—the flowers are orange with brown spots—are blooming now in the mini marsh at the west end of the Lincoln Park bird sanctuary.

They are tall plants with pale green leaves. Their stems are translucent, and according to some authorities you can actually see the sap running in the vascular tissue inside them. These same authorities differ on the source of the plant's name. Some say it refers to the flowers. Some say it comes from the fact that water forms gleaming beads on the leaves, and some say it comes from the silvery sheen on submerged leaves.

Gardeners will recognize the name *Impatiens.* Several Old World species of the genus are planted as ornamentals. We have a patch of pink ones in our backyard that has been blooming continuously since June.

Jewelweeds have a number of other common names. Touch-me-not is the most widespread of these. If you want to show off your classical training, you can call it *noli me tangere*, which is touch-me-not in Latin. I have a vague memory of Christ saying those words to somebody in the Bible and much more vivid memories of the girls I dated in my youth telling me the same thing in slightly different words.

The name touch-me-not and a related name, snapweed, are both derived from the jewelweed's method of spreading its seed. The fruits of the jewelweed are tiny capsules whose walls are formed of strands that are under tension like compressed springs. Touch one and it pops, scattering seeds up to several feet away.

The seeds are important because jewelweeds are annuals, plants that germinate, flower, set seed, and die in a single season. If they seeds don't survive, there won't be any jewelweed next year.

Jewelweeds grow in a variety of habitats, including forests, where annuals are not very common. Most of the annuals in this part of the world are weedy species, invaders that push their way into habitats that have been opened by disturbance. Tear up the soil in some way, and you get ragweed and other annual opportunists moving in to fill the vacant space.

Life is much harder for an annual in a woodland because nearly all the available space is already taken up by perennials. A germinating jewelweed seed is like a man opening an independent hamburger stand right across the street from a McDonald's. The seed sends out its tiny probing rootlet and instantly encounters heavy competition from root systems that have been established for years.

However, jewelweeds are most common in wet forests, and they are especially abundant on floodplains where nature provides periodic disturbances that open things up for struggling annuals. You may have noticed that the Des Plaines River is overflowing its banks right now. The flood is drowning out all sorts of plants along the river as well as laying down a heavy new deposit of mud. Next spring, that fresh mud should be prime jewelweed habitat.

The juices of a jewelweed are said to be an excellent remedy for poison ivy. If you think you have brushed up against a poison ivy plant, just pluck a jewelweed leaf, crush it between your fingers, and rub it on the affected portion of your anatomy. The poison in poison ivy is carried in an oil, and jewelweed juice seems to break up that oil and remove it from your skin with less violence than such recommended remedies as unleaded gasoline.

If you are fearful of running into poison ivy when no jewelweed is available, you can gather leaves and stems, throw them in a pot of water, and simmer them until the water is reduced by half. Strain the resulting broth and keep it around for emergencies. Euell Gibbons recommended freezing the broth in ice cube trays. It will keep indefinitely that way, and when you need some, you can just pull a cube from the tray and rub it on.

Jewelweed juice is also an effective fungicide. If you are afflicted with athlete's foot, just rub a little between your toes.

You can probably eat the stuff too, but this may be a bit risky. Plants of the genus *Impatiens* do produce raphides, microscopic, needlelike crystals that may be quite irritating to anything that eats them. M. L. Fernald, the author of the eighth edition of *Gray's Manual of Botany* and therefore the ultimate authority on the plants of this part of the world, writes—in his book *Edible Plants of Eastern North America*—that the plant is supposed to be poisonous to livestock. However, Fernald is just passing along hearsay evidence.

Euell Gibbons actually ate some—cautiously and in small portions—and suffered no ill effects. He always urged people to confine themselves to eating very young plants in spring.

I am always a little nervous about detailing the uses to which wild plants can be put. Around Chicago, and indeed in most parts of the country these days, wild plants are likely to be growing only on protected ground. Encouraging people to pick some jewelweed for their athlete's foot or their dinner could be considered an incitement to crime. Even worse, it could lead to the destruction of yet another wild plant.

I also don't like to offer any support to the idea that plants have to justify their existence by being useful to humans. Jewelweeds are absolutely essential to other jewelweeds, and that is all that matters.

Finally, I get depressed around people whose major interest in wild things is gastronomic. They are like caterpillars. They relate to the world only through their stomachs.

So use Desenex for your feet, Caladryl for your poison ivy, and Boston lettuce for your salads. If you come across a patch of blooming jewelweed, just sit down and watch it for a while. You may see a hummingbird or, even better, a robber bee purloining some nectar. And in late fall when the flowers are gone and the fruits are ripe, you can walk through the patch and enjoy the sight of the seed popping out all over the ground as you touch the touch-me-nots.

Hazels

Once Our Most Abundant Shrub

October 11, 1996

When the General Land Office surveyors were laying their perfectly square sections on the round earth in northeastern Illinois around 1820 they came across a lot of hazel bushes. American hazel grew in dense thickets scattered across the prairies; it grew in coppices at the edge of woodlands and in the shade of oaks inside the woods. Analyses of survey records suggest that American hazel grew in nearly all our woods and savanna groves and was several times more abundant than any other native shrub.

Hazels are still around, but they are much reduced from their previous abundance. Their thickets are small and widely scattered and many a woodland in our region has none at all.

Most people are familiar with the taste of hazelnuts. Hazels are the small, round filberts in a can of mixed nuts, and the nuts are also popular as a flavoring for coffee. Out in the woods, squirrels love 'em, blue jays love 'em, deer love 'em, and if we ever manage to reintroduce wild turkeys into these parts, the turkeys will love 'em.

The decline of American hazel from the most abundant shrub in the region to relative scarcity follows the same general path that can be traced for hundreds of other native species. And like other besieged natives, hazels are beginning to get some attention from restorationists.

American hazel, *Corylus americana,* is one of two species of hazel native to the eastern U.S. The other, beaked hazel, *Corylus cornuta,* has been found in at least one location in the Chicago region, but it is far more common north of here. In the second-growth aspen woods of northern Wisconsin, beaked hazel is all over the place.

Both of these hazels are shrubs. In a relatively shady situation in the woodland they grow only about four feet tall, but in woodland openings where more sun is available they can get up to ten feet tall. Some Eurasian species of hazel are really small trees, and these are the source of the commercial crops.

Hazels spread through their roots, sending out lateral root sprouts that in turn produce vertical stems. The dense thickets created by this growth pattern make hazels excellent sites for the nests of a considerable assortment of woodland and brushland birds.

Hazels belong to the same plant family as birches and alders. One of the family traits of this group is that the male and female flowers are separate, but each plant produces both kinds. The staminate flowers, the ones that produce pollen, hang in long, slender catkins. The pistillate flowers, the ones that will produce the nuts, are at the tips of branches.

The catkins form late in the growing season and stay on the plant through the winter. As early as March they turn a bright yellow as the pollen is released and carried by the wind to the pistils. Bright yellow hazel catkins are a welcome assurance in the dreary late winter that spring is truly coming.

The decline of American hazel is a subject that hasn't drawn much attention until quite recently. Endangered species, plants that are hanging on by their metaphorical fingernails, are the obviously desperate cases. They inspire the creation of habitat-manipulation schemes, captive-breeding programs, and hand-pollination efforts. But the decline of a once-abundant species has to be a matter of major concern. Especially since the decline is obviously not over. Marlin Bowles of the Morton Arboretum has been monitoring tree and shrub densities on plots laid out in oak groves at the Middle Fork Savanna in Lake County over the past ten years. In that time the number of living hazel stems has declined by 19 percent. Losing one-fifth of the population in a decade is not good.

Part of the reason for this loss is easy to find. Bowles's counts show during the same ten years an increase in European buckthorn—an imported tall shrub—of 550 percent. Tatarian honeysuckle, another imported pest, increased its stem count by 88 percent. So as a first guess, we can select competition from these exotics as a factor in the losses suffered by American hazel.

The fragmentation of the landscape enters into the mix too. Buckthorn produces small berries that surround hard seeds that can pass undamaged through the digestive system of a robin. So robins and other birds serve as seed scatterers for this species. Because they can fly, they can provide the buckthorn with the means to overcome the problems created by fragmentation.

Hazels have a harder time. You could say that they have adopted a different kind of reproductive strategy. Their heavy nuts are far less likely to be carried any great distance, and if they get eaten the seed is destroyed. The gain from this kind of strategy comes from the large amounts of food stored in the seed. If the nut survives long enough to sprout, the young growing hazel bush has a substantial reservoir of calories available to get it through the difficult early days of life.

In the past hazels probably did most of their reproducing with their root sprouts. Large thickets seem to have been a regular feature of the landscape in savanna groves and open oak woods. A clone of shrubs *can* move, but it happens very slowly. If you had the temporal perspective of a white oak you could see the root sprouts on the edge of the clone where conditions were getting better begin to survive at a much higher rate than sprouts from elsewhere. And where things got worse, hazels would die out. A green ultra-slo-mo amoeba, the clone would creep toward good times. Excellent in 1800 but hard to apply on I-90.

Grazing hit hazels hard too. Cows eat the plants; pigs eat the nuts. Fire suppression then chipped in by creating lots of dense, very shady woods that are too dim for hazels.

I think hazels fit into the category of creatures that the biologist E. O. Wilson called "obligate fugitives." An obligate fugitive can survive only in the presence of disturbances that do it considerable harm. The classic human counterpart would be the peasant farming the slopes of Mount Vesuvius. Every once in a while a big lava flow is going to come through, but between times, the land is rich.

Hazels are very thin-barked. Their stems are easily killed by fire. And it takes three years for new stems to mature enough to produce nuts. But without fire the woods become too dark for hazels. So "no fire" is catastrophic. As we say in Chicago, you take the good with the bad.

Marlin Bowles has been planting hazels in places where they used to be but haven't been lately. His sites include Waterfall Glen Forest Preserve in Du Page County, Hickory Creek Barrens in Will County, the Fermi Lab, and Morton Arboretum.

The plantings in these sites were done in a variety of conditions: open ground, woodland edge, grove, shady woods. The plants did well under a variety of light conditions, but competition from other plants had a significant effect on the fortunes of the hazels. Particularly harmful was Hungarian brome, an exotic weed that grows on open ground. Hungarian brome forms a dense sod, and that may be what hurts the hazels.

Marlin Bowles's hazels are still alive and growing, and their relative success in varying circumstances will tell us something more about this plant and about where we might hope for it to live in the future.

Shrubs are becoming a hot topic among people interested in ecological restoration and preservation. Our biggest single problem in protecting natural areas has been coping with European buckthorn. When your biggest problem is too many shrubs, you may not think a lot about how to get more shrubs. However, clearing out the competing buckthorn had to be helpful to our remaining hazel clones. Perhaps with a little push from us, hazels could be available to help feed the wild turkeys that we are certainly going to get—someday.

Hazels were important pieces of our landscape not long ago and they could be—and should be—again.

Raspberries
205 Species and Counting

July 17, 1998

This is a great year for raspberries. The little patch in our backyard is producing a dessert every night, and out in the woods the canes in the bramble thickets are heavy with fruit. I make plans for our backyard berries, plans for raspberry tarts and for berries dressed with sweetened yogurt drained of its whey and enlivened with lime juice and mint leaves. Somehow I never get to these plans. Fresh raspberries—picked, washed, and drizzled with honey—are better than any of my raspberry-gilding ideas. The old saying goes, "Doubtless God could have made a better berry than the strawberry, but doubtless God didn't." The saying is, of course, wrong. He did make a better berry—the raspberry.

When I was a kid we had a good-size raspberry patch in the backyard. My mother used to send me out to pick berries for supper. I had to pick a ton, because most of what I collected I ate on the spot.

Twenty-some years ago, my wife Glenda and I used to spend long periods of time on 40 acres of scrubby second-growth woods we owned in Taylor County, Wisconsin. Raspberries grew beside the gravel roads in the neighborhood. The roads carried maybe 12 cars a day. We could pick quarts of berries without ever breathing the dust of a passing car.

When we lived in Douglas County, Wisconsin, one of our neighbors had a small herd of Guernsey cows. Guernseys don't produce as much milk as Holsteins, but what they do produce is very rich in butter fat. We used to trade fresh berries for fresh cream so both households could enjoy the combination.

What I am saying is that I really like raspberries. However, my love for them is as nothing compared to the regard botanists feel. For botanists, raspberries are not just a wonderful dessert. They are a career.

Gray's Manual of Botany lists 205 species of the genus *Rubus*, which includes raspberries, blackberries, thimbleberries, and other brambles. (For the sake of convenience I will use the term "raspberry" to cover the lot.) The manual deals only with eastern North America, and *Rubus*

grows throughout the northern hemisphere and in mountains as far
south as South America. The worldwide species total must be enormous. Just thinking of names for all these plants would be a considerable undertaking.

Many of our eastern *Rubuses* were given their names by Liberty Hyde
Bailey, a botanist born in 1858 who wrote voluminously on the genus. Bailey was careful to give credit to the discoverers of the various species he
described, so we have *R. maltei*, named for a Swedish botanist, *R. rosagnetis* for a nun named Sister Rose Agnes Greenwell, and *R. whartoniae* for
Mary E. Wharton. We also have assorted geographical names, including
indianensis, wisconsinensis, michiganensis, and, even more localized, *kalamazoensis.* Bailey could also get positively whimsical, attaching the name
licens (unrestrained) to a spreading species, *temerarius* (ill-advised) to a
species he had originally misidentified, and *compos* (master of its domain)
to a species that tended to form extensive thickets. Bailey was himself
honored by the designation of *Rubus baileyanus,* given to a species found
in open sandy woods. All of these many names are attached to plants that
produce five-petaled flowers—almost always white—that give way to

fruits called drupelets. Drupes are fruits, like peaches and olives, with single hard stones at the center. Drupelets are aggregations of very small drupes. In raspberries the stones are small enough to be readily edible but hard enough to give a noticeable rasp to the sensation of eating a berry.

Raspberries are mostly herbaceous, but some of their canes can get a bit woody. First-year canes (primocanes) carry only leaves. The second-year canes (floricanes) carry flowers and fruit. In some species the canes are erect, in others they grow in arches, and in still others they lie along the ground. In some species the plants spread by sending up shoots from roots that spread horizontally underground. In others the arching canes take root at their tips. Either way, raspberries can form dense thickets that crowd out other plants, provide shelter for rabbits and other small animals, and offer concentrated food sources for everything from small birds to bears. Most raspberries are prickly and are therefore protected from both grazing and browsing animals.

You might reasonably ask why there are so many different kinds of plants belonging to the genus *Rubus*. The answer is complex, incorporating as it does both botanical and historical factors. We could simply blame the splitters.

Taxonomists, the people who classify plants and animals, have traditionally been divided into splitters and lumpers. Splitters tend to see tiny differences as significant enough to justify the naming of a separate species. Lumpers accept considerable variation within a single species. Maybe the genus *Rubus* is just a case of splitters going wild.

However, M. L. Fernald, the author of *Gray's Manual of Botany,* describes the genus *Rubus* as a "most difficult group." His reading of the situation is that "our few original wide-ranging, essentially unvarying and ancient species have greatly commingled since extensive clearing of the land and have crossed, producing somewhat localized but rapidly spreading offspring." He calls these offspring "incipient 'species.'"

Even the indefatigable Bailey admitted that when he used the term "new species" in connection with the genus *Rubus* he was not using the term in "its old formal, final sense." In other words, the dramatic changes we have produced in the landscape have thrown together previously separated populations and created hybrids that never could have existed before. Fernald expected that these new forms would "increase with time and new crossings."

The changes we set in motion are a long way from over. Textbooks define species as reproductively isolated groups. Even if *R. kalamazoensis* and *R. indianensis* encounter each other they shouldn't be able to reproduce. If they can, then maybe those "ancient species" were themselves only "incipient." Though separated by circumstances, they might, if thrown together, produce offspring as readily as a Frenchman and a Potawatomi.

Complicating the issue is the fact that *Rubus* is a genus in the rose family. It is a difficult group within a larger difficult group. The family includes hawthorns, a group of shrubs that may include 103 species—or far fewer or far more. Members of the rose family seem to have a strong tendency to create apparently sterile hybrids that reproduce by vegetative means such as root suckers but not through seed. Plants have an edge here. Mules, for example, have to be produced each generation by the crossing of a horse and an ass. If mules were plants, they could send up root suckers that would produce a new individual, without all the rigmarole associated with sex.

Swink and Wilhelm, in *Plants of the Chicago Region,* treat the brambles about as simply as one can. They lump several different forms into each species, ending up with ten natives. They place both *R. baileyanus* and *R. rosagnetis,* along with some others, in a species they give the common name "one-flowered dewberry." This humane approach greatly simplifies the lives of field botanists. The most visible of their species is the common blackberry, which is currently feeding birds and passing hikers on natural lands throughout the region.

For land managers in the Chicago area, brambles include everything from aggressive weeds that drive out every other plant to rare and endangered species that need protection. No fewer than three of the ten species described by Swink and Wilhelm are on the endangered or threatened lists in Illinois. Even the ability to hybridize freely and form dense, self-protecting thickets has not been enough to keep all the brambles safe.

Wild Onions
Official History Revisited

January 31, 1992

A check of my phone book reveals four listings under the name "Wild Onion." They include a restaurant and a yoga center. And though it's not in the phone book, there is also a group called the Wild Onion Alliance, whose goal is to promote bioregionalism.

All of these are named in honor of Chicago, which, according to a variety of sources, is named after a wild onion plant that was called *chicagoua* by the Miami and Illinois Indians, and the Indian town that was named after the plant. For some time there has been general agreement that the specific wild onion involved is *Allium cernuum,* nodding wild onion, a plant of the prairies with lovely pink flowers. Nodding wild onion does indeed grow in abundance on the few remaining prairies in the Chicago area.

But according to an article in a recent issue of the *Illinois Historical Journal,* the identification of Chicago with the wild onion is false. Not only that, but the city is not even located in the place the Indians call Chicagoua. In fact, the correct plant is *Allium tricoccum,* which is usually called wild leek in these parts but is also called wild garlic or, in the southern Appalachians, ramp. And the place called Chicagoua was not on the lake plain but along the Des Plaines River, probably somewhere around present-day Palos Hills.

The discoverer of the true *chicagoua* is John F. Swenson. He describes himself as a "lawyer by profession and a historian by choice," and he has unmasked two completely separate cover-ups of the truth about the name of our fair city.

Chicagoua first entered history in the late 17th century, when French missionaries and explorers entered this region. Maps dating from the 1680s show a place at the southwestern tip of Lac des Illinois (Lake Michigan) that is designated by such a name. Swenson's major source is a manuscript written by a man called Henri Joutel, a retired French soldier who accompanied La Salle on his final expedition to the North

American interior. After La Salle was murdered by one of his own men in Texas, Joutel—along with La Salle's brother and nephew and three other men—fled north, hoping to reach Quebec. They arrived at Chicago in September 1687 but decided to return to Fort Saint Louis—at present-day Starved Rock on the Illinois River—to spend the winter.

In late March or early April 1688 they returned to Chicago, and while waiting for favorable canoeing weather on Lake Michigan they explored the region. Joutel wrote of "Chicagou" that it "has taken this name because of the quantity of garlic which grows in the forests in this region." That spring they gathered the edible bulbs of this wild garlic in a maple forest and tapped the trees for sap to make syrup.

The habitat points plainly to *tricoccum* as the plant. Nodding wild onion is a prairie species, but *tricoccum* grows only in woods. There is also the question of taste. *Tricoccum*, according to everyone who has ever eaten its bulb or its leaves, tastes like garlic and not like onion. Frenchmen traveling in Illinois had sometimes survived on the bulbs of this wild garlic (*ail sauvage*), and if you can't trust a Frenchman to be able to tell onion from garlic, who can you trust?

As additional evidence, the nodding wild onion has a small tough bulb that is not very good eating. The wild leek—or wild garlic or ramp—is an excellent food plant. Its leaves and bulb are edible, and they are both good sources of vitamin C. When techniques of food preservation were poorly developed an early-spring shot of vitamin C was very important. In the Appalachians people still gather ramps in March and April. Several towns now have ramp festivals to attract tourists. According to John Swenson, these festivals are so popular that ramps are being driven to extinction in many areas. Some towns now have to send ramp hunters out as far as 100 miles to gather all the bulbs they need to feed the tourists.

Joutel and several other sources also record Illinois and Miami names for both *cernuum* and *tricoccum*, as well as for *Allium canadense*, the only other wild onion native to this region. *Tricoccum* is called *chicagoua*, while the other two have names that are quite different: *ouabipena* or *ouiscapesioua* and assorted variants.

The Miami also used the word *chicagoua* to describe skunks, though the etymological connection here is not the bad smell of skunk but the spray. The word is associated with meanings like weep, rain, spill, splash, and pour rather than with bad smells, but there is no doubt that if you step on a wild leek and crush a leaf, a rather skunklike odor results.

Joutel also wrote a careful account of his wild garlic, describing its leaves as wider and shorter than the leaves of the domestic garlic of Europe. This description fits *tricoccum*, but it does not fit the slender, grasslike leaves of *cernuum*.

From Joutel's description of the area where the *chicagoua* plants grew, it is obvious that he was in the woods along the Des Plaines River looking across the plain toward the lake. Which means that the Miami village called Chicagoua was not on the lakeshore but somewhere near the western end of one of the portages that connected Lake Michigan with the Des Plaines River. One of those portages was through the South Branch of the Chicago River and Mud Lake; the other was through the Calumet River and the Sag.

The evidence from the time makes it fairly obvious that Indians did not live on the Chicago lake plain. Marquette spent a winter in a cabin in what is now Bridgeport and reported no Indians there. Of course there probably aren't any Indians in Bridgeport now, but for somewhat different reasons.

The lake plain would have been a very inhospitable place. It was mostly prairie, and Midwestern Indians did not live on prairies. There was no firewood on prairies, the sod was so tough they couldn't plant their crops, and when the winter wind blew there was nothing to break its force. Add to that the strong tendency for the whole Chicago plain to be underwater every time it rained, and it is easy to see why the Miami stayed inland.

They may have visited the lakefront at certain times of year, but both archaeological evidence and early accounts suggest they spent more time along the Des Plaines and in the marshes around Lake Calumet than they did on the Lake Michigan beaches.

So with all this evidence pointing toward *tricoccum* as the true *chicagoua*, how is it that we have all sorts of historical authorities claiming that *cernuum* is the true plant? The historical problems begin with La Salle. The chevalier was a real promoter. He got financial backing for his expeditions by promising to produce fabulous profits for his investors. In fact, he claimed that they would double their money if they sank cash into his enterprises. The man was a true Chicagoan.

Joutel had put his life savings into La Salle's projects, and when the chevalier was killed Joutel was left without a sou. He went back to France and managed to find a job with the city of Rouen. His manuscript was "edited" by two men—Pontchartrain and Iberville—who were involved with French colonization of the gulf coast. They cut large sections out of the manuscript—mostly, Swenson thinks, because these sections might have revealed French plans to set themselves up near the lightly defended Spanish silver mines in Mexico. At the time Louis XIV was attempting to place his grandson on the throne of Spain, so it was important to the French that nothing be published that might offend the Spanish. Joutel needed his city job, so he wouldn't be likely to do anything to upset the authorities; his manuscript was published in a truncated version that left out much of importance. For his research Swenson went back to surviving manuscripts rather than relying on published versions.

The second historical cover-up dates from the last century, when historians such as John F. Steward and J. Seymour Currey decided, against the clear evidence in their source material, to anoint the nodding wild onion as the true Chicago eponym. Their decision was apparently based on their desire to claim that the present location of Chicago was also the original location of Chicagoua. Since nodding wild onion grew in the prairies on the lake plain, it had to be the plant. If it wasn't, then Palos Hills was really Chicago, and Chicago would become a city with no name. Personally, I'm thinking of opening a restaurant called the Wild Leek.

Eastern Prairie Fringed Orchid
Hand Pollinating an Endangered Plant

October 1, 1993

If you are a hawk moth, you pollinate an eastern prairie fringed orchid on a soft, warm night in early July by hovering in front of it and inserting your long proboscis past the sexual organs of the flower and deep into the long spur that hangs from the rear of the blossom. A pool of nectar as much as a centimeter deep awaits you there, and as you suck up the sugary syrup, the pollinium, the little packet of pollen in the flower, attaches itself to the side of your proboscis. When you probe another flower the pollinium will attach itself to the stigma of that bloom, allowing the pollen to grow into the ovary and fertilize the ovules there.

If you are a human being, you pollinate an eastern prairie fringed orchid by searching through likely habitat on a hot day in early July carrying a stack of Styrofoam cups and a box of toothpicks. If you find an orchid in flower you get down on your hands and knees in front of it and insert a toothpick into one of the blossoms. The pollinium sticks to the toothpick. You place an upended cup on the ground and insert the free end of the toothpick into the cup's bottom. When you have finished removing the pollinia from the dozen or so blooms on the average orchid, your cup is crowned with a little palisade of toothpicks.

You find another flowering stalk and repeat the process. Then you carefully insert the pollinated ends of the toothpicks from the first plant into the blossoms on the second plant, one at a time, and allow the pollinia to attach themselves to the stigmata in each blossom. Then you take the pollinia from the second plant and insert them, one at a time, into the flowers on the first plant.

Somehow the way the moths do it sounds like more fun. Of course we humans are capable of having fun once removed. Even the most arduous task can become a source of joy and satisfaction if we can honestly tell ourselves that the work is doing some good. This year a group of about 20 Chicago-area volunteer human pollinators got a chance to tell themselves exactly that.

They were working on one phase of a recovery plan for the eastern prairie fringed orchid, *Platanthera leucophaea,* a plant that has fallen on such hard times that it is listed as endangered in Illinois and threatened nationwide. It didn't use to be a rarity. It grows across a fairly broad segment of the moisture gradient, showing up occasionally right in the middle of the gradient in mesic prairies. It is most common in wet-mesic and wet prairies, but it can also be found in the even wetter sedge meadows and fens.

All these habitats used to be widespread in northern Illinois, and it seems likely that our area was the heart of the plant's historic range. You can still find eastern prairie fringed orchids in Michigan, Ohio, Wisconsin, and southern Ontario. West of the Mississippi the western prairie fringed orchid—the two were thought of as a single species until recently—takes over.

Illinois has 21 known populations of the orchid, more than any other state. Michigan is the runner-up with 14. Eighteen of Illinois' sites are in the northern part of the state.

The recovery plan for the species was drawn up by Marlin Bowles of the Morton Arboretum. Its major emphasis is on management of sites where the orchid now grows to improve conditions for the species. The measures recommended are familiar practices on prairies and wetlands around here: keep brush out, control exotics like purple loosestrife, burn from time to time, keep the deer population within reasonable limits. It is a regime that is likely to benefit the entire native plant community.

On some of the sites management will be handled by members of the Volunteer Stewardship Network. The state Department of Conservation is doing major management work on sites it owns. If these efforts have

their expected effect, the existing 21 populations will be vigorous, healthy, and able to sustain the species for some time.

But wouldn't it be nice if we could establish more populations? What if we could saturate northern Illinois with eastern prairie fringed orchids? We live in an area where the art of ecological restoration is entering a golden age. Thanks to the efforts of our restorationists, we have more potential sites for this plant than we did ten years ago, and each year adds to the list. Why not spread the orchids so widely that we can take them off the lists for good?

This is where the two-legged hawk moths come in. Back in 1981 Steve Packard of the Nature Conservancy hand pollinated some eastern prairie fringed orchids on a site along the North Branch of the Chicago River. The plants produced abundant seed, which he scattered on the site. Five years later—it takes that long for the orchids to mature—the plants that grew from the seeds he scattered produced flowers.

That experience provided the basis for a small grant from the U.S. Fish and Wildlife Service to the Nature Conservancy for a joint project to help restore the eastern prairie fringed orchid. The project would use volunteer labor to hand pollinate the plants in July. The volunteers would return in late September and early October to gather the mature seed capsules. The seeds would be scattered either on the same site or in a new location.

It is not a wild exaggeration to say that this kind of project could happen only in the Chicago area. The Volunteer Stewardship Network and all its associated restoration efforts along the North Branch of the Chicago River, at Poplar Creek, in the Palos area, around the Sand Ridge Nature Center, and at dozens of other places have created an army of hundreds—perhaps thousands—of dedicated, knowledgeable field botanists. Chicago is a place where a discussion of the ecology of prairie grasses can fill a college lecture hall with 300 schoolteachers, mail carriers, dentists, and carpenters, all of whom will understand every word that is said—including the long strings of scientific names. Scientists who come from elsewhere to give talks in Chicago are always amazed to encounter this level of knowledge and enthusiasm among laypeople.

Amelia Orton-Palmer, an endangered-species biologist with the U.S. Fish and Wildlife Service office in Barrington, talks of the "incredible commitment and knowledge" of the local volunteers. "This area is really special in that regard. The citizenry is really tied in."

The tied-in citizens who pollinated the orchids in July are now out collecting the mature seed capsules. According to Bowles, leaving the matter entirely to the hawk moths would result in pollination of about half of the 12 or so flowers on each plant. Hand pollination approaches 100 percent. The reproductive strategy of orchids involves producing very large numbers of very small seeds. Each flower produces a capsule that contains as many as 5,000 seeds.

Part of the high-powered scientific equipment provided for each volunteer—along with the toothpicks and Styrofoam cups—is a small white bowl. The volunteers are instructed to count out 25 tiny seeds into the bowl and eyeball the 25 so they know what 25 seeds look like. Then they can pick up approximately that number, one pinch at a time, and scatter them.

Some of the capsules will be tied to tall grass stems with gray thread (more sophisticated scientific equipment—of course if the Pentagon were buying this stuff the thread would cost $100 a foot). As the capsule deteriorates, the wind will carry the seeds away just as it would if the capsule were still on the orchid.

So far the seeds have been dispersed to 17 sites. Most of these either have populations or have had populations in recent times. All are protected sites where active management will give the orchids a reasonable chance of survival.

No one knows yet whether the orchids require special mycorrhizal fungi to thrive. All plants enter into symbiotic relations with fungi that live on their roots. Most of these mycorrhizal fungi can spread their spores without any aid. But if the orchids require something special, the seeds will need to be mixed with soil from places where the plants already grow. Bowles is currently examining this question.

The outcome of this project will only begin to be revealed five years from now, when this year's scattered seeds begin to produce flowers. Until then our two-legged hawk moths will be out in July with their toothpicks.

[This successful program continues, mostly in the area served by Chicago Wilderness.]

6 › People and Places

Field Guides
Nature Is a Process, Not a Vista

September 8, 1989

In the last decade, the field guide has become the most common type of book about nature. Field guides are not new, of course. In one form or other, they have been around for at least a century. Roger Tory Peterson's *A Field Guide to the Birds,* originally published in 1934, played a major role in creating the sport of birding, and its success inspired not only other bird guides but a whole series of Peterson Guides that covered practically every visible aspect of nature, from stars and planets to seashells.

Peterson was directly involved only in his bird books and in a wild-flower guide, but all the many volumes in the Houghton Mifflin series used his identification system wherever possible. The Peterson system, which is copyrighted, uses a small number of field marks to differentiate entities of similar appearance. I can't use a word more precise than "entity" because the Peterson system has been applied to everything from mollusks to white dwarfs.

The Peterson bird guides—the original described only eastern birds, but a volume covering western birds was published in 1941—had little true competition for several decades. Richard Pough of the American Museum of Natural History published a two-volume Audubon guide to North American birds in 1946. A two-volume work is a bit cumbersome for field use, but it did allow Pough to include some information on nesting habits and behavior that wouldn't have fit into Peterson's more compact books.

Golden Books published a one-volume guide to North American birds in 1966, with Chandler Robbins of the U.S. Fish and Wildlife Service as principal author. The Golden guide pulled some customers away from Peterson.

But the typical nature book of the late '60s and the '70s was either a how-to account of outdoor activities like backpacking or an introduction to ecology, an inspirational look at the way nature works. The leader in the former category was *The Compleat Walker* by Colin Fletcher. The first edition became a best seller and something of a publishing phenomenon in 1968. A thorough revision followed in 1974. Fletcher is an engaging writer who can make backpacking in summer in Arizona sound appealing, and his books helped set off a backpacking boom that soon overcrowded trail systems from Georgia to the Brooks Range.

This boom, like most of the other recreational booms of the past 30 years, was fueled by the ultimate boom: babies. Further force was provided by remarkable advances in equipment. The backpacker of the '50s carried a canvas tent and wooden poles in a pack mounted on a flat board that bore no relationship to the contours of the human back. If you have ever tried to roll up a wet canvas tent, you can appreciate how much easier things got when synthetics like nylon replaced canvas as the tent makers' choice.

The equipment shift created a major change in the relationship between humans and the wilderness landscape. When I was in the Boy Scouts way back when, the camping techniques we learned all fell into the general category of woodcraft. We were taught how to cut down saplings to build temporary shelters and how to make comfortable beds out of spruce boughs. By 1970 such skills were not only unnecessary, they were positively harmful. The backcountry was so full of wilderness trekkers that if all of them had cut spruce boughs for beds, the forest would have looked as if it had been dosed with Agent Orange.

With aluminum cookware, a stove fueled by white gas, a nylon tent, and a sleeping bag filled with polyester, a backpacker could "take only pictures, leave only footprints," as the motto of the times advised. Of course, treading lightly on the wilderness required oil fields on Alaska's North Slope and vast bauxite strip mines in Jamaica, but that irony was something nobody liked to think about.

The new ethic and the new equipment also severed the intimate relationship between backpacker and wilderness. If you were going to rely on spruce boughs for bedding you had to know what a spruce tree looked like, but the modern trekker with his house on his back and his skin coated with Deep Woods Off could see the world as a show, a flattened image like the picture on a movie screen. As long as his equipment held out, he didn't need to know anything about the world he was traveling through.

That was an ultimately unsatisfying way to relate to nature, and its shallowness was beautifully revealed in books like Aldo Leopold's *Sand*

County Almanac, a wonderful work that popularized the science of ecology.

Things are happening out there, Leopold told us. It's not just a vista, it's a process, or more precisely, a whole bewildering set of processes whose operations sustain the lives of all the individuals and all the species on earth. We can't hope to understand these processes completely, but if we are willing to learn about them, we can comprehend some pieces of this complexity and get at least a vague, general sense of the whole. But like Adam in the garden, we can't discover a new world until we can put names to things. And that's where the field guides come in.

My wife, Glenda Daniel, and I lived through this evolution. In the early '70s we wrote two where-to guides to backpacking, one describing trails in the Midwest, the other covering the southern Appalachians. Then in 1977 Glenda wrote *Dune Country,* a field guide to the Indiana Dunes, and in 1981 we wrote *A Naturalist's Guide to the North Woods* for the Sierra Club books.

The latter book grew out of our experiences on some land we bought in Taylor County, Wisconsin. Our 40 acres was an absolutely undistinguished second-growth woods pocked with alder thickets that were underwater every month except August, when they were just muddy. Our land was not the sort of place that got selected as a nature preserve, but we had nesting marsh hawks, American bitterns, barred owls, and rotted-out white pine stumps so big the two of us could stand inside them.

We cleared a space big enough for a 10-by-16-foot tent and took advantage of our freelancers' status to spend a big piece of every summer exploring our land and other interesting places in the neighborhood. We waded through acres of bogs, compared spring wildflowers in pine woods with the ones that grew in sugar-maple forests, and searched for boreal chickadees and Connecticut warblers.

We began to get a feel for the region. The flat, movielike image, the meaningless jumble of shapes, textures, and colors, became coherent; the rare species we used to miss suddenly jumped out at us. Our new view allowed every plant and animal its individuality while combining each separate organism into a whole whose beauty was levels beyond what any movie image could show.

The search for that kind of experience of nature has provided a large part of the impetus behind the explosion of field guides, especially the habitat guides that have followed the Sierra Club's pioneering efforts. One of the best of these has just been published by NorthWord Press, of

Minocqua, Wisconsin. Called *Northwoods Wildlife: A Watcher's Guide to Habitats,* it was written by Janine Benyus with substantial assistance from members of the staff of the U.S. Forest Service's North Central Forest Experiment Station in Saint Paul.

The beauty of the book is its specificity. It covers only the transition-forest region that dominates the northern portions of Michigan, Wisconsin, and Minnesota. Since late in the last century, the cool woodlands of that region have been prime vacation destinations for those of us living in the hotter, duller parts of the Midwest. The book divides these woods into 18 separate habitat types and describes the prominent vertebrates likely to be found in each.

Each species gets a general introduction, followed by detailed tips on exactly where to look, what to look for, and what to listen for. So we learn that LeConte's sparrows can be found in sedge meadows, that they seldom fly very far, that their nests are usually found on or near the ground at the dry edges of the meadows, and that their song is a single, repeated "thin, husky, and insect-like" note.

We learn that dawn and dusk are the times to look for meadow voles, that their nests are balls of dried grass hidden under rocks and logs, that their runways are paths about an inch wide usually roofed over with grasses, and that early spring, when the grasses are matted down, is the best time to look for them.

If you are looking for deer, hunt for scrapes—patches of bare ground scraped clean by a buck's hoof and then urinated on as a message to rival males and possibly interested females.

The guide also includes a list of hot spots, places where wildlife watching is likely to be particularly productive, a month-by-month almanac describing what you can see and when you can see it, and a listing of state ornithological groups and other organizations involved with conservation in the north woods.

The thing I like best about this book is its emphasis on sitting down and shutting up. The best way to see animals is to find a likely spot and then make yourself as inconspicuous as possible. The animals are there, if you have the patience to let them come to you. Nature rewards silence and immobility.

[*Northwoods Wildlife: A Watcher's Guide to Habitats* by Janine M. Benyus is out of print.]

Surveying Illinois
How Humans Shaped the Landscape

June 21, 1996

I have been studying what was here before we current inhabitants of Chicagoland arrived, what lived on the land before we transformed it into cornfields, pastures, Norwood Park, Floodplain Manor, the Ford assembly plant, and the Proviso rail yard.

Early accounts of life in the Prairie State often described the landscape in general terms. The most detailed come from the survey reports of the U.S. government's land office, made between about 1820 and 1840. In those days the federal government was essentially a real estate agency. Taxes were almost nonexistent, because much of the revenue the government needed came from land sales. But before they could sell it they had to survey it. Using a system devised by Thomas Jefferson, the land office subdivided every survey tract into six-mile-square townships and one-mile-square sections.

The surveyors had one of the worst jobs in the world. They waded through swamps under clouds of mosquitoes, lived on hardtack and bacon when they couldn't get game, and had to work hard to meet their quota of section lines surveyed. They also had one of the best jobs in the world. They wandered over northeastern Illinois through prairies decorated with blazing stars and bobolinks, stopped for lunch under the gnarled limbs of giant bur oaks, and nodded off to sleep while wolves sang in the distance. It would beat the hell out of staring at a computer screen all day.

An ecologist looking to learn as much as he could and as fast as he could about a new place would set up transects, straight lines like those Jefferson's system demanded. Our ecologist would then study the vegetation along the transect lines, assembling a picture of the whole landscape by extrapolating from that sample.

The surveyors did essentially the same thing, walking Jefferson's lines and recording every significant shift in vegetation along the way. So we read of section lines that were so many chains of "prairie fit for cultivation," followed by "well-timbered" land for a few more chains, and then maybe some marshland (chains were the surveyors' standard unit of measure; each chain was 66 feet long, and there were 80 chains to the mile). The surveyors marked each section corner and half-mile point on each section line by locating it in relation to nearby "witness trees." These trees were marked with blazes, and the surveyors' notes record their species, size, and direction and distance from the point.

We can learn a lot about what was here then by studying these witness trees. The surveyors would pick the largest and nearest trees, so if they had to go 50 feet and the tree they chose was only eight inches in diameter we can safely conclude that timber was sparse and trees were small on that spot. On prairies where there were no trees at all the points were marked with heaps of charcoal.

The species of the witness trees tell us something about the kinds of woods that surrounded these points. In a paper presented at the fifth Midwest Prairie Conference in 1976 Robbin Moran constructed a map of the presettlement vegetation of Lake County, Illinois, based on surveyors' reports. The surveyors recorded 2,240 witness trees of 21 species in the county, though 90 percent were bur, black, and white oak. Trees that are now common, such as black cherries and basswoods, were evidently quite scarce then. Only 11 basswoods show up as witness trees and just two black cherries.

The map strongly supports the idea of a landscape shaped by fire, with the fire-resistant oaks dominating the wooded lands and the fire-sensitive cherries and basswoods confined to areas where the topography provided fire protection. Much of the county was open savanna. The surveyors used terms like "scattering timber" to describe these open groves. On average they had to go 30 meters from the surveyed point to find a witness tree in this sort of surroundings.

Philip Hanson of the Field Museum did a study similar to Moran's of the Chicago lake plain, the flat former lake bottom where most of the city stands. Early travelers wrote that you could see the trees along the Des Plaines River from the lakeshore at the mouth of the Chicago River, and Hanson's map bears out that description.

If you had started west from the lakefront along the section line that became North Avenue you would have begun in a black oak savanna on the sands near the shore. The savanna would continue west to a point just past Clybourn. There, on low ground protected from fire by the river just to the west, you would enter a floodplain forest of silver maple and basswood. When you reached the bank of the sparkling clear

Chicago River you could look at prairie—much of it wet—stretching to the Des Plaines River.

Crossing that prairie, you could look north to around Foster and Pulaski, where the Bohemian National Cemetery is now, and see what was probably the only patch of sugar maple forest on the plain. Beyond it, stretching all the way to Wilmette, was an oak-hickory woods.

The local history I was taught paid little attention to the native landscape. We were given a vision of darkness illuminated briefly and intermittently by the writings of Marquette and Joliet, La Salle, and an assortment of other French, English, and American visitors who gave us glimpses of what was here between 1673 and about 1800. Real history began with Fort Dearborn and ended in massacre. It rose again in the 1830s when an assortment of hustlers—all convinced that Chicago was going to be a very lively location—began buying and selling large tracts of underwater real estate.

In places where the major scenic attractions are 10,000-foot pointed rocks you can get away with some reckless disregard for the rest of nature. Here in northeastern Illinois local history nearly obliterated the local landscape. We lost all but one of our big mammals. Only white-tailed deer survive from a fauna that included bison, elk, black bear, timber wolf, and puma. We lost wild turkeys, sharp-tailed grouse, prairie chickens, passenger pigeons, bald eagles, ravens, and swallow-tailed kites. No one could begin to guess how many insects departed. Many of our native plants have been reduced to the status of rarities. They hang on in a few lucky spots that have escaped the general carnage but are missing from hundreds of locations where they used to thrive.

As a culture, we haven't even kept that landscape alive as memory. Indeed, it vanished so quickly we don't have any memories to keep alive. We look on fields of Hungarian brome and Queen Anne's lace and white sweet clover and begin to see those botanical refugee camps as nature. Having no memories or attachments to the particularities of this place, we look on trees and fields as generic. Bur oak or Lombardy poplar, a tree is a tree. The people with memories—the Native Americans—were rounded up and shipped off to reservations west of the Mississippi. Aside from the moral quality of that act, intellectually it was the equivalent of burning down a library.

We now, belatedly, realize that the beautiful, rich, enormously diverse natural landscape of northeastern Illinois depended on human action for its survival. The fires that shaped the land were, to a considerable extent, set by human beings. The Potawatomi and their predecessors on this land were engaged in managing natural areas. The pernicious national myth that North America was an empty continent just waiting for us to supply it with people has prevented us from seeing this.

We also think of nature as a thing we encounter only on the battlefield. We are at war with nature. We intervene only to destroy. Our ignorance of a local history before the French came combines with our bellicose attitudes about humanity and nature to create a fatal estrangement. Our attempts to reestablish the connection that used to exist between people and the rest of nature in northeastern Illinois, and in the process to rescue the great natural beauty and diversity that ought to be our heritage, can become a matter of controversy. When plans are announced to restore savanna conditions to a forest preserve, people in the area often start screaming, mostly because they don't have any idea what savanna conditions are. They demand to know why restorers seem to worry so much about oak trees, which is like demanding to know why northern Californians get so worked up about redwoods or why people in Tucson get excited about saguaro cactus.

My own biases in this area should be clear to anybody who had been reading my columns over the years. I have been involved in ecological restoration for close to 20 years, sometimes as a paid worker but mostly as a volunteer. I have seen the results of restoration in preserves all over the region. I would invite everyone to go look at the land. Restoration works, and if you take the time to look you can see it working.

Inland Marsh

Brush and Savanna Birds

January 5, 1996

The place the National Park Service calls Inland Marsh is a complex landscape of high dunes and broad, low marshlands. It is a remnant of an earlier stage in Lake Michigan's development. When the winds were piling up these dunes the water's edge was about a mile south of the present shoreline.

Inland Marsh is part of the West Beach Unit of the Indiana Dunes National Lakeshore. Between it and the present shore are U.S. 12, a set of railroad tracks, Long Lake, and the high dunes and interdunal ponds of West Beach. The upland portions of Inland Marsh are covered with an oak savanna, and black oak is the most common tree. A rich understory combines prairie species like little bluestem and switchgrass, southern forest shrubs like sassafras, and northern species like blueberry. These black oak savannas growing on sandy soils are among the distinctive features of the vegetation of the Indiana Dunes.

I've been very fond of Inland Marsh for a long time. Thirteen years ago I did my first surveys on nesting birds there, getting a taste of an activity that now seems to have taken over much of my life. Doing censuses is obviously a seasonal project, but organizing them and compiling them can eat up most of the year.

I knew almost nothing about savannas in the spring of 1983. In those days prairies were the center of attention. We were studying prairie remnants and restoring prairies on old fields or on lands that had been invaded by box elders and other low-status woody vegetation. You could say there was a lot of generalized antitree feeling around, and even oaks—now objects of almost druidic admiration—were looked on with some suspicion.

I took a walk around Inland Marsh last Saturday, and what I saw brought back some memories and also raised some interesting questions for future study. Some weird stuff was still present, like the ancient car hulk that is slowly rusting away between steep sand hills. It must have been a real project getting that thing through the deep sands to this remote spot. You wonder why anybody would want to go to all that trouble just to get rid of a car.

When I first surveyed Inland Marsh I was most interested in the possibility of finding some neat wetland birds. I did find—or at least hear—one such marsh species. Twice in the predawn darkness I heard the unmistakable call of the king rail, a very nice bird indeed. But in my fantasies I was finding nests of king rails or maybe the female (queen rail?) slipping through the reeds accompanied by eight or ten downy chicks. Just hearing the bird off in the distance was way short of the experience I was after.

Aside from the distant rail, the wetlands produced very ordinary species, mostly redwings and marsh wrens. But the savannas, the upland portions of Inland Marsh, were beginning to tell me a story, though I didn't fully recognize it at the time. The story was about the birds of savannas, the avian community that lived in the landscape that occupied a major portion of northeastern Illinois before settlement. Nearly all that landscape has been destroyed.

The story of its bird life, like the story of its plant life, has to be assembled from various sources, and Inland Marsh was the first of my own sources. Scarlet tanagers were part of the story. My estimate was that four or five pairs nested there in 1983. At the time I was somewhat surprised to find them in such an open situation. Not only are the trees scattered, but the steep slopes put the crowns of adjacent trees at very different levels, making the canopy seem even more open. I expected tanagers to live in dense forests. However, all the books do say that these birds have a strong affinity for oaks, so maybe that was the attraction.

Inland Marsh was also the first place I heard the nest call of the Cooper's hawk. This high-pitched *ki-ki-ki-ki* is a sound they make only around their nest, so just hearing it was enough to confirm nesting. This species is scarce in most places. It is on the endangered list in many states, including Illinois, so finding a pair nesting is a big deal. Again I was somewhat surprised to find this species in such an open situation.

I would be much less surprised to find either of these species there now. Now we are thinking in terms of savanna birds, and both the tanagers and the Cooper's hawks seem to be candidates for the savanna bird list. You can see some logic in that in the case of the hawk. It is primarily a bird eater and typically perches quietly on a limb while keeping an eye out for movement below. The open understory of the savanna offers less cover for potential prey than the shrubbier conditions of a forest.

Down at ground level at Inland Marsh I found bobwhites. Our only eastern quail is essentially a southern species that hits the northern end of its range at the Indiana Dunes. In the pine forests of the southern coastal plain this species is typically found where soil conditions—and frequent fires—produce a sparse understory. Another prime candidate for savanna bird status.

In 1983 Inland Marsh had not been burned in some time, and portions of it had been taken over by thickets of aspen. In those dense thickets I found yellow warblers, yellow-breasted chats, towhees, field sparrows, and other species of brush birds. Except then I wouldn't have called them brush birds. I would have called them edge birds and assumed they were there because they liked being at the edge of groves of larger trees. Now we realize that brush is the attraction and that these birds will find islands of brush out in the middle of a prairie. They don't actually need edges.

We are thinking a lot about the place of these brush birds in our natural areas. As a group these species are in some trouble because their favored habitat is so dependent on human intervention in the landscape. Most available brushy areas were once something else; they're former woods or old fields that are simply passing through a brush phase while we figure out what to do with them. You can get some emotion behind a campaign to save the prairies or preserve the stately oak woods. But a campaign to save brushy thickets somehow doesn't seem like the sort of thing that would inspire much passion. Most of our ecological restoration efforts involve removing brush—usually exotic species—so probrush opinion is hard to find.

On my visit to Inland Marsh last Saturday I did notice some changes in the landscape, changes that are probably the result of fires. There have been prescribed burns in the area in the past decade, and I believe there was one wildfire as well. The fires and, I suspect, some cutting have reduced the area covered by the aspen tangles. This means less habitat for the brush birds.

My impression was that more prairie plants are growing at Inland Marsh now than were there 13 years ago, but this is only an impression. The most startling change was the presence of dense thickets of black oak on many of the hillsides. Fires often kill the aboveground parts of trees, but the roots can survive the flames. In the spring following the fire these roots produce new shoots—often many new shoots. The presence of many trees with multiple trunks is a strong clue that a hot fire burned through sometime in the past.

The young black oaks at Inland Marsh are virtually all multitrunked.

They range in height from less than 2 feet to about 15 feet, and their shrubby shapes form lovely brushy thickets. I found this rather startling because restoration efforts over the past couple of decades have usually involved removing brushy thickets so oaks can get enough light to reproduce, but here the oaks were the brushy thickets. It was a real treat to see them aggressively taking over the landscape.

Next June I will have to go back to find out if brush birds are nesting in these oak thickets. If they are we could have a solution to a vexing management problem. We tend to think that management—especially fire management—will produce a landscape of prairies alternating with stately groves of large oaks. The flames will keep down the brush, reduce the understory, and maintain the open oak groves that early travelers encountered in northeastern Illinois. But that vision leaves no room for the brush birds. Inland Marsh suggests that the effects of fire can be more varied—that fires can produce brushy tangles as well as destroy them. And that there will be space for yellow-breasted chats in a restored landscape.

Women Naturalists

Eighteen Forgotten Writers

July 25, 1986

I developed a crush on Cordelia J. Stanwood while reading Arthur Cleveland Bent's multivolume series *Life Histories of North American Birds.* She is especially prominent in the two-volume set on wood warblers, the tiny, usually brightly colored insect eaters that mostly nest in the forests of the northern U.S. and Canada.

The bibliography lists three articles she wrote on wood warblers, two published in the *Journal of the Maine Ornithological Society,* one printed in the *Auk,* the journal of the American Ornithologists Union. All are dated 1910. But most of the citations and quotes in the two volumes are credited to unpublished manuscripts or to private correspondence.

To give you an idea of what attracted me, I quote a portion of Miss Stanwood's account of a pair of black-throated green warblers building a nest in a fir tree near her home in Ellsworth, Maine:

> First they laid knots of spider's silk and little curls of white birch bark in the shape of the nest, on the horizontal fork about midway of a branch six feet long. Next bits of fine grass, a little usnea moss, and cedar bark fibre. Both the male and female worked on the nest, . . . the female shaping it with the breast each time they added a bit of material. Around the top were carefully laid the finest gray spruce twigs. These were bound together with masses of white spider's silk. . . . The lady bird continued to shape the nest with her breast, turning around and around, as if swinging on a central pivot, just her beak and tail showing above the rim. If I came too near, she stood up in the nest as if to fly. If I withdrew to a respectful distance, say three yards, she went on with her work of shaping the nest. . . . On the second day the rim of the nest seemed about completed. . . . On the fourth day, by touching the inside of the nest with the tips of my

fingers, I judged that the lining was about finished. It consisted of rabbit-hair and horse-hair, felted or woven together
so as to be very thick and firm.

The beauty of this passage may not be immediately apparent. The
prose is no more than workmanlike. It does avoid—as do all her writings that I have seen—the excessive cuteness that mars nature writing of
the second rank. There is no talk of maids and swains, no attempt to turn
birds into characters in a medieval romance. She is a careful and precise
observer who records exactly what she sees.

What impresses me is that she spent so much time just sitting and
looking, sitting quietly enough to avoid disturbing a skittish pair of
birds building a nest. Other excerpts from her work show that she was
equally quiet and attentive while recording the actions of adults feeding
young in the nest and young birds preparing to leave the nest.

Now you may think that sitting still and paying attention is no big
deal, but perhaps you have never been in a northern spruce-fir forest in
June. As it happens, I have been in several, and I can tell you that they

are in many respects terrible places. The weather is either cold and damp or hot and humid. The thick foliage deadens the liveliest breeze. And the bugs! Mosquitoes buzz around your ears, fly into your mouth, land on your eyelids. Assorted carnivorous flies chew on every bit of exposed skin. Ticks crawl up your legs.

If you are walking at a brisk pace and free to slap when necessary, you can endure this assault. But sitting still, not slapping, not even waving your arms to fend off the most aggressive bugs, takes patience of a saintly order. Reading Cordelia Stanwood's detailed accounts of the lives of wood warblers, realizing what she had gone through to gather this information, I thought: this is my kind of woman.

But she was a total mystery to me. I knew nothing of her beyond what Bent allowed me to guess. Now thanks to an interesting new anthology called *Birdwatching with American Women,* edited by Deborah Strom and published by Norton, I have learned a bit more about her life and about the lives and work of 17 other American women who wrote about nature.

Strom's interest is in tracing the evolution of nature writing by women. Her earliest selections were published prior to the turn of the century, and nearly all were printed before World War II. She avoids such recent and well-known practitioners as Rachel Carson and Annie Dillard.

Most of the work in this book comes from the era of the first great awakening of interest in conserving nature in North America. It seems strange to us now that in those times no species of bird was protected in any way. Frank Chapman, the first editor of *Bird Lore* magazine, recorded a list of 40 species of North American birds fastened to women's hats on two walks around lower Manhattan in 1886. The adornments ranged from single feathers to wings to whole stuffed birds and included such unlikely species as the saw-whet owl, the northern shrike, and the pileated woodpecker. Small boys routinely sharpened their skills with slingshots, BB guns, and thrown stones by slaughtering songbirds.

Many of the women represented in the anthology both recorded and contributed to the change in our attitudes that has come about since Chapman did his hat birding in Manhattan. Sarah Orne Jewett, a writer of fiction, is represented by a story called "The White Heron," about a little girl who decides not to tell a bird collector the location of a rare New England nest of the snowy egret, the white heron of the title. The girl is offended by his desire to shoot the bird, stuff it, and mount it in his collection. To her, the bird is only beautiful alive.

Several of the 18 writers were active in the nature education movement. Anna Botsford Comstock, the first woman to be named a full professor at Cornell, is represented by curriculum materials she wrote to teach nature study in the primary grades. School nature study programs became commonplace in the first conservation era, and millions of children learned to identify birds and wildflowers through them. Even Roger Tory Peterson got his start this way.

Inevitably, there is some silliness represented, especially by Neltje Blanchan Doubleday, the wife of Nelson Doubleday, founder of the publishing firm. Mrs. Doubleday wrote a number of books on birds aimed at both children and adults. Her works sold well, but they were often more fanciful than true, and some of her attitudes toward natural things were absurd. She hated bird-eating hawks like the sharp-shinned hawk and the goshawk, and happily, and ignorantly, urged their extermination. According to Theodore Dreiser, Mrs. Doubleday was instrumental in suppressing the Doubleday edition of *Sister Carrie* because of its supposed indecency, so apparently she made a habit of being wrong.

Several wives are represented in the collection, women like Helen Cruickshank and Eleanor Pettingill, who wrote popular accounts of their husbands' fieldwork in ornithology. Florence Merriam Bailey was married to Vernon Bailey of the U.S. Biological Survey, but she did distinguished scientific work on her own. Her brother, C. Hart Merriam, was for many fruitful years the director of the survey, and Mrs. Bailey shared his love of nature. She founded the District of Columbia Audubon Society, and on expeditions with her husband she studied the birds while he examined the mammals. Her *Handbook of the Birds of the Western United States,* published in 1902, went through several editions and became the standard work in the field.

She is represented by a charming reminiscence of a summer spent birding in San Diego County, California, in 1894. The piece is sharply observed and witty, and makes you wish you had been there with her.

The big discovery for me was Mary Austin, a writer whose work I had not previously seen. She was born in Illinois and moved to California after finishing college. She lived for three years in the San Joaquin Valley, and a book about that place called *Land of Little Rain* made her famous, and rich enough to spend the rest of her life writing. She lived in a cabin in Carmel for a time, hanging out with Ambrose Bierce and Jack London, and then moved on to New York and New Mexico. She was an active suffragette and a lecturer on birth control.

The anthology excerpts a chapter called "Scavengers" from *Land of*

Little Rain. Ostensibly about the buzzards and vultures (she seems to use the former term for turkey vultures and the latter for California condors) of the San Joaquin, it is really about the horrors of a prolonged drought that killed cattle by the herd. It is powerful writing, and it made me want to read the whole book.

Cordelia Stanwood is represented in this compilation not by any writings but by photographs. It turns out that she was a splendid bird photographer. Her pictures, mostly of young birds, are filled with joy and life. There is a photograph of her too, taken in 1894 when she was 29 years old. Her dress and hair are in the stern New England style, but her gaze is cool and intelligent, her eyes full of sympathy.

The sad facts of her life are summarized in a biographical sketch. Born in 1865, the daughter of a successful merchant sea captain, she taught school in various New England towns for 17 years, but retreated to the family home in 1904 to recover from a nervous breakdown brought on by overwork and—according to Strom—"the difficulties of being an isolated spinster."

She remained there for the rest of her long life, studying the birds of the neighborhood. She could not find a publisher for a manuscript of *The Birds of Maine.* She had the respect of a few ornithologists who knew her work, but to her neighbors she was a strange, reclusive old lady. Local children called her a witch. She died in 1958, in what state of mind, I wonder? Was she embittered by her loneliness and lack of recognition? Or did nature sustain her through the trials of her life? That I still don't know.

[*Birdwatching with American Women: A Selection of Nature Writings,* edited by Deborah Strom, is out of print.]

Bird-Watchers
How the Sport Got Started

August 28, 1987

Charles J. Pennock was one of the finest birders in the country around the turn of the century. A prosperous Philadelphia businessman, he was also a longtime president of the Delaware Valley Ornithological Club, the snootiest birding club in North America, a group so exclusive that it refused to admit women until 1982.

Pennock was in every respect a solid citizen: a justice of the peace, a member of the board of the Philadelphia Academy of Sciences, a volunteer curator at the academy's museum, a devoted husband and father.

But on the night of May 15, 1913, he disappeared. His frantic family notified the police. But a missing persons bulletin about a gray-bearded man, 55 years old, wearing a dark suit with gray stripes and a stand-up collar, produced no responses.

The years went by. The Delaware Valley Ornithological Club began listing him as a "Deceased Member." His wife, despairing, donated his huge collections of birds, eggs, and ornithological books to the Philadelphia Academy.

But not long after Pennock's disappearance, a new name began to appear in the ornithological journals. A John Williams was filing excellent reports from the tiny village of Saint Marks on the gulf coast of Florida just south of Tallahassee. Mr. Williams did splendid work, full of careful observation, and since he lived in one of the richest birding areas in the country, editors welcomed his submissions. He was elected, sight unseen, to the American Ornithologists Union and the Wilson Ornithological Club, and even became a fellow in absentia of the Delaware Valley Ornithological Club.

Skilled ornithologists were not exactly as common as house sparrows in the U.S. 70 years ago, but somehow Mr. Williams's excellent writings didn't arouse any curiosity as to where he came from and how he came to know so much about birds. Finally, his handwriting betrayed him. He sent a manuscript to an old friend, who tipped off his family. His brother-in-law traveled to Saint Marks and discovered that John Williams was in fact Charles Pennock. He had tried to vanish. He had shaved his beard, changed his name, moved far away, but he couldn't get over his fascination with birds, and that had exposed him.

Mr. Pennock's strange story is one of a wealth of tales contained in *A World of Watchers* by Joseph Kastner, a history of both professional and amateur bird-watching in America from the Indians to the present day.

This is social history of a high order, a tracing of changes in attitudes and actions over time and a gallery of portraits of some intriguing characters who were in the thick of those changes.

Mr. Kastner begins with the Indians. His information is necessarily sketchy. He has some bird names that suggest the unsurprising idea that Indians were quite familiar with the songs and habits of the birds, and he has an anecdote about an ornithologist who went birding with some Apaches in the 1870s. The Indians saw so many more birds than the ornithologist that they decided that white men must be blind.

The rest of the book is about the discovery of America by Europeans, a process that took more than 300 years, and the changes in attitude that the discovery produced. The story starts with very early reports, such as Captain John Smith's first sketchy account of eagles, "hawkes of diverse sorts . . . wild turkies, . . . blackbirds with red shoulders," and "some other strange kinds unknown by name" around the Jamestown settlement, and continues through Margaret Morse Nice's intimate history of the life of the song sparrow. It runs from John James Audubon's remark that "I call birds few when I shoot less than 100 per day" to the strict protection laws passed under the inspiration of the society that bears his name.

This story has been told before in various ways and in various places, but Kastner brings it all together. And he has a very nice feel for the people involved, the forceful and often contentious personalities who created the situation we have today, with bird protection a settled fact and millions of people spending time outdoors watching birds.

Conservatives may be dismayed to learn it, but the U.S. government played a central role in all this from very early in the game. In fact, in the last half of the 19th century, during the golden age of American ornithology, much of the most important work was accomplished by the U.S. Army Medical Corps.

The man behind that development was Spencer Fullerton Baird.

Appointed assistant secretary of the newly created Smithsonian Institution in 1850 and promoted to secretary in 1878, he remade the study of natural history—as field biology was then called—in North America.

His years at the Smithsonian could also be called the golden age of American imperialism. With army units setting out to the west to pacify and explore the vast territories newly stolen from Mexico and/or the native Indians, Baird had an opportunity to fill in some very large empty spaces on the ornithological map.

Thanks to his lobbying and his superb connections—his father-in-law was the inspector general of the army—he managed to make natural history collecting a part of the army's duties in the new lands. George McClellan, later commander of the Union armies in the Civil War, was one of his better correspondents.

But most of the work was done by doctors, the only military men with scientific training, and the only military men who could dissect a specimen and make sense of what they found inside.

So from isolated frontier forts, and from the expeditions that explored the routes that the railroads would later follow west, Baird's doctors sent crates of specimens to the Smithsonian. They came from William Alexander Hammond (after whom Hammond's flycatcher is named), from Elliott Coues (Coues' flycatcher), from Charles Bendire (Bendire's thrasher), from Janos Xantus (Xantus murrelet), and from William Anderson, whose wife is honored in the name of Virginia's warbler.

The interested amateur has always played an important role in ornithology, and a bit over a century ago, the amateurs began to organize. The first birding society was the Nuttall Ornithological Club of Cambridge, Massachusetts, formed in 1873 by a group of well-connected Bostonians. A Nuttall member was expected to have "good moral character, genuine interest in bird study, a reputation for accuracy, and qualities of heart and mind that make a man clubbable." The Nuttall Club did not admit women until 1974.

The Linnaean Society of New York was founded in 1878 for the study of natural history, and particularly birds. Like the Nuttall Club, it drew its members from leading families. Several Vanderbilts belonged and so did various Roosevelts, including, at different times, both President Roosevelts.

But about 70 years ago, the Linnaean Society began to change. The change was initiated by Ludlow Griscom, the prophet of birding with field glasses rather than shotguns, and it was carried on by a bunch of high school kids from the Bronx, lads of obscure origin with very little money. Their main guidebook had been salvaged from a garbage can by one of their members.

These smart-assed teenagers—they called themselves the Bronx County Bird Club—astounded their stuffy elders with the sightings they reported and their ability to defend the accuracy of those sightings at meetings of the Linnaean Society. As Kastner puts it, the Bronx, "like Boston Harbor when the patriots dumped tea into it or the Finland Station when Lenin arrived there . . . became a starting point of a historic revolution, which was to turn bird watching from the pastime of a relative few into the pleasure of a great many."

Several of these kids—Joseph Hickey, Allan Cruickshank, William Vogt—went on to distinguished careers in ornithology. A young art student from Jamestown, New York, an honorary member of the Bronx County Bird Club, became the Thomas Paine or Marx and Engels of this particular revolution. That was Roger Tory Peterson, whose bird guides made the game accessible to almost everyone.

Kastner points out that Peterson was uniquely qualified for this work. Even at age 19, he was among the most skilled birders in the country, and his training in art included study at the Art Students League under John Sloan, a realist of the Ashcan School, and at the more traditional National Academy of Design.

Today, according to a survey cited in Kastner's closing chapter, one out of four Americans does some bird-watching. Most of these watchers know little, but about seven million Americans can identify at least 30 species and two million can identify 100 or more. Bird-watching has become, behind hunting and fishing, the third most popular outdoor sport in America.

[*A World of Watchers* by Joseph Kastner was reprinted by the Sierra Club in 1988 but is now out of print.]

Henry Chandler Cowles

Father of Ecology

November 6, 1998

The year 1999 marks the 100th anniversary of the publication of a series of scientific papers under the general title "The Ecological Relations of the Vegetation on the Sand Dunes of Lake Michigan." Written by Dr. Henry Chandler Cowles of the University of Chicago, the papers were a major contribution to the young science of ecology, a major shaper of what we now think of as the commonsense view of the structure and functioning of natural communities.

The story that has been handed down says that Cowles got interested in the dunes while on his way to Chicago to take up his position at the university. His train stopped somewhere in northwestern Indiana, and he became intrigued by plants he could see growing near the tracks. His subsequent investigations centered on the Indiana Dunes but also extended up the Michigan shore of the lake to Sleeping Bear Dunes and beyond.

The naturalists of the 17th and 18th centuries studied a world they considered quite young. There was creation, the catastrophe of the Noachian flood, and ever since things had been pretty quiet. All species were created in the beginning, and one of the satisfactions of the study of nature was discovering how beautifully individual species fit into their environments.

The 19th century brought time and change into the picture. Geologists kept increasing their estimates of the age of the earth. Fossils came to be understood as records of plants and animals that had once thrived but were now extinct. Darwin and others showed how new species could be created by the interactions between organisms and their environment.

As Cowles studied the flora of the dunes, he came to realize that a walk through the dunes was a walk through time as well as space. By studying the vegetation of the contemporary dunes, he could decipher the history of the place.

"The ecologist," he wrote, regards "the flora of a pond or swamp or hillside not as a changeless landscape feature, but rather as a panorama, never twice alike. The ecologist, then, must study the order of succession of the plant societies in the development of a region, and he must endeavor to discover the laws which govern the panoramic changes. Ecology, therefore, is a study in dynamics. For its most ready application, plants should be found whose tissues and organs are actually changing at the present time in response to varying conditions. Plant formations should be found which are rapidly passing into other types by reason of a changing environment."

At the dunes Cowles found perfect examples of plant formations "rapidly passing into other types." The basis for the change was the extreme youth of the landscape. Our whole region was under ice until 14,000 years ago, and much of the land near the present shore of Lake Michigan was underwater until only 4,000 years ago. The history of the lake's retreat to its present size is written in a series of beach ridges that curve around the southern shore. The oldest of these ridges are as much as ten miles inland. Depending on the slope of the terrain, the youngest ridges may be only a few hundred yards from the present shore.

The vegetation of the present-day beaches is quite sparse. On the lower beaches, where the waves of summer storms regularly disrupt things, no plants grow. On the upper beach, where only the more violent storms of winter strike, a few scattered annuals can survive. Yet on old beach ridges just a short distance inland, forests thrive. Cowles recognized that the beach environment is a difficult one. On the Indiana shore, winds sweep across the water before striking the land with immense force. Cowles recommended that people lie on the sand facing into the wind to get a real sense of how much sand is landing on the beaches. You can follow his advice today. The beach environment is subjected to a nearly continuous low-level sandblasting, an onslaught only the most thick-hided plants can survive.

Half a mile inland, conditions are much more benign. Cowles's own research highlighted the contribution of the plants themselves to this more comfortable situation. You can study an example of this contribution at Montrose Beach. In 1994 an Illinois endangered species called sea rocket was found growing on the beach. The plant is a thick-skinned annual that specializes in life just above the summer-storm line. The Chicago Park District erected a fence around the plant, and ever since the fence has protected a small piece of the beach from human disturbance. Cottonwoods in great numbers have invaded the protected space.

These are true dune builders. Their roots and trunks capture blowing sand and hold it near them. If the sand around them grows too deep, the trunks can sprout new roots.

Cowles noted the importance of cottonwoods, marram grass, and a few other pioneering plants as builders of dunes. The sand piles up around them. The plants grow new roots to stay above the deepening sand, and eventually you have dunes nearly 200 feet above the waterline. These dunes grow only along the southeastern and eastern shores of the lake. Prevailing northwesterly winds carry the sand to these shores. On the lake's eastern shore the dunes are low. The lake deposits sand along the shore, but the winds do not carry it inland.

In the lee of every high dune is a sheltered space, a low spot that the winds seldom reach. Here wetland plants less specialized for life on the windy dunes can find a home, and woodland and prairie species can thrive.

At every step in this process, Cowles discovered, the plants are active agents in the changes taking place. Their roots help stabilize the sand. Their shade moderates the shifts between hot and cold, between wet and dry. Their decomposing remains enrich the soil, turning sterile sand into fertile ground.

I visited Indiana Dunes State Park twice last month and was reminded of how strongly Cowles's research influences my view of the landscape. Walking the trails between the nature center and the beach, I stepped through every stage from sugar maple to marram grass. The dunes near the beach were cold and windswept. The bark of an ironwood tree growing on the foredune had been bleached from brown to gray by the wind. In the basins and on the slopes of the high dunes that have been built in the 4,000 years since the lake receded, sugar maples and basswoods grew under a canopy of oaks. Witch hazel, sassafras, and flowering dogwood formed a dense shrub layer. On the crests of the high dunes, where conditions were drier and windier, black oaks dominated the landscape and blueberries covered the ground under the shade of the oaks.

Cowles taught us to see these differences as moments in time. We should expect change, and if we study the landscape carefully we can predict the likely direction of that change. If things are not changing, there is a reason. Some forces are pushing the land in the direction of stability, and we can study those.

One of Cowles's students at the University of Chicago was May Thielgaard Watts. She popularized the work of Cowles and others in the fledgling science of ecology. Through a series of books with the general title of "Reading the Landscape" and through generations of classes at the Morton Arboretum, she taught laypeople that landscapes are ordered in both space and time. She taught that we can understand what is happening in these landscapes if we study their history and learn to interpret their present state as the product of that history.

Ray Schulenberg, who planted the first prairie restoration in Illinois at the Morton Arboretum, and Floyd Swink, senior author of the best book on regional flora in North America and a superb educator, both learned from May Watts. They in turn educated the educators who are working as naturalists in the local forest preserves, planning exhibits at local zoos and museums, and creating curricula for local schools. Cowles's insights guide land mangers responsible for sustaining natural communities in parks and preserves. They have become local traditions, like 16-inch softball. His work, completed 100 years ago, is still helping protect our remaining natural communities.

Poplar Creek Preserve
Two Approaches to Restoration

September 6, 1991

When the Cook County Forest Preserve District acquired the Poplar Creek Preserve near Hoffman Estates, most of the property was old cornfields growing up to weeds. The preserve is a big piece of land. It measures about 3.5 miles east to west and about 2.5 miles north to south. Only four roads run through it, two from north to south and two from east to west.

It had one high-quality natural area, a small hilltop prairie, Shoe Factory Road Prairie, which is an Illinois state nature preserve. And it had a grove of large oaks thickly infested with European buckthorn shrubs. Both of these features are near the western end of the preserve.

Poplar Creek Preserve first attracted attention in 1984, when a consortium of suburbs tried to get the County Board to approve the construction of a garbage dump on the land. The board refused, but the battle did get conservationists thinking about the preserve.

In 1989, the Cook County Forest Preserve District and the Nature Conservancy put together a joint-management proposal that called for a major restoration affecting the 600 acres of the preserve that lie west of Route 59. Both Shoe Factory Road Prairie and the oak grove are on this land.

Work began in the summer of 1989, when two interns paid by the Nature Conservancy began clearing the invading buckthorn out of the grove. Volunteers were solicited from neighboring towns to carry on the work on a long-term basis. Today more than 100 people are regularly involved with various aspects of the project.

I took a look at Poplar Creek a few weeks ago. It was my first visit since 1989. Significant changes are already visible there, although parts of it look like weed patches that only a real prairie zealot could love. However, I know that the weedy look is only temporary—an unavoidable awkward stage, like adolescence, that will soon pass.

The cleared areas under the huge old spreading oaks are still open, and substantial growths of savanna grasses and wildflowers are filling in the spaces left by the removal of the buckthorn. Bottlebrush grass was in flower when I was there, and woodland brome and silky rye grasses are also thriving.

On the open grasslands, the places that will be prairie someday, I could see some signs of the prairie future peeking through the weeds. In the past, prairie restorations have followed one of two patterns. Some, like the restoration at Fermilab, have started from bare ground. The soil is plowed and disked and then seeded with a mixture of prairie plants. Emphasis is on the more aggressive species, things like big bluestem grass and Indian grass.

The other method, called successional restoration, has been used on the North Branch prairies. With successional restoration you scatter seeds or plant individual seedlings on an existing grassland.

There are advantages and disadvantages to both. With successional restoration, you can establish populations of conservative prairie species without waiting for big bluestem or Indian grass to get big enough to provide a prairie matrix. It is difficult to use successional restoration on large sites, however, because the work all has to be done by hand. Beginning from bare ground allows you to use tractors and other mechanized equipment and plant substantial acreage.

At Poplar Creek, they have decided to combine the two methods. Long narrow strips have been plowed and seeded. These strips are separated by unplowed land where seeding and planting were done by hand.

Right now, the plowed strips are some of the ugliest places you'll ever see. The dominant species on the strips are Queen Anne's lace and white sweet clover. Both of these are aggressive, weedy aliens that have moved in to take advantage of the disturbance created by the plowing. Fortunately, we know that time is on the side of the prairie. Prairie plants take a very cautious approach to growth. A big bluestem a few centimeters tall may have roots extending a couple of feet into the soil. Only after the plant has a root system substantial enough to ride out an Illinois drought will it expand its holdings aboveground. The root system is also the part of the plant that survives the winter. You can burn a prairie in late fall or early spring when everything aboveground is dead and do no damage at all to the native plants. Aliens, accustomed to longer growing seasons, don't do as well. Fire and competition will eventually squeeze out aliens like Queen Anne's lace and leave the prairie species in control of the field.

Keeping track of the changes that restoration brings to Poplar Creek is the job of a crew of plant monitors led by John Navin, a mailman from Roselle. Navin was recruited for the project by an appeal to Nature Conservancy members mailed out two years ago. He came out to the first few workdays, and that got him hooked. "I started with a blank page," he says now. "I could recognize dandelions and that was about it." With some help from professionals working on the project and a lot of study on his own, he has turned himself into the man the monitors consult when trying to identify the difficult species. The monitoring crew, which has 15 to 18 regulars, will be keeping track of all the plants growing in one-meter-square plots scattered across the 600-acre restoration site.

A project like Poplar Creek provides a focus for many people with an interest in nature. Judy Mellin was a casual birder for several years until she took on the job of monitoring bird populations at Poplar Creek. Working with Duane Heaton, an active birder with long experience, she compiled a list of 69 species as confirmed or probable nesters at the site this year.

The list includes such prairie specialties as eastern meadowlark, bobolink, and savanna sparrow, wetland birds like the sedge wren, and in the oaks, the blue-gray gnatcatcher. Poplar Creek is also the only known nesting site in Cook County for the common snipe.

Judy Mellin now birds every week at Poplar Creek, and her casual interest has expanded into a passionate study of bird behavior. "I want to know why they do the things they do," she told me.

Involvement in projects like Poplar Creek changes people's lives. Coming to work again and again on the same ground, noticing tiny changes in plant life, the appearance of a new bird species, or the arrival of a butterfly never seen at the site before, creates an intimate attachment to the natural world. The science of applied ecology is giving late-20th-century Americans a way to touch nature without trying to pretend that we are Potawatomis. The project can also foster other kinds of intimate attachment. A couple who met on Poplar Creek workdays will be married at the site later this month.

Poplar Creek, the North Branch Prairie Project, and the extensive ecosystem management now under way in the Palos preserves are helping return the Cook County Forest Preserve District to a leadership position in the administration of natural areas. So it seems an appropriate time to say something nice about Arthur Janura. After 30-some years as general superintendent of the district, he announced his plans to retire at the end of 1991. Richard Phelan, the new County Board president, decided to give him the ax at midsummer. Since then we have been reading stories about eccentric administrative procedures Janura carried on for reasons known only to him. And the *Sun-Times* revived the old story about patronage drones on the forest-preserve staff living free—or nearly free—in houses on preserve property. Stories like this are as much a tradition of Chicago journalism as photos of polar bears at the zoos trying to stay cool on the hottest day of the summer.

Janura made all the decisions about who got to live in those houses, and his choices seem to have been almost as quirky as his administrative procedures. I'm sure there are patronage drones in some of those houses, but running down the list of lucky employees that the *Sun-Times* published, I also find staff naturalists I know to be highly qualified and dedicated. I'm sure that their presence in houses near the nature centers they run does help maintain security and improve service to the public.

So, like Janura himself, the issue is complicated. He seemed to feel perfectly comfortable operating in a system where patronage was a fact of life, but he also tried to do some good. He could be very difficult. The first words he ever spoke to me were not "Hello, how are you?" but "Why are you trying to destroy the forest preserves?"

Despite all that, he did decide to let the North Branch Prairie Project use volunteers to carry out a management plan that included both cutting down trees and setting fire to preserves. And he decided to let similar groups of volunteers play major roles in the Poplar Creek restoration and the management of the Palos preserves. Not many bureaucrats would have that much nerve. We owe him some thanks.

Lichen Scholar

111 Species in Cook County

November 3, 1995

Rich Hyerczyk and I sat down at a picnic table in Harms Woods to discuss lichens. He had an assortment of books, information sheets, hand lenses, and bottles of calcium hypochlorite and potassium hydroxide to help with species identification. I thought, OK, here is all the equipment, where are the lichens? He pointed at the tabletop. The dark weathering wood was coated with a film of pale green.

"This is *Lecanora*," he said, naming a genus of crustose lichen. "I can't be sure of the species." Looking through a hand lens, I could see tiny saucerlike structures scattered over the green surface of the lichen. These are apothecia, reproductive structures that send out spores ready to create a new generation of lichens—possibly on this tabletop, possibly on the rail fence at the edge of the picnic ground, possibly on a fallen log.

I had seen that greenish film before on wood left outdoors, but I had always thought it was just an alga or perhaps a moss. When I lived in Seattle we had railroad ties in our backyard as landscaping elements, and they were covered with the stuff. *Lecanora* gets slippery when it's wet, and one of my most vivid memories of my time in the great northwest was a fall I took on a soggy railroad tie that led to arthroscopic knee surgery—which is my absolute most vivid memory of the northwest.

The rail fence at Harms Woods harbors several kinds of lichens, and it is a major reason why the lichen flora of Harms Woods is richer than that at any of the other preserves along the North Branch of the Chicago River. We know this because Hyerczyk has surveyed every one of these preserves in search of lichens.

You have seen them as green films on wood or yellow patches on tree bark or gray disks on rocks. In areas recently uncovered by melting glaciers they are the first colonizers of bare rock. In more stable circumstances lichens specialize in particular substrates. Corticolous species live on tree bark; lignicolous species live on wood—including picnic tables—saxicolous species live on rock or concrete, and terricolous species live on soils. And, according to Rich Hyerczyk, species that live on reeds are called reedicolous. A little lichen humor.

Lichens are a perfect argument against reductionism. They are wholes that are much more than—and much different from—the sum of their parts. The parts are a fungus and an alga. Algae are green plants. They contain chlorophyll. They make their food by capturing the energy of sunlight and converting it to sugar. Fungi do not make their own food. In the great ecological scheme of things they are usually decomposers who make a living by feeding on organic matter both living and dead. They help reduce wood and other complex chemicals to their constituent elements, returning them to the ecosystem and making them available once again to living things.

In lichens the fungi provide a structure, a protected environment for the algal cells. If you were to slice open the pale gray body—called a thallus—of *Physcia millegrana,* a common species growing on tree bark in our area, you would find that the upper and lower layers are fungi. Between these upper and lower cortices is the sheltered environment where the algae live.

It is possible to grow the algae and the fungi of lichens separately in laboratory conditions. But the fungi will not assume their lichenous form without the algae. Living by themselves they grow as shapeless blobs, and they do not reproduce.

Out in nature they reproduce in a couple of different ways, none of them involving sex. The spores in those saucer-shaped apothecia I saw on the *Lecanora* are created vegetatively by the single parent plant. Other forms of vegetative reproduction happen too, but to a considerable extent, to quote *How to Know the Lichens* by Mason E. Hale, "the reproduction of lichens in nature is a mystery. Sexual reproduction in which spores germinate and recombine with algae is theoretically possible but no one has been able to follow these steps in nature."

It strikes me that Hale's words provide all the reason anyone would need for getting interested in lichens. Here is a group of organisms familiar enough to grow on picnic tables and fence posts and still so mysterious that we don't really know the details of how they reproduce.

A thought rather like that seems to have struck Rich Hyerczyk a few years ago when he took a course in lichens in pursuit of a degree in botany. He already had a degree that prepared him for a career in the computer-assisted design of machine parts. The botany courses were purely for the love of it, a love stoked by Hyerczyk's involvement in ecological restoration at the Palos forest preserves.

Restoration work is often an open-ended kind of thing. You start out pulling a few weeds, and the next thing you know you're studying for finals in lichenology. Early this year Hyerczyk completed two major reports: one on the lichen flora of the North Branch preserves, the other on the lichen flora of the Palos and Sag Valley preserves. He has also done extensive fieldwork in Putnam County, which is along the Illinois River southwest of La Salle-Peru.

A century ago William Wirt Calkins wrote a report on the *Lichen Flora of Chicago and Vicinity,* which was published by the Chicago Academy of Sciences. Calkins described 125 species of lichens he had collected in Cook, Du Page, and Will counties in Illinois and in Lake County in Indiana. Current thought would lump some of these together, producing 109 total species.

Hyerczyk's fieldwork, combined with work done by Gerould Wilhelm of the Morton Arboretum, has discovered 111 species in Cook County. This total is very near Calkins's, but the numbers disguise a major shift in the lichen flora. Forty-nine species found by Calkins have not been found in recent years. The new species discovered recently are mainly organisms that grow on concrete. The species lost have almost certainly been done in by air pollution. Lichens, perhaps because they get their mineral nutrients from air and rainwater, are extremely vulnerable to pollution.

Wilhelm has been both a mentor in Hyerczyk's pursuit of lichens and a grateful beneficiary of his fieldwork for his own report, *Lichens of the Chicago Region,* which is currently in preparation. "A lot of young people think that everything is already known," Wilhelm told me, "because that's the way it is presented to them in school. But Rich found an area to work where very little is known. Everything he collected in Putnam County is a new record, because nobody every looked for lichens there before."

You might ask why anybody would decide to devote so much attention to lichens. They are very obscure members of natural communities. Those

33 species at Harm's Woods account for only a tiny fraction of 1 percent of the biomass of the preserve. Lichens are not major shapers of the community. They are not an essential food source for much of anything. Blue-gray gnatcatchers do build their nests with a gray lichen called *Parmelia sulcata,* and there is some reason to believe that parula warblers won't nest in places that don't have a lichen called *Usnea* sp., which the birds use for their nests. On the stony ground of the tundra the fruticose lichen called reindeer moss is a major food of reindeer and caribou.

And while lichens seem like small potatoes around here, when you get south of the regions that were once glaciated they get much more important. According to Wilhelm, on barren, rocky slopes in the Ozarks the ability of lichens to colonize bare rock makes them a major component of the ground cover. "You can't really understand what is going on in those communities without studying the lichens."

One of the things going on in those communities is a successional pattern. Lichens on bare rock collect dust. The dust combines with dead lichens to create a sort of soil that might support a flowering plant that could continue the soil-building process.

Of course the real reasons for studying lichens are first, that they are there, and second, because it's fun. And then there is that symbiosis. If you remember anything about lichens from biology class, you remember their unique hybrid nature. But is it unique? Wilhelm thinks it is more like a pattern that is repeated throughout nature. "Fungi typically have a relationship with another organism," he says. Fungi of decay have these relationships with dead organisms, but many fungi are symbiotes with living ones. Flowering plants have mycorrhizal fungi growing on their roots that play a major role in the absorption of minerals from the soil. The fungi can't live without the plant, and the plant can't live without the fungi. "Should we think of the white oak as a separate, independent organism?" Wilhelm asks. "Or should we think of it as part of a combination of fungi and green plant?" In other words, are oaks in their relationship to fungi just very large versions of the lichens that grow on their bark?

Meanwhile Hyerczyk continues to collect and continues to find intriguing things. Lichens are usually more common in open sunny areas and less common in shady woods. But when a large oak fell at Black Partridge Woods Forest Preserve, Hyerczyk examined the crown of the tree and found 13 species of lichens growing in it. They had been up where the sunlight was. I suggested he needed the sort of rigs used to study the canopies of rain forest. He just smiled. I'm wondering if he might try it.

Dinosaurs and Birds
Fossils That Link Them

November 9, 1990

I went to see the Field Museum's new bird fossil on Monday. They were still setting it up when I got there, so I waited around for a half an hour or so for the privilege of being one of the first to see it.

It was worth the wait. It is very tiny of course. The living bird, I would guess, would have been about starling size. The legs are the easiest part of the fossil to see. The rest of the body is somewhat scrunched up and the rock surface around the rib cage is not as smooth as that around the legs.

But if you look carefully, you can see the stubby tail and the keel bone, two very birdish traits. You can also see the clawed fingers on the forelimbs, the teeth in the jaws, and the long extension on the ischium, one of the bones of the pelvis. These are characteristics of the dinosaurs that are now almost universally regarded as the ancestors of birds.

People have been fascinated with dinosaurs ever since the first specimens were dug up in the early 19th century. In 1852 a British sculptor named Waterhouse Hawkins even got a government grant to erect life-size statues of dinosaurs and other ancient beasts in Sydenham, a London suburb. Richard Owen, the British naturalist—as biologists were then called—who coined the term "dinosaur" ("terrible lizard" in Greek), worked closely with him to ensure the authenticity of the re-creations.

Of course they got almost everything wrong. Specimens were few in those days. In some cases Hawkins had nothing but a skull, so he had to imagine the rest of the body. He produced an amphibian called laby-rinthodont—which in life looked rather like a crocodile—as a giant frog. The largest dinosaur, the iguanodon, came out looking like a rhino. We now know that this animal, like many other dinosaurs, was bipedal. It carried its weight on its huge hind legs, and its forelimbs were much reduced.

When the restorations were complete, Owen gave a celebratory dinner for 21 dignitaries. The dinner was held *inside* the iguanodon model. The festivities went on for most of the night, becoming increasingly hilarious as toast after toast was raised to the glorious success of the models.

In the late 19th century the major action in the dinosaur field shifted to the U.S. The Great Plains turned out to be one of the richest dinosaur beds in the world. Geologically, the rocks there were of just the right age, and the dry climate meant that the land wasn't all haired over with trees. There was, and is, a lot of exposed rock, so the fossils are much easier to see than they would be in a wetter climate.

As early as 1854 a geologist named Ferdinand Hayden, who was accompanying a U.S. Army surveying expedition to the Judith River in Montana, picked up some very large teeth. At the time the Plains Indians were still very active and inclined to contest the passage of army surveyors. They gave Hayden a name of his own, "he who picks up stones while running," that suggests the conditions under which he had to work. However, Hayden gained protection because his actions seemed so bizarre that the Indians decided he was crazy. Lunatics were regarded as touched with divinity and were therefore left alone.

Hayden's finds aroused considerable interest, and by 1870—six years before Custer's defeat at Little Bighorn—there were paleontologists out on the plains of Kansas digging up fossils.

The two most notable paleontologists of the era were Edward Drinker Cope of Philadelphia and Othniel Charles Marsh of New Haven. They hated each other. (I've been toying with the idea of writing a screenplay about their rivalry. The story has both the romance of intrepid scientists in the old West and the absolute silliness of otherwise sensible, intelligent men acting like three-year-olds.)

Cope and Marsh set spies on each other. They tried to steal each other's fossils. They sent agents west under assumed names in order to avoid each other's spies. At the end of a field season they—or their hired diggers—would destroy bones they didn't have time to remove to make sure they wouldn't fall into the hands of the hated rival.

Their battle culminated at the Como beds in eastern Wyoming, some of the richest fossiliferous rocks in the world. Both men had crews on the scene at the same time, and on some occasions the two groups actually came to blows over the right to dig in particularly promising locations.

Fame was the spur to some of this rivalry. Then as now, dinosaurs made headlines. Most paleontologists live lives of great obscurity. They chronicle the rise and fall of trilobites, mollusks, or flowering plants, and nobody who is not in the same field ever hears of them.

Two kinds of paleontologists can get famous: those who study the evolution of human beings, and those who study dinosaurs. Our fascination with our own forebears is easy to understand, as is our almost equal interest in fierce animals as big as houses. Kids love dinosaurs. They are so wonderfully creepy and enormous.

In the past couple of decades paleontologists have gotten even more interested in dinosaurs than they were before. Beginning in the '60s, a new conception of these huge old beasts began developing.

The old interpretation, which dates back to Richard Owen, was that dinosaurs, in their behavior and physiology, were very much like the reptiles of today. Their body temperature fluctuated with the temperature of their surroundings, and they depended on the sun to get them warm enough to move around and be active.

The new interpretation says they were warm-blooded, like birds and mammals. Their body temperature was controlled internally, remaining at a constant high level regardless of the air temperature around them.

The switch from cold-blooded to warm-blooded has lots of implications. Reptiles spend most of their lives sitting still and doing nothing. Their energy requirements are very low. A Komodo dragon, the enormous Indonesian lizard, eats the equivalent of its own weight every 60 days. A cheetah needs to eat its own weight every nine days. Maintaining a constant high body temperature uses up a tremendous amount of energy. It takes a lot of food to keep the furnace fed.

So warm-blooded dinosaurs would have been active animals. They would also have been fast growing. Reptiles grow slowly throughout their lives. They don't have the physiology to handle fast growth. Birds and mammals grow very fast until they reach adulthood. Then they stay the same size for the rest of their lives.

Warm-bloodedness would also make large size advantageous. When an animal gets bigger, its volume grows faster than its surface area. Small animals have lots of surface and very little volume. They lose heat rapidly from all that surface, so they have to eat furiously. Shrews, the smallest mammals, need to eat more than their own weight every day just to stay alive. Big animals, with more heat-generating volume and less heat-losing surface, can get by with less. We know from fossilized skins that dinosaurs had no hair or other insulating coverings, so their large size would have been especially helpful.

The newest famous paleontologist, a Montanan named John Horner, has added another new wrinkle to our view of dinosaurs. He has dug up strong evidence that at least one species of hadrosaur—a large herbivore—laid its eggs in nests, that the nests were grouped in colonies, and that the adults fed the young in the nests until they were big enough to fend for themselves. Parental care on this level is not a feature of reptilian life.

The connection between birds and dinosaurs has been known for more than a century. One of history's most famous fossils, the archaeopteryx ("ancient feather") was dug out of a limestone quarry in Germany in 1861. The bones of this creature were those of a small dinosaur. It had heavy jaws studded with teeth, claws on its forelimbs, and a long, bony tail. But on the fine-grained limestone, one could plainly see the outline of feathers. Depending on how you interpreted the fossil, this was either the first bird or a dinosaur on its way to becoming a bird.

Archaeopteryx would have been too heavy to fly much. It might have glided some, but its hind feet are those of a terrestrial animal and wouldn't have been very useful for perching on a tree limb. If the feathers weren't so plainly visible, this fossil would be thought of as a small dinosaur.

The new fossil at the Field Museum is ten million years younger than archaeopteryx, and much more birdlike. Its hind feet could fit a limb. Its tail vertebrae have been reduced to a stub, one of many changes in the direction of lighter weight that came with flight. It also has a keel bone on its breast where the heavy muscles needed to power the wings were attached.

If dinosaurs were truly warm-blooded and if some of them had evolved a high level of parental care, then the shift from dinosaur to bird would not be very large. In fact, two paleontologists have suggested that we need to reclassify these animals. Instead of a class Aves and a class Dinosauria, we need only a class Dinosauria, with birds as one of the groups within it.

In other words, dinosaurs didn't become extinct. They just changed with the times. If you want to see one, you don't need to go look at a skeleton in a museum. Just walk outside and look up, and you can see the dinosaurs flying by.

[The fossil, which came from China, was on loan to the Field Museum and has been returned.]

Roger Tory Peterson
Irreplaceable

August 16, 1996

Roger Tory Peterson died on July 29, 1996. There was no one else like him while he was alive, and no one like him is apt to come along.

If there is anyone we can compare him with it is the great artist-ornithologists of the 18th and 19th centuries. The list of such men is short. It starts with Mark Catesby, who visited the southern colonies and the Bahamas in the 1730s and '40s. Alexander Wilson is the next great figure in this line, and John James Audubon is the culmination of the type.

These men were explorers. Each of them found species unknown to European science, and their books were both a way to make the scientific world aware of these new finds and a way to pay for the expeditions that found them.

By the time Peterson's first *Field Guide to the Birds* was published in 1934, scientists had pretty well delineated North America's avifauna. Peterson directed his work to a nonscientific audience, and thanks to modern printing methods—which could reproduce paintings in full color—his field guides were accessible to an audience much poorer than the genteel amateurs of the natural sciences who had supported Audubon's efforts. Teenage boys could afford a Peterson.

Wilson and Audubon were both scientists and popularizers. Peterson was a popularizer whose contribution to science was more indirect. His books helped teach generations of scientists how to identify free-flying birds in the field, and that skill helped make their contributions possible.

Peterson led an enviable life. He grew up in Jamestown, New York, at the extreme western end of the state. His childhood interests were birds and art, and in his adult life he became rich, famous, and widely admired by pursuing those interests. He left his hometown to study at the Art Students League and the National Academy of Design in New York City. In New York he hooked up with a small group of teenage bird nuts who called themselves the Bronx County Bird Club. The membership included several young men who went on to notable careers in ornithology, including Joseph Hickey, who became a professor at the University of Wisconsin, and Allan Cruickshank, who was associated with the American Museum of Natural History.

Peterson was teaching at a high school in Massachusetts when he completed *A Field Guide to the Birds of Eastern North America* in 1934. It was a skimpy work by today's standards. Many of the plates were in black and white, and the color plates squeezed as many as 15 species onto one seven-by-four-and-a-half-inch page. Four publishers turned down the book before Houghton Mifflin decided to take a chance on an edition of 2,000 copies. That edition sold out within two weeks, and the subsequent editions of the work have been doing a brisk business ever since.

Peterson's genius lay in a rigorous suppression of detail. His birds were schematized, stripped to essentials. He invented a system of identification that selected two or three features of each species as the field marks that set that species apart from similar birds. These field marks were highlighted in the paintings with straight lines that served as pointers. Anything that was not absolutely required was left out.

My favorite bird from Peterson's early period is the male canvasback duck. A real live canvasback seen in good light has a dark gray beak, a rusty-red head and neck, and a black breast. Most of its body is white. Its wings are white tinged with gray, and its hind parts are black.

Peterson renders the swimming bird in black and white as four almost featureless solid blocks. The beak and the head and neck are gray, with the beak slightly darker than the head. Below that is a solid black block representing the breast. Another black block at the rear shows the tail. The body and wings are a simple expanse of white with no demarcation of folded wings from body. In fact, the bird apparently has no wings.

I can testify that this minimalist rendering works in the field. I identified the first canvasback I ever saw with the aid of Peterson's painting.

It has been said that Peterson's paintings were a perfect fit for the optics available in the '30s. Most birders were using four- to six-power binoculars of somewhat less than astronomical quality. On a gray morning a distant canvasback sitting on a lake, perceived though those binoculars, would look very much like Peterson's schematic painting.

If you want to succeed you need to be in touch with the zeitgeist, and Roger Tory Peterson was. His book not only sold well, it founded an industry. Look in any of today's bookstores and you will find shelves full of field guides to birds, mammals, reptiles, insects, mushrooms, trees, wildflowers, fossils, rocks and minerals, and everything else under the sun. And thanks to star guides, everything beyond the sun as well.

Most Americans grow up in the city or suburbs, where nature is a distant rumor. Our grandfathers tend to know more about accounting or plumbing than they do about scarlet tanager nests. Field guides are the way we learn about nature, and Roger Tory Peterson was the best field-guide creator ever. Almost all of those shelves full of guides feature works done by committee. Except for Peterson's, the bird guides all have several fathers. The National Geographic Society's *Field Guide to the Birds of North America* doesn't even have an author's name on the cover. Inside you can find a list of more than 50 editors, researchers, writers, and artists who contributed to the work. They remind me of the armies of presidential speechwriters who labor mightily to produce stuff that is not as good as the speeches Lincoln wrote for himself.

Peterson's work earned him just the right degree of fame. Fame is a very tricky commodity in contemporary America. People who have too much, people who are, for example, known to both Sam Donaldson and John Tesh, can get caught up in nightmarish existences. They simultaneously live their own lives and the lives of fictional characters loosely based on them. Peterson was known and admired by a relatively small group. They loved him, but they wouldn't be inclined to tear his clothes off or steal his garbage before it was picked up.

I had the privilege of going birding with Roger Tory Peterson at an American Birding Association convention ten years ago. He was enjoying his ideal degree of fame at the convention. He was surrounded by intelligent, knowledgeable people who held him in great esteem. He could bask in the glow of their admiration and still know that if he left the ho-

tel and walked into a 7-Eleven just down the street he would be just another elderly gent.

On the field trip that we shared with about 20 other people he was just another birder. A very good birder, but only one of several very good birders. His interest then was in seeing birds and enjoying the fellowship of other people who also liked looking a birds. He was obviously not thinking too much about being the famous Roger Tory Peterson.

The doors that Peterson's books opened have enriched the lives of millions of people, and they have made a significant contribution to the protection of the environment. It was birders armed with Peterson's who first noticed the decline in bald eagle numbers that followed the introduction of DDT. Many of the tallgrass prairie remnants around Chicago were discovered by people using his guide to wildflowers. More broadly, he helped people realize what was at stake in the environmental struggle. You can't care about something if you don't know it exists, and Peterson's books made it possible for us to care. He is irreplaceable.

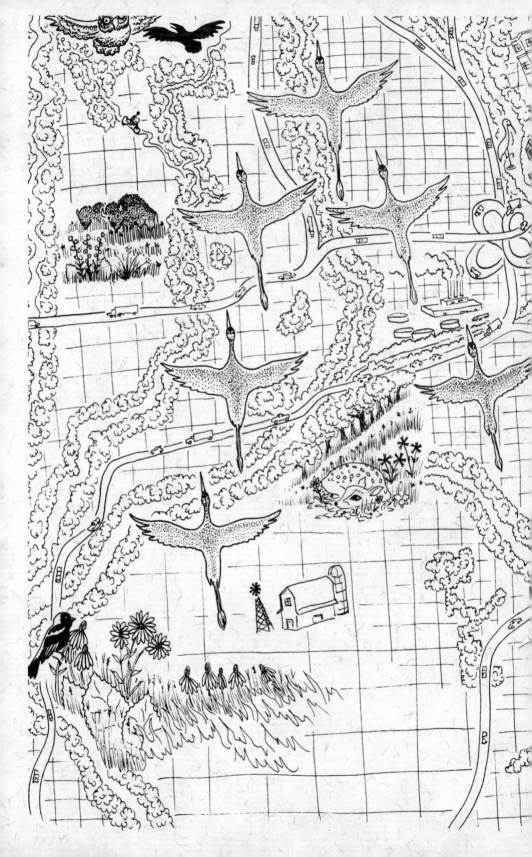